Memorable Moments
in a Long Rabbinic Career

Rabbi Bernard Lipnick

Memorable Moments
in a Long Rabbinic Career

Rabbi Bernard Lipnick

Foreword by Rabbi Jack Riemer

Edited by Lester H. Goldman

The Rabbi Bernard Lipnick Foundation for Conservative Judaism
Affiliated with Congregation B'nai Amoona

St. Louis, Missouri

ISBN: 978-1-7345292-0-3
Library of Congress: 2020902804

Printed in the United States of America
Book design: Peggy Nehmen and Gary Kodner, n-kcreative.com

The Rabbi Bernard Lipnick Foundation for Conservative Judaism
Affiliated with Congregation B'nai Amoona
324 S Mason Road, Creve Coeur, MO 63141

bnaiamoona.com/rabbilipnickbook

This volume of sermons by Rabbi Bernard Lipnick
is dedicated with profound appreciation
to the Congregants, *Klei Kodesh,* and Staff, past, present,
and future, of Congregation B'nai Amoona.

CONTENTS

Supplemental audio and video to enhance your appreciation
of the career and person of Rabbi Lipnick are available at:
bnaiamoona.com/rabbilipnickbook

Foreword

What Made Bernard Lipnick Such a Special Rabbi?

By Rabbi Jack Riemer

Three things:

First is that he stayed at the same synagogue for his entire career. Not very many rabbis do that anymore, not only because of our ambitions and not only because of *shul* politics, but simply because synagogues nowadays do not always last for a generation. But he chose to stay at one synagogue for his entire rabbinate. I am sure that he could have gone to other places over the years if he wanted to, but, if he had, he would have ended up being far less effective a rabbi than he was. He lived long enough to see some of 'his boys,' as he liked to call them, go up the ladder. . . from being president of USY to being president of the synagogue. And he lived long enough to preside over the *simchas* and the sorrows of the children and the grandchildren of people at whose *simchas* and sorrows he had presided. That is why he meant so much to so many people in his old age, and that is why there was such genuine grief in the congregation when he died.

Second is that every rabbi is like a one-armed paperhanger. When a rabbi is faced with a problem that he does not know how to solve, all he has to do is wait a minute and the phone will ring with another problem that will take his mind off the first. A rabbi has to be—at one and the same time—concerned with the needs of the young and of the old; concerned with the needs of the congregation and concerned with the needs of the community; able to share in joyous events and then move on to share in sad events—all in the same day. Wise rabbis learn to do many different things at the same time, but major or concentrate on the part of the rabbinate that means the most to them. For me, it was preaching and writing. For other rabbis it is pastoral work, or social action, or scholarship or something else. For Rabbi Lipnick, it was education that was the central focus of his rabbinate.

For me and for many other rabbis whom I know, involvement in the nitty-gritty of working with young children—children who came to the synagogue school after a whole day at 'real school'—was never very appealing. But that was Rabbi Lipnick's first priority. He was a talented and innovative educator who came up with many ideas: ideas like taking kids away once a month and spending a weekend at a campsite with them—living Jewish life instead of just talking about it. Others sent their graduating classes to Israel for a summer. He was the only one I know who sent them to a carefully selected *moshav*, that had children their ages, and who thereby created a deep and a lasting relationship between them and Israel that lasted for many years. A child who becomes bar or bat mitzvah at B'nai Amoona to this day reads the Torah at *Minchah* the Shabbat before, leads the *Birkat Hamazon* at the *seudah shlishit*, and makes *Havdalah* that night, puts on *tefillin* and leads part of the service the Monday before, and acquires synagogue skills that last a lifetime.

Third, I never understood the importance of management skills in the rabbinate until I met Bernie Lipnick. I thought that managing a synagogue was for executive directors to worry about, not for rabbis, and I thought that people who cared about the details of budgets or the work of committees were pencil pushers or pedants. I learned from Bernie Lipnick that what a rabbi accomplishes is directly related to his management skills. I would give a sermon in which I would say: "I think that we should do 'X,'" and then sit down. The people would nod their heads in approval, and forget the idea by the time *Mussaf* ended. Bernie would conceive of a project, choose the leaders to carry it out with him, plan the strategy by which to get it approved, and the last thing he would do, only after all the ducks were in a row, as he would say, was announce it from the pulpit and persuade the people to buy into it.

These are three of the qualities that made Bernard Lipnick such a very special and effective rabbi. Qualities like his total integrity, his compassion, his intelligence, and his God-given and unforgettable voice cannot be taught. But these qualities—sticking to one place all the days of his life instead of moving from place to place; choosing education as the center of his rabbin-ate and making it work; and management skills that could have made him the CEO of any large company—these are the things that I believe made him the giant of the rabbinate that he was.

Here you will find collected a small sample of some of his favorite sermons. Read them and remember what it was like to sit in that sanctuary on Trinity, and later in the sanctuary that he helped design and create on Mason Road, and listen to that voice and to these words. Remember how they gave grace and dignity to the service. Remember how they came out of the long and noble tradition that he revered, and that he strove to apply to the new world in which we live.

Remember as you read these sermons. Remember—and be grateful.

Rabbi Jack Riemer

Preface

A Rabbinic Introduction

By Rabbi Bernard Lipnick

One fine day, quite out of the blue, I was approached by a certain member of B'nai Amoona with the suggestion that I put together some of my sermons in book form. That person was Ed Balk, who is a long-time friend of mine, and an honored and devoted member of B'nai Amoona. To say the least, I was taken aback by the idea, and told him that I would think about it and let him know. During the following weeks, a number of others came to me with the same suggestion, and so I had to come up with an answer, one way or the other.

Part of me said: "Does my work really have the lasting significance that would deserve preserving it within a book?" Another part of me said, "If so many people are telling me to do it, how can I say no?"

I turned to Rabbi Jack and Sue Riemer, who have been my close friends and advisors for over thirty years, and asked them what they thought of the idea. Rabbi Riemer is known throughout the country as a creative and talented preacher, and Sue, his wife, is a great editor and a very smart lady, and so I felt that they would give me good advice.

Rabbi Riemer said, "Bernie, do not attempt to judge the eternal significance of what you have spoken and written. Leave that to the future generations to decide. The reason so many congregants have asked you to do this book is that for all these many years, you have been central to their spiritual lives. They want to preserve your words, because these words have guided them and have helped them to understand themselves, and to understand the meaning of their times. By all means, give them this gift to treasure as a witness to your rabbinate. They will be truly grateful."

I realized he was right. There is plenty of good literature available for people to read. But the people of B'nai Amoona, especially those who came to Shabbat morning services regularly, wanted a record of what they lived through together, and how the pulpit made the resources of the Jewish tradition available to them, so that they could find meaning in their lives in confusing times.

And so the whole project took on a different cast. These good people, with whom I had spent much of my life, wanted a permanent record of what we had lived through together, and how could I say no to this request?

I thanked the Riemers for putting the purpose of this book in a clear and compelling form, and then I went a step further. I asked them and Harriet: "Would you be willing to help me, if I undertake this project? After all, no one is really objective about his own writing. Would you go through the sermons that I have compiled, and tell me which ones you think are worth printing and which ones are not? And will you promise to do so with complete honesty?"

Without a moment's hesitation, the three of them agreed, and so the idea of *Memorable Moments in a Long Rabbinic Career*, which you now hold in your hand, began.

We began by going through some sixty years of sermons. I asked myself about each one, "Is the event which occasioned this sermon important enough to be remembered, and was my response to it adequate enough?" I read and reread my files, trying to determine, as best as I could, which ones were dated and which ones still have significance. Our first paring resulted in about one hundred and twenty-five sermons—obviously far too many for a book that would be of a manageable size. A second paring brought the number of possibilities down to sixty, and a third run-through brought the number down to twenty-eight.

There you have it—the story of how this book came about, the names of some of the people who persuaded me to do it, and the hope that I have as to what it may accomplish.

Before I close this introduction, however, there are some important "thank yous" that I must express. First, to the people of B'nai Amoona, with whom

I have shared a close relationship for almost sixty years: I have been around the world, but I do not know of any congregation anywhere that has in it people of more *mentschlichkeit* than this congregation has, and I am forever grateful that God cast my lot in this place.

In my nearly sixty years at B'nai Amoona, I never had more than a one-year contract, because I believed that ours was a covenantal relationship, and not a business one. I believed, and still do, that I worked for God and the Jewish people, not for the congregation, and that principle served me in good stead. The people of B'nai Amoona were not my bosses, but no rabbi ever had a better congregation, one which was and is filled with good people; people who took and who continue to take seriously the task of becoming good Jews, and of raising their descendants to continue the goals of their ancestors.

Beyond the congregation, I want to single out my secretary/colleague for some twenty-five years, who committed to paper most of the messages that are found in this book. She was Mrs. Harry (Miriam) Friedman, *zichrona livracha*, a member of the distinguished Sandmel family. No rabbi ever had a more faithful and a more competent co-worker than she. May her memory be a blessing to her children, her grandchildren, and to all who knew her.

Finally, I want to take this occasion to express my undying gratitude to my dear wife of thirty-six years, Harriet. The truth is that my personal life was not always smooth. It had its full share of challenges. It was the relationship with Harriet, who is an extremely competent and resourceful person, which enabled me to pick myself up and continue to live in tough times. If not for her, some of the accomplishments that I may have achieved would not have been possible. Beyond being the love of my life, she has been the quintessential partner in all that I do and am. I owe her everything.

I write these words on a cruise ship as we approach Singapore. There is much more that comes into my mind and could be said, but there has to be some limit to an introduction. Before closing, I want to mention Harriet's and my beloved children: David and Becca, Jayme and Mark, Mark and Nancy, Tammy and Alan, Jesse and Corrine, and the son who has predeceased me, Daniel. And I want to acknowledge their wonderful children who mean so much to me: Joshua, Emily and Rachel, Michael and Abby, Marisa and Bennett, and Chaim and Dassi.

Finally, I want to thank God for all of the many, many blessings which have been showered upon me in this life. In the words of our father, Jacob: "I am not worthy of the least of all the steadfast love, and all the faithfulness that God has shown to me."

Bernie
On the High Seas
February, 2010

Acknowledgements

This book would not have been possible without the support, skill, and generosity of:

The Rabbi Bernard Lipnick Foundation for Conservative Judaism, founded and supported by Sanford and Gloria Spitzer.

Rabbi Jack and Sue Reimer, who helped Rabbi Lipnick select the sermons collected here from the hundreds of sermons delivered over the course of 60-plus years, and for Rabbi Reimer's heartfelt foreword.

Rabbi Irwin Kula whose inspirational words honors Rabbi Lipnick.

Rabbi Carnie Shalom Rose for his thoughtful word of appreciation.

Professor Ron Wolfson, whose epilogue provides a fitting closing to the sentiments and uncommon wisdom expressed in these sermons.

Harriet Lipnick who was instrumental in helping select the sermons and photographs for this book, and the driving force behind its publication.

Zach Dalin, for his technical skill and creativity in preparing the audio and video supplements to this book found at bnaiamoona.com/rabbilipnickbook.

Drew Selman, for his early work with Rabbi Lipnick in preparing this book.

Ellen Cohen, for her skill and untiring effort in preparing the typed manuscript of Rabbi Lipnick's selected sermons.

Teressa LeBaube, for her expert proofreading, formatting, and editing.

Beverly Chervitz and Jan Baron for skillful proofreading.

Peggy Nehmen and Gary Kodner, the principals of Nehmen-Kodner, for their indispensable aid in designing and guiding this book through the intricacies of successful publication.

A Resonate Voice

By Rabbi Irwin Kula

Maaseh Shehaya—Three Stories that Happened

I had the privilege of working with Rabbi Bernard Lipnick at B'nai Amoona from 1982-87. On my first day at the shul, Bernie called me into his office. He took out a calendar and began to divide up the speaking responsibilities for the entire year. As a young assistant rabbi, in my first position, at a major congregation where somewhere between 500 and 1000 people showed up every Shabbat morning, I assumed I would speak every six weeks, perhaps once a month, but Bernie had other ideas. Calendar in hand, he simply assigned our speaking alternating between us each week. When Kol Nidre fell out assigned to me, I said with a mix of trepidation and incredulity, "Are you sure I should speak on Kol Nidre?" "Irwin," Bernie responded, "the congregation may have hired you as the assistant rabbi but to me you are just rabbi. I can do it if you don't want to but it's your turn." From my first day at BA, Bernie treated me as an equal in ways no assistant rabbi experiences. Confident in his own remarkable ability in every single facet of the rabbinate —teaching, writing, speaking, preaching, educating, pastoral work, life cycle, programming, running a meeting, strategizing, fundraising, leadership—he trusted me with the opportunity to do everything and anything with one caveat. He always demanded excellence. No one had higher expectations of me than Bernie and no one's approval as a rabbi was more important to me than his—from that first day until literally the day he died.

Later, that same first week at BA, we were talking in his office. He stood up and asked me to come behind his imposing, impeccably neat and orderly mahogany desk. Bending down he opened two massive drawers at the bottom of a book case that reached to the ceiling. In the drawers was every sermon he had written since the early 1950s cataloged by portion of the week, holidays, and special events. There must have been more than a thousand sermons, most in multiple iterations, each typed up perfectly, some with a relevant article or a text attached to it. It was overwhelming. "Feel free to go through these files and take anything you want, just make sure to make copies and put the original back in exactly the right place," he said. Bernie was open source before there was open source. His Torah was not proprietary, it was free flowing always to be offered. I read every one of those sermons. I learned that being smart is easy. The hard job of a rabbi is to always make Torah—Jewish wisdom and practice—accessible and usable, to always respond to serious questions and genuine problems in people's lives with Torah that adds insight and value to help them have better lives and become better people. Yes, Bernie had that indomitable gift of a perfect, deep, rich, resonant voice but he did the intellectually serious, disciplined, hard work to create Torah that was real, alive, contemporary, rooted, courageous, and wise. He trusted himself and the Torah and he trusted me—in fact he always trusted young people—to take his Torah and metabolize it in any way I saw fit.

A few months later, with a mix of enthusiasm, confidence, and ambition, I shared with Bernie some new creative idea I eagerly wanted to institute. I don't remember the idea but Bernie's response has impacted my life to this day. He took out a writing pad, gave it to me and told me there were 27 lines on the pad and that I was to fill in each line with some step I thought necessary to make my idea happen. The steps did not need to be in any order but every line on the pad needed to be filled out. When finished, we would review the steps, see what was missing, and determine the feasibility of my idea. There was only one rule: Getting funding was not to be one of the steps on my list. I will never forget what he said. "Money is never the issue in realizing your ideas. If your idea is good and well-thought out, the money will always be there." Bernie was a true leader with an absolute unique blend of unbridled idealism and realism, impatience and perseverance, vision and pragmatism, unquenchable spirit and determination, creativity, resilience, energy, and love for God, Torah and the Jewish people. He never blamed the people for what couldn't get done or didn't happen. He took responsibility. He—and therefore I—could always work harder, do better, think more clearly, communicate more effectively, execute more wisely, lead more passionate, and serve more deeply, and then nothing was impossible.

Three stories from just the first six months of the five most formative years of my rabbinate or as Bernie would often tease me—"the most luxurious years" of my rabbinate.

Rabbi Bernard Lipnick made me the rabbi I am and though I disappointed him by not staying at BA and becoming his successor, we metabolized that disappointment and remained profoundly connected from the day I left BA to the day he died. Less than an hour before Bernie died I was holding his hand. We had had an amazing conversation a few hours earlier about the good life he led, his love for his remarkable life affirming Harriet, his accomplishments, and the wild and productive times we shared decades earlier. Privileged to be holding his hand in the awesome moments between life and the next world, I suddenly remembered how Bernie had the firmest handshake of anyone I ever met. With trembling and playfulness I whispered to him, "Bernie you always had the strongest handshake if you hear me squeeze my fingers. I want you to know how much I love you and I hope you were proud of me." His eyes were closed. He squeezed my fingers four times so hard I yelled ouch and I laughed. He died just a few minutes later.

A Word of Appreciation

By Rabbi Carnie Shalom Rose

Shalom!

I begin with, most appropriately, the fulfillment of the oft-underappreciated and thus oft-overlooked Mitzvah, *hakarat haTov*, the recognition of the multitude of blessings bestowed upon us in our lifetimes. Among those blessings, for me, was my association with and deep debt to Rabbi Bernard Lipnick (sorry folks, no matter how often and how hard he tried to get me to do so, I could never bring myself to call him Bernie). Rabbi Lipnick, as Rabbi Emeritus of our congregation, was so self-aware and so committed to *tzimtzum*, conscious self-restraint for the sake of making space for others to shine, that he always deferred to me and not once in our five years of daily contact did we ever share a cross word. Rabbi was not only the consummate rabbinic professional; he was also a *Mentsch* of the highest order. I loved him dearly and miss his steady guidance, his reassuring voice (and what a beautiful voice it was!), and his wise insights. I—like all who knew him—was enriched by his presence.

The first teaching Rabbi Lipnick ever shared with me, when I became Senior Rabbi, back in 2005, was drawn from the words of his teacher—and ours—Rabbi Abraham Joshua Heschel:

"Song is the most intimate expression of man. In no other way does man reveal himself so completely as in the way he sings. For the voice of a person, particularly when in song, is the soul in its full nakedness. When we sing, we utter and confess all our thoughts. In every sense, religious singing is Hishtapkhut Hanefesh *(outpouring of the heart)."*

The great symphony of the life of Rabbi Bernard Lipnick was most assuredly a transcendent and sacred song that we all still need to hear. I hope we will all listen, hear and assimilate into our own lives the song of Rabbi's life, captured through his stirring words contained in this volume.

May the memory of our beloved teacher—a man who gave so selflessly and so freely from the depths of his being—ever be a source of comfort, consolation, and inspiration. *Yehi Zichro Baruch*! And in remembering him, may we continue to be blessed by him, just as we were during the many years of his earthly sojourn and holy service.

Rabbi Carnie Shalom Rose
The Rabbi Bernard Lipnick Senior Rabbinic Chair
Congregation B'nai Amoona

Introduction

By Lester H. Goldman

As a young man in 1949, while a rabbinic student at the Jewish Theological Seminary, Bernie Lipnick resolved to help build the new state of Israel...with his own hands. And so he left his studies and traveled to *Eretz Yisroel*. As a mature man in the early 1990s, in retirement, he resolved to build a home for himself and his dear wife, Harriet, on a mountain in Idyllwild, California...with his own hands. And so he did. During the 40 and more years in between Israel and Idyllwild, as a rabbi and a teacher, he resolved to build a congregation of committed Jews and to reimagine Jewish education. And so he accomplished it...with all his strength and all his heart. This is the legacy of Rabbi Bernard Lipnick *z"l*.

The Formative Years

Bernie, as his family and friends called him, was born in Baltimore, Maryland, on April 29, 1926, to Thomas and Augusta "Gussie" Lipnick. His mother, Gussie, came to this country when she was about nine, having fled the infamous Kishinev pogroms. Every Passover, she would tell how she and her siblings hid, trembling, under the bed as her father stood at the door with an iron bar ready to defend the family from the marauding hooligans. Bernie's father, Thomas, was born in America. His family was learned and devoted to Judaism. His father's father had migrated from Lithuania and eventually was one of the founders of a Baltimore Synagogue. Bernie had a brother, Jerome, who was eight years older and a strong role model. The family was affected adversely by the depression. Thomas lost his furniture business and found employment selling insurance for Metropolitan Life. While they never lacked for necessities, money was scarce. Bernie used to ask to see his father's paycheck each week; rejoicing when it was substantial and grieving when it was meager. The male family members went to *shul* regularly. Theirs was a kosher, observant home. He remembers a happy childhood.

Baltimore, at the time, had a very large Jewish population. One of the leaders of the Jewish community was Dr. Louis L. Kaplan who was the executive director of the Baltimore Board of Jewish Education and president of the Baltimore Hebrew University. In later years he was on the Board of Regents of the University of Maryland and served as acting Chancellor of the Baltimore branch of the University of Maryland. Dr. Kaplan was a profound influence on the young Bernie Lipnick who spent many Shabbat afternoons at Dr. Kaplan's home.

Bernie was an excellent student in secular and Judaic studies. He finished 2nd in his high school graduating class of over 1000 students. Characteristically, he took on a daunting schedule in his teenage years. He recalled leaving home in the early morning with his lunch and his dinner because after high school was over he would teach (beginning as a 16-year-old) at the afternoon Hebrew school and then would take classes at the Baltimore Hebrew University. He would not get home until after 10 p.m. when he did his high school homework before being able to go to bed for just a few hours of sleep. He also found time to take singing lessons and conduct a choir. This experience convinced him that he could accomplish anything that he wanted by working harder and putting his every being into the task. A lesson that he carried with him throughout his life.

His high school years were the war years. He graduated in January 1944, and started Johns Hopkins University with the plan to enter the Jewish Theological Seminary (JTS) after college, as his brother, Jerome, had done. He was granted a theology deferment from the draft but early into the first semester, all theology deferments were canceled so, rather than wait to be drafted, he left Johns Hopkins and enlisted in the Navy. Before starting his enlistment the government, under pressure from the Protestant community, reinstated the theological deferments, but he had already enlisted and had left school. At this point his mentor, Dr. Kaplan, took charge. They appealed to the draft board for him to be released from his enlistment. The draft board agreed on the condition that he was back in school. When they left the draft board it was already Friday evening and Shabbat had begun. It was the first time that he recalls ever driving on Shabbat. Monday morning Dr. Kaplan and Bernie visited each of his professors seeking permission for him to return to class. By now the semester was more than half over and he had lost many weeks of classes. The professors cautioned that he would likely fail his courses but they let him back into class. Bernie took on the challenge and worked day and night to catch up. He recalls that that semester he got his best grades of all. He had many great teachers but most noteworthy was William Foxwell Albright, the foremost archeologist of his generation. Bernie was the only undergraduate admitted to Dr. Foxwell's courses. He finished Johns Hopkins in three years, with a major in Semitic Studies, and started JTS in 1947.

When Bernie entered JTS, its faculty consisted of some of the most renowned Jewish scholars of any age. There was Abraham Joshua Heschel, Mordecai Kaplan, Alexander Marx, Saul Lieberman, Louis Finkelstein and others. All with whom he studied. But by the end of his first year he was ready to quit. Rabbinics was not for him. What he had always wanted was to be an educator like his mentor Dr. Kaplan. At the same time, he so admired his brother Jerome, who had gone into the rabbinate, that he was torn between these two vocations. He reluctantly started his second year at JTS. It was a momentous year. Israel was becoming a state. For the first time in 2000 years there would be a real homeland for Jews. But Israel had to fight the surrounding Arab nations for its survival. Bernie tried to organize some of his fellow JTS students to go to Israel and join in the battle for its existence but the school administration vetoed the idea. This was the last straw. He told Chancellor Finkelstein that he was quitting. The Chancellor made him an offer; finish the second year and go to Israel for your third year and study at Hebrew University and then return for your fourth year, take the comprehensive exams and be ordained. This was an extraordinary proposal. Not only did it usually take five and sometimes six years of study for ordination, a year of study in Israel was rarely if ever part of the curriculum at that time. Bernie accepted and spent the academic year 1949-50 in Israel.

His year in Israel was remarkable and profoundly influenced the rest of his life. The first sermon in this book recounts his encounter with the very raw and very new State of Israel, its people and it's mystic.

In 1951 Bernie was ordained and from then on was known as Rabbi Lipnick.

The Years of Achievements and Challenges

Having been ordained but not interested in finding a pulpit, Rabbi Lipnick sought enlistment in the Navy as a chaplain. The Korean War was then in progress. He said that he always felt guilty that he had not fought in World War II. His best friend had died in the battle for Guadalcanal. It is likely that the Navy appealed to him, in part, because he had grown up in Baltimore, a major seaport where many of the Liberty Ships, that helped win the war, were built. Unfortunately, though he tried several times to enlist, his blood pressure was too high for him to pass the physical. Later, in retirement he realized his dream, many times over, of sailing on the high seas. [See the sermon titled "Insights Gained in Retirement."]

Since he could not enlist and since he did not want to look for a position as a rabbi, he joined the staff of Camp Ramah in Wisconsin and was appointed head counselor for the 1951 summer session. He had been a counselor at the Ramah camp in the Poconos the year before and was impressed with how effectively Judaism was experienced and imbibed by the teenage campers in an informal camp setting. Always the educator, as head counselor in Wisconsin, he was able to try out new and imaginative ways to teach Hebrew and the rituals and beliefs of Judaism. It was a very happy summer but, as it was drawing to a close, he needed to think about his future. At the time, the Assistant Rabbi of B'nai Amoona, Simcha Kling, was leaving and the congregation was looking for a replacement who would be responsible for its religious school program. Rabbi Lipnick was asked to apply. He had met two girls form B'nai Amoona who were campers at Ramah, Libby Seltzer and Estelle Goldberg, and was highly impressed with their demeanor and knowledge of Judaism. He thought that if B'nai Amoona had such fine young people as students this might well be the place for him.

He traveled to St. Louis and was interviewed by the president of the congregation and Rabbi Halpern. He learned that the religious school program consisted of a four day a week after school Hebrew School and a Sunday school, and its enrollment totaled about 750 students. This was one of the largest religious school programs in the Conservative Movement. During the interview weekend he was taken to a Men's Club ball game. He joined the game and impressed everyone with his youthful vigor and athletic prowess.

He even hit a very long home run. But what clinched the deal was his desire to be the education director and not the assistant rabbi. This fit very well with Rabbi Halpern's desires not to have an assistant rabbi. Rabbi Halpern became the congregation's rabbi in 1917, and by 1951 was a powerful force in the St. Louis Jewish community and a person who felt very comfortable being in sole charge of the spiritual life of his congregation and its members. What he wanted and what he needed was a young man who could relate to the youth and run a very large and complex religious school program and, truth be told, not be a second rabbi. This was a perfect fit for Rabbi Lipnick and B'nai Amoona. So began a relationship that lasted, formally and informally, for 60 years.

In the 1950s the Conservative Movement was growing rapidly and was the largest of the three principle Jewish denominations, and B'nai Amoona was one of the preeminent congregations in the Movement. Immediately Rabbi Lipnick saw that the formal after school and Sunday program was not effective enough to develop committed Jews. In fact, it had the opposite result. It caused resentment. The youngsters wanted to quit as soon as they could. The mindset of the School Board, at the time, assumed that the children would always be affiliated Jews when they grew up and that the main purpose of the religious school was to teach them how to daven in Hebrew and a little pediatric Jewish history and culture. The rest would take care of itself. Rabbi Lipnick saw the futility of this approach and quickly went to work to bring in new ideas. While he could not readily change the after school program, he tried to interest the post bar and bat mitzvah teens into staying connected by bringing to B'nai Amoona the very new youth group program known as United Synagogue Youth (USY) that provided a social and informal educational outlet for high school students. He also worked hard encouraging children to attend Jewish summer camps like Ramah. He established a high school education program and even a College of Jewish Studies led by Dr. David Reiss, a great scholar and educator. In the 1960s, 1970s and 1980s, he never tired of finding new and better ways of educating the youth of the congregation. He started what was then called a nursery school that has developed into an Early Childhood Center. He imagined and created two Jewish day camps, B'nai Amee for younger campers and Ramot Amoona for older campers. He was able to convince the congregation to purchase 33 acres of undeveloped land, in west St. Louis County, that could become a camp site. (It later, in the 1980s, became the site of the congregation's school and sanctuary.) He brought into being a community Jewish day school affiliated with the Solomon Schechter Day School movement, the first non-orthodox day school in St. Louis, an enormous accomplishment. But perhaps the innovation in education that he was most proud of was the "*Vov* Class." [For the details of this innovation see his sermon titled "The *Vov* Class."] He earned his doctorate in education from Washington University with his dissertation on the "*Vov* Class" which later became a book "The Experiment That Worked."

In 1953 Rabbi Lipnick met, fell in love with and married Stephanie Friedman. Stevie, as she was known, was a member of the congregation and the daughter of a prominent and successful businessman in St. Louis. Rabbi Lipnick, always the educator, felt that his bride needed a deeper Jewish education and knowledge of Hebrew, so he told Rabbi Halpern that he was leaving B'nai Amoona for one year and going to live in Israel with Stevie. Rabbi Halpern said that if you leave we will replace you and you will not have a job when you return. This was alright with Rabbi Lipnick, and so they left and spent ten months in Israel where he studied at the Hebrew University and worked for Israel Radio as an announcer broadcasting to the European countries. While in Israel, Harold Tober, the chair of the congregation's School Board, traveled with his wife to Tel Aviv to let Rabbi Lipnick know that they wanted him to return to B'nai Amoona after Israel. They had not replaced him. Rabbi Halpern had managed the school in his absence. So when he and Stevie returned to St. Louis, he resumed his duties as education director of B'nai Amoona.

By 1960 Rabbi Halpern's health was diminishing and Rabbi Lipnick took on more rabbinic duties. He was elevated to Associate Rabbi with the expectation that he would succeed to the senior position at some point in the future. In 1962, after 45 years as rabbi of B'nai Amoona, Rabbi Halpern died suddenly of a heart attack and Rabbi Lipnick became the Rabbi of B'nai Amoona.

The 1960s into the 1970s were a turbulent time. Segregation had ended and neighborhoods and schools were changing. The Civil Rights Movement was gaining momentum. President Kennedy, his brother Robert, and the Rev. Martin Luther King were all assassinated. Protests over the United States' involvement in the Vietnam War were splitting the nation in to hawks and doves. There were urban riots and a rising crime rate associated with illegal drugs. Feminism became a force for equality at work, in the home and in Judaism. The Hippie culture, with its slogans of "Don't Trust Anyone over Thirty" and "Make Love not War," separated the generations and families. The Cuban Missile Crisis and the Cold War caused fear of nuclear annihilation. The plight of the three million Soviet Jews and the "Refuseniks" was becoming desperate. The Six-Day War and the Yom Kippur War deepened the distrust between Israel and the Moslem world. The Watergate scandal shook the nation. The divorce rate, even among Jews, was increasing. Interfaith marriage was becoming acceptable and more common. All of these concerns found their way into the life of B'nai Amoona and into the sermons of Rabbi Lipnick, of which a representative sample are included in this volume.

In the late 1960s Rabbi Lipnick's marriage to Stevie was failing. They had three children, David, Daniel and Jesse. It was a very painful and very stressful time for all of them. His would be the first divorce of a rabbi in St. Louis in modern times. He was always grateful to the congregation for not allowing this personal tragedy to affect his position as rabbi.

In the early 1970s, Rabbi Lipnick and Harriet Sophir began seeing each other. They fell in love and were married in 1973. She had three children from a previous marriage; Jayme, Mark, and Tammy. Harriet was the consummate Rebbitzin and a great partner and helpmate throughout their very happy, loving marriage which lasted 36 years, until Rabbi Lipnick's death.

By the mid-1970s it became apparent that B'nai Amoona was in the wrong location. The building at Washington and Trinity in University City was a landmark, having been designed by Erich Mendelsohn, a world renowned architect. But even by the time it was dedicated in 1950, people were starting to move to the suburbs and driving to *shul* was the norm. Within the next twenty-five years most of the members lived many miles from the synagogue and their children were going to schools far from the congregation. With many women working it became increasingly more difficult to get the children from public school to Hebrew school. With very limited parking, services on Shabbat and especially on the High Holidays created major inconveniences. The congregation, by this time, owned 33 acres of prime real estate on Mason Road, in a perfect location for a new school and sanctuary, but the cost of relocating was very high and there were many who thought that leaving University City would be viewed very negatively as "White Flight." Rabbi Lipnick was ambivalent about moving but understood the practical need to do so for the survival of the congregation. A compromise was worked out. A school would be built on the Mason Road property but the Sanctuary would stay in University City and efforts would be made to acquire land for parking. In 1981, just shy of the congregation's 100th anniversary, the new school building was dedicated.

The compromise did not work out. It became increasingly obvious that the sanctuary needed to be relocated to Mason Road so a capital fundraising campaign was begun and the architectural firm HOK was engaged to design a new sanctuary. Rabbi Lipnick worked very closely with Gyo Obata, one of the world's most outstanding architects, to create a worthy successor to the Mendelsohn sanctuary. In 1986 B'nai Amoona's new sanctuary was dedicated, to rave reviews.

Rabbi Lipnick advised the congregation that he would retire in 1991 when he was 65 years old, having served B'nai Amoona for 40 years. At his retirement weekend enough money had been raised so that the mortgage on the school and sanctuary could be "burned"—which he gleefully did. He had accomplished much for B'nai Amoona and now it was time to devote his energies to making a more private life for Harriet and himself. The congregation gave him and Harriet the gift of a 36-foot motorhome and so they began a new adventure.

The Years of Exploration and Reflection
For the first two years of retirement they lived in their motorhome on the side of a mountain in Idyllwild, California, while Rabbi Lipnick and a helper built their home from the ground up. It was a magnificent home when finished, fit for an active retirement. Shortly before the home was finished, however, Rabbi Lipnick was engaged by the Cunard Steamship Company to be its Jewish Chaplain on a Chanukah cruise to Spain, Morocco, and

the Canary Islands. Finally his dream of sailing on the high seas would be a reality. All in all, Rabbi Lipnick served as the Jewish chaplain for Cunard, Holland America, Crystal, Princess, Royal Caribbean, and Regent. In that capacity he and Harriet took many short cruises for the companies and also completed 6½-around-the-world cruises. In between cruises, he managed to start a new congregation, Beth Shalom, in Bermuda Dunes, California, which continues to thrive to this day. In 2004, he and Harriet returned to St. Louis because he needed expert medical attention for a condition known as bronchiectasis. The care he needed was not available in or around Idyllwild. B'nai Amoona was between rabbis at that time so Rabbi Lipnick filled in as interim Rabbi for one year until the congregation engaged Rabbi Carnie Shalom Rose. Thereafter, Rabbi Lipnick served as Rabbi Emeritus. At age 83 he celebrated his second bar mitzvah with his beloved family at his beloved B'nai Amoona. He and Harriet continued cruising and enjoying life until he passed away on April 20, 2010.

The *Klei Kodesh* Who Served with Rabbi Lipnick

During the years of Rabbi Lipnick's association with B'nai Amoona, he was privileged to share the bimah with five Hazzanim. Hazzan Jacob Gowseiow was from the "old school" of European Cantors who knew all the traditional hazzanut and composed original melodies. He served 40 years with the congregation (1920-1960) and was Emeritus until his passing in 1972. Hazzan Jacob Renzer (1960-1965) and Hazzan Joseph Levine (1966-19680) served for short periods and were succeeded by Hazzan Leon S. Lissek (1969-1998), who had a very beautiful and powerful tenor voice. He led the congregation in the traditional melodies and encouraged newer expressions of the liturgy. He also enjoyed entertaining the community with songs from the musical theater repertoire. Hazzan Sharon Nathanson (2003-present) served with Rabbi Lipnick when he was the Congregation's interim rabbi from July 2004 to June 2005.

Each of Rabbi Lipnick's assistant and associate rabbis went on to serve other congregations or the wider Jewish world with great distinction. Those rabbis and their years at B'nai Amoona are:

Rabbi Arnold Asher *z"l*   1963-67
Rabbi Sheldon Switkin   1967-73

Rabbi Sanford Tucker   1974-76
Rabbi Jeffrey Cohen   1980-82
Rabbi Irwin Kula   1982-87
Rabbi Neil Sandler   1988-89

Rabbi Lipnick was fortunate to share the bimah and pulpit with Rabbi Jack Riemer, who was B'nai Amoona's Scholar in Residence for two years (1978-1980). Rabbi Riemer brought his insightful understanding of the Jewish faith and lived experience to the congregation through brilliant sermons and interactive discussions. Rabbi Riemer and his wife, Sue, have been very close friends of the Lipnick's for many years.

Rabbi Irwin Kula, one of the assistant and later an associate rabbi of B'nai Amoona, served at a particularly creative time when its day camps and other informal educational initiatives were being developed. He also was part of the leadership team that guided the congregation as it transitioned from University City to Mason Road. He left B'nai Amoona to join the National Jewish Center for Learning and Leadership and is currently serving as its president. He has also been recognized by *Newsweek* as one of the country's 50 most influential rabbis.

A protégé of Rabbi Lipnick's, though not a rabbi or rabbinic student, was Ron Wolfson, who served the congregation as an educator from 1967 to 1974. Dr. Wolfson earned his Ph.D. at Washington University and wrote his dissertation based on his experiences at B'nai Amoona as the lead teacher during the "*Vov* Class" era. He and his wife, Susie, led the first B'nai Amoona group to live like Israeli teenagers in *moshav Nir Galim* during the summer of 1972. He is currently the Fingerhut Professor of Education at American Jewish University in Los Angeles, president of the Kripke Institute, and the author of fourteen books on Jewish education, Judaism's lessons for living a meaningful life, and how the Jewish community can reimagine itself for the 21st century.

Rabbi Lipnick returned to B'nai Amoona in 2004-5 as interim rabbi while the congregation searched for a senior rabbi. The congregation chose Carnie Shalom Rose. Rabbi Lipnick, as emeritus rabbi of B'nai Amoona, had the pleasure of mentoring and assisting Rabbi Rose whenever called upon. They enjoined cordial and respectful collaboration during the remaining years of Rabbi Lipnick's life.

A Word About the Sermons

The 28 sermons in this book were selected by Rabbi Lipnick from hundreds of sermons he delivered over his career. Those who were privileged to hear the sermons were as captivated by the delivery as by the messages. Rabbi Lipnick was gifted with a sonorous baritone voice which he coupled with a dramatic presentation that would make even his reading the telephone book spellbinding. In truth, what he has given us are much more than sermons; they are stories, essays, lessons, entertainments, and inspirations that can guide us toward living a better life, being a better Jew, and being a better person.

Photo Gallery

Rabbi Bernard Lipnick

Lipnick Family

Thomas (father), Jerome (brother), Bernard,
Augusta "Gussie" (mother) (1936)

Daniel, David, Dad (Bernie), & Jesse (1970)

Bernie at about 10-years-old

Lipnick Family

Wedding to Harriet Sophir (December 18, 1973)

Children and spouses with Harriet (center): Jayme, Tammy, Mark, Jesse, Corinne, Mark, Alan (2014)

Israel

Radio announcer for Israel radio (1949)

On the same tank in Israel
(1949 & 2003)

Rabbi Lipnick and Harriet in an Israeli tank
or armored vehicle

Civilian volunteer for IDF Sar-El program (2007)

Praying at the Kotel (2008)

Educator

Boy Scout leader and educator (1954)

Teaching a group of young people about blowing the shofar at the Kotel (1976)

Receiving his Ph.D. in education from Washington University (1972)

Cruise Ship Chaplin. He provided Judaic programs on 6 ½ World Cruises and numerous shorter cruises in his "retirement"

Dr. Ron Wolfson and Rabbi Lipnick (1986). Rabbi Lipnick mentored Dr. Wolfson when he was a student at Washington University (1967-74)

Civil Rights: USA and USSR

Clergy leaving for Selma Alabama to march with Dr. King. Rabbi Lipnick is second from the head of the group on the plane stairs (see arrow). Sister Ebo is the first Nun in the line (March, 1965)

Sister Ebo and Rabbi Lipnick receiving Civil Rights awards in 2006 from *Jews United for Justice*. He was assigned to protect her in case of violence when they marched in Selma Alabama as part of a Civil Rights protest in 1965

In the USSR, attempting to contact Jewish "Refuseniks" who were being denied their civil rights because they wanted to practice Judaism and move to Israel (1984)

Harriet Lipnick showing a "refusenik" *Tzitzit* for a *Tallit*, smuggled into the USSR in a ball of yarn (1984)

Rabbi of B'nai Amoona

Studying

Writing

Chanting Torah

At the installation of Rabbi Lipnick as senior rabbi of Congregation B'nai Amoona (1963).
Thomas Lipnick (his father), Rabbi Jerome Lipnick (his brother), Rabbi Louis Finkelstein
(Chancellor of the Jewish Theological Seminary), and Rabbi Lipnick

Rabbi of B'nai Amoona

B'nai Amoona in University City where he began in 1951 as Education Director
under Rabbi Halpern and was installed as senior Rabbi in 1963

Moving the Torahs from the synagogue in University City to the new synagogue on Mason Road.
(November 25, 1985). Ed Balk, Harold Guller, Frank Raisher, Rabbi Lipnick, and Harriet Lipnick

The Mason Road. synagogue sanctuary he inspired and designed with Gyo Obata of HOK

Idyllwild, California

Building their home with his own hands

They lived in the motor home for 18 months while their home was being built

Front view

Idyllwild, California

Finished home (1992),
side & back view

Rabbi Lipnick's study with
a stained glass window
from the Synagogue built in
1919; the first of the three
synagogues built by the
congregation

Dining Room with the needle
point Chagall Windows, a
gift from some women of the
congregation, for his office in the
new synagogue on Mason Road

At Leisure

Counselor at Camp Ramah (1951)

Camping out (1972)

Backpacking through 11 countries in Europe in 30 days (1975)

Parasailing above the Red Sea by Eilat, Israel, facing Jordan (1994)

At Leisure

On the beach in Puerto Rico (1978)

Fishing in the Pacific Ocean (1974)

Sailing on Hudson Bay, N.Y. (1997)

His favorite island: Raiatea, in the
French Polynesia (2008)

On the road in their 36-foot
motor home, a retirement gift
from the congregation (1991)

Merntors and Colleagues

Rabbi Abraham E. Halpren
Rabbi of Congregation
B'nai Amoona 1917-1962
Mentor and Colleague

Dr. Louis Kaplan, President of
the Baltimore Hebrew University
and Chancellor of the University
of Maryland, Baltimore, at the
installation of Rabbi Lipnick
Mentor

Rabbi Jerome Lipnick
Mentor and older brother

Rabbi Louis Finkelstein, Chancellor
Jewish Theological Seminary
Mentor

Dr. Ron Wolfson, Fingerhut Professor of
Education, American Jewish University
Protégé and Colleague

Merntors and Colleagues

Rabbi Jack Riemer
Colleague

Rabbi Irwin Kula, President
of the National Jewish Center for
Learning and Leadership
Protégé and Colleague

Hazzan Leon Lissek,
Hazzan Emeritus,
Congregation B'nai Amoona
Colleague

Rabbi Carnie Shalom Rose,
Rabbi Bernard Lipnick,
Senior Rabbinic Chair,
Congregation B'nai Amoona
Colleague

Cantor Sharon Nathanson,
Congregation B'nai Amoona
Colleague

Starting Out and Summing Up

The two sermons in this section are like bookends to a life well lived.

In the first one, given in 2009, a year before his passing, Rabbi Lipnick tells the story of his vital and energetic young manhood. He was a student at the Jewish Theological Seminary in 1948 when the State of Israel became a reality after over 2000 years of longing by the Jewish people. He tells of his yearning to go immediately to the new State and help build it "with his own hands". He tells how he arranged to leave his studies and how he spent a life-changing year in *Eretz, Yisrael*.

The second sermon, given in 2001, ten years after he retired, reveals the perspective of the mature man who has lived a full life of rewards and challenges, of many joys and some sorrows. He offers us a philosophy of life that is both enduring and inspiring.

The Joyful Digging of Ditches

I am especially grateful to Rabbi Rose for the invitation to speak to the congregation today on this theme because, as is known by anyone who knows me, Israel is and always has been very close to my heart. I was tempted to use this occasion to try to dissect some of the numerous problems facing Israel today—problems which are at the forefront of my concern and probably yours as well. But as I thought more deeply, it occurred to me that if I have anything special to offer, if I am to make a contribution to our understanding and appreciation of Israel, the best that I can do is share some of my personal experiences with you. Experiences from the early days of the state; during a time when life was somewhat simpler than it is today and when the miracle that is Israel was, perhaps, more clearly in focus.

Actually, this decision to share my personal story was suggested to me by my good friend Herb Bilinsky, our congregational treasurer, who, when he heard some of what I want to share with you, said that this is what I ought to do. Tell my story, he advised. Which hopefully will have the effect of reminding us of the importance of what is surely the most significant event in all of Jewish history during the past two thousand years: The creation of the independent, sovereign state of Israel.

Israel became a state on May 15, 1948. At that time, I was a student living in New York, just finishing up my first year at the Jewish Theological Seminary of America. In the buildup to May 15th, it was evident that the Arab world was not going to take kindly to the declaration of Israel's independence; that the Arab world would do everything in its power to thwart the state, even as it was coming into existence. Indeed that proved to be the case. Seven Arab armies invaded the young state in an effort to kill off the 600,000 Jews who lived there and destroy the state before it could take its first breath. As a staunch supporter of the state, I felt that I, and the rest of the Seminary student body, should lend a hand in the war effort by providing either a fighting contingent or a support group which would journey to Israel and participate in what was obviously Israel's war of survival. I broached the idea of forming such a group to the then-President of the Seminary, Rabbi Louis Finkelstein, and he declared the idea to be a bad idea; that it was my job, and the job of the rest of the Seminary student body, to study Torah—even or especially during this critical period. Needless to say, as a lowly freshman, and without any kind of a military background, I accepted his judgment which, in the wisdom of hindsight, may have been correct. I desisted from carrying the idea forward. Well, as we all know, Israel won the war without my help and succeeded in establishing itself as an independent state.

Yet, I will admit that the experience of being turned down caused me, perhaps unjustifiably, to be resentful... to the point where, after my first year and around the beginning of my second, I began to have thoughts of chucking my whole rabbinic education and leaving the Seminary. Ultimately, I did return for the second year. But, eventually, about midway through, I resolved that I had had enough and that I would withdraw. It was at that point that some very kind people in the Seminary administration took a personal interest in my situation and urged me not to act hastily. They proposed what turned out to be an extremely generous offer, an almost unbelievable offer, as I think back to it now. If I would agree, they said, to finish out this, my second year, I would be allowed to spend my third year in the state of Israel. Assuming that I would complete certain study assignments that they would give me, I would receive a full year's credit and be allowed to return for my fourth and final year, half of which would be consumed with studying for comprehensives, which was the practice in those days. An offer that I couldn't refuse and which I eventually accepted. So, I successfully completed the second year and began to prepare to leave for a year in Israel.

It was July of 1949, just one year after the founding of the state. I gathered all of my resources, financial and otherwise, and secured a ticket to Haifa aboard a ship called the *Gierison*. It was a former Liberty Ship which was being given to Turkey and which somebody had the bright idea to outfit with dormitory bunks and schedule a stop in Haifa. Passage on that ship, from New York to Israel, cost me all of $150. Also, it was well known at that time that there was very little to eat in Israel. So I bought a case of canned tuna fish to take along, and a case of George Washington Instant Coffee. I also acquired an eight-inch Bowie knife, a pair of combat boots, a backpack, and enough cash for a return ticket to America if things would not work out. As to spending money, I possessed a grand total of $85 which I hoped would carry me through the year. I was prepared to go to Israel, at this rather late date from my point of view, resolved that I would spend the year making whatever small contribution that I could to the welfare of the young state.

My parents, who lived in Baltimore, Maryland, some 200 miles south of New York, decided to come and to see me off. My mother, in particular, loved to come to New York. One, to visit me; and also because she enjoyed visiting a favorite cousin there by the name of Morris Bublitsky, whom she invited to dockside to see me off. We gathered at the dock that morning. I loaded my stuff aboard the ship and I said a somewhat emotional goodbye. But, as I was going up the ship's gangway, Morris Bublitsky grabbed me by the arm and said, "You know, Bernie, I have a brother living in Haifa. I will write him an airmail letter," (a big thing in those days), "and tell him that you are coming." I thanked Morris, and promptly forgot what he had said.

Thus it was that I and several hundred other people began slowly, very slowly, to make our way across the Atlantic Ocean in an old tub of a ship to the new state of Israel. Most of the passengers aboard the ship were Jews, but not all. A fair number were Christians to whom the founding of the Jewish state represented the fulfillment of their own theological commitment. One group, for example, had manned the Exodus '47, two years earlier, and were now returning to cast their lot with our people in the Promised Land.

As for the Jews, most were Holocaust survivors who had escaped with their lives and little else. They had ended up either in the Americas, North and South or, in some cases, the Far East, and were now edging their way back to the new Jewish state.

Many were seeking family members—parents, children, and spouses; other relatives—from whom they had been separated during and after the war, and with whom they now hoped to be reunited. If you can imagine, emotions ran very high during the journey. This was no ordinary tourist group and certainly not a pleasure party. Most of these people had suffered unimaginable horrors and were now embarking on what they prayed would be a whole new start in life. . . especially if they could do it in the company of long-lost family and friends.

Those of us with some camping and youth group background soon swung into action. We organized anyone who was amenable into an Israel-bound "learning community." Soon we had daily classes going in all sorts of subjects with Jewish content—classes in dance, in music, discussion groups on Israel politics and culture. I taught a course in beginner's Hebrew—subsisting, because I kept kosher, on *ekmek* (the Turkish word for bread) and *su* (the word for water), with an occasional can of the tuna fish thrown in. Sufficient to keep me going, but not much more. The ship slowly plied its way across the Atlantic towards Gibraltar and the Mediterranean. The voyage was supposed to take two weeks. But one of the three engines quit in mid-Atlantic so that overall the trip took 20 days. There was one stop in Algiers where the whole Jewish community, including the venerable Rabbi, came out to greet us and to wish us well. They brought us presents and sweets because they had heard that we were on our way to a new/old place called Israel. We slept during that voyage not at all. Nights were spent forward on the ship's bow under the stars, talking and singing and napping, as the prow of the *Gierison* cut through the water, bringing us closer and closer to the land of Israel.

And then the day scheduled for arrival came. Not a wink of sleep that night for anyone. As dawn began to break, everyone gathered forward for that first glimpse of land. First, in the far distance, you see clouds, and as the ship gets closer and closer, you make out what you think is land fall. Gradually, ever so gradually, you approach the shore line. I shall never forget when the Israeli pilot came aboard, just outside of Haifa. He climbed up the ship's ladder and bounced onto the deck. We had, of course, prepared a welcome, in Hebrew no less. I remember vividly how he was wearing a nautical hat decorated with gold braid on the bill, and a *Mogen David*, also out of gold braid. Our first contact with a real live Israeli! And then the ship hove to and swung around the break water of Haifa, as it slowly sidled sideways, towards the dock. At this point, every single person aboard the ship was lined up on the deck along the side rail. Squinting and straining to make out the faces of the people who were gathered on the dock five or ten feet below. Hoping to recognize a father or a mother, a sibling, or a spouse, and in the process being overcome as they cried and screamed, fainted and swooned, I remember that the scene became so intense that I had to leave. I went down below to get away from what was quickly becoming a virtual maelstrom of emotion. And as I sat on my bunk, an even scarier realization suddenly hit me. These people, most of them, were looking for loved ones. But I was arriving in a strange country, half way around the world, knowing not a soul, having no idea where I would go or where I would lay my head that first night. With a bankroll of only $85, I felt alone and, if you will forgive me, more than a little sorry for myself.

Soon I heard someone calling down the stairwell, "Lipnick, Lipnick, come up here." I climbed the stairs and some of my friends made a path through the crowd and pushed me up to the railing. There, not 20 feet from where I was standing, at about eye level, I saw a man sitting on a pile of sacks, and he was saying in Hebrew, "I am looking for Lipnick." So I answered sheepishly, "I am Lipnick." And the first words out of his mouth were, "Where have you been all of this time? I have been sitting here five days and nights waiting for you. Where were you? I am Dudek Bublitzky." Then, I muttered something about the ship breaking down, and he said in one of his favorite expressions, "Never mind. Where is your stuff?" The next thing I know, a big ten-ton truck backed up against the ship, opened its back doors and received my trunk and duffle bag and cases of food. It so happens that Dudek was a truck driver, a person who owned his own truck, which put him at the top of the social and economic heap in those days and also gave him access to the Haifa docks. Thus it is that for a guy who didn't have anyone to meet him and who didn't know a single soul, I ended up being the first person off the ship. Sitting like a king in the front cab of a big truck on my way to a section of Haifa known as Hodar, where Dudek lived.

We arrived at his apartment, and then I shall never forget what happened. After depositing my stuff in his place, Dudek handed me a key to the apartment and said, in Hebrew, "This is your place for as long as you want it. I will be back at eight o'clock to pick you up for dinner."

Let me tell you a little bit about Dudek. He was born in Russia, in Kishinev, where my mother and her family were from. He had come to Israel about ten years before, from Russia, by bicycle! Yes, that was his mode of transportation—all the way from Russia to Israel! He worked hard, acquired a truck, and made his living ferrying people and material from the docks in Haifa, mostly new immigrants and their possessions, to the tent cities which had been erected for them. Many of them, pitiful remnants of the Holocaust who were coming to a place they had never before seen—but which was the only place in this wide, wide world that wanted them and welcomed them. I know because later I worked on Dudek's truck, especially during Operation Magic Carpet, when the young state brought in the Jews of Yemen, primitive and uneducated people for whom the doors of Israel were thrown wide open.

The first blessing then that Israel represents, that I want to derive from my own personal experience and should never be forgotten, is that Israel, for the past 61 years, remains the one place in this wide planet where a Jew is welcomed home as a member of the tribe, who is entitled to life and liberty and protection. Without excuses and without apologies—the one place in this vast earth where a Jew is accepted, not by sufferance, but by right. I witnessed it in 1949, and it remains true to this day.

Now, it soon became obvious to me since my "bankroll" was not going to last all that long, that I would have to find gainful employment. Yet in those days, I should point out, that if you were able-bodied and willing to work, which I was, one could always exchange a day's labor for a bed and three-square in a *kibbutz,* which I did on more than one occasion.

The first job I got was as a correspondent for the Jewish Agency, attached to the Israel Defense Forces, or more precisely what was a fighting force of young men and women who spend part of their time in agricultural or building projects in addition to their military training.

My first assignment was to join a contingent which traveled to and was stationed in Eilat on the Red Sea, which, at the Rhodes Armistice Agreement just a couple of months before, had been awarded to Israel. Our job was to fortify the place. It consisted of only three mud huts and not a single blade of grass or anything else that grew from the ground. The one thing that Eilat represented in those days was "potential." It was to become Israel's outlet to the Indian Ocean by way of the Gulf of Eilat or Aqaba. So we arrived at Eilat, known by its Arabic name of *Umm Rashr Rash.* We set up our tents and proceeded to dig trenches, as well we should have, because the British, who were still ensconced in Aqaba, just across the bay, maintained there a gunboat which would shell the hills behind us each morning. Not to kill us, God forbid, but to remind us on a daily basis of who was still in charge.

Eilat was tough duty because it was unbelievably hot. We lived in tents; we had no refrigeration and precious little water, all of our water being purified from sea water. Everyone was soon plagued by dysentery.

But I shall never forget that when I left Eilat, on my way back to Tel Aviv, I traveled by command car through the desert. There were no roads in those days, only camel paths. The trip took 19 hours to traverse about 100 miles. I remember arriving at civilization around evening time, hungry and caked with the dust of the desert... but mostly hungry. I picked out a house, knocked on the front door and invited myself to dinner. And the lady of the house—I tear up as I recall what happened—seeing that I had just come from the army through the wilderness, the lady of the house gave me an egg to eat for dinner. Surely her only egg, and how precious that egg was. Yet, she gave it to me, a perfect stranger. I remember spending that night sleeping on the beach in Tel Aviv.

This experience then leads me to a second conclusion regarding what I consider to be the greatness of Israel. Not only does Israel represent the one place a Jew can go to and be admitted without question, but it is also the one place where Jews, after they arrive, are cared for and shared with, indeed as members of one family. In our day, this kind of warmth is extended mostly to Jews but not only to Jews. It is extended to non-Jews as well. Numerous Sudanese, Thais, and Vietnamese and others, are recipients of Israel's largesse and willingness to care for people who are in need.

With the first third of my year behind me, I decided to seek other employment. I applied for and got a job as a common laborer in a work crew which was building a naval station outside of Haifa in a place called *Bat Galim*. They offered me a job to teach the young cadets; but I preferred this kind of work since it spoke to my fantasy of building the state with my own two hands from the ground up. And indeed, we did build it from the ground up. We did all sorts of work—building fences, laying concrete sidewalks, construction and numerous other projects, including cleaning out sewers!

Therein lies a story. Our crew was under the jurisdiction of a Chief Petty Officer whose name was Ovadiah. He was a Yemenite Jew, strong as an ox and a bit of a slave driver. I remember once being lowered into a sewer, actually a catchment tower of the sewer, and being given the job of cleaning the walls of the tower. Another man would lower a bucket into the sewer and I would fill it with the crud that I scraped off the wall. It was very unpleasant, foul-smelling work, to say the least. But one thing that that tower had was great acoustics—something like a shower at home. So while I was working, in order to ease the burden a bit, I began to sing. In those days I had a pretty good voice, and singing gave me some comfort. Soon, I looked up and I saw a pair of feet dangling from the manhole, and soon another set of legs and feet, until my fellow workers ringed the whole manhole listening to my singing. So I stopped singing. But what I didn't know is that two of the feet belonged to Ovadiah, who ordered me to keep singing. When I had exhausted my repertoire, Ovadiah ordered a stool lowered into the sewer and then he said, "*Baruch*, as long as you sing, you don't have to work. But the moment you stop singing you are going back to work." So, for the next two or three days, I arrived at work, was lowered into the sewer, sat on my stool, and spent the whole time singing, not working.

There are many more stories to tell, but suffice it to say, the naval base was built and continues to operate to this day as the home base for Israel's small but powerful Navy.

So once again, not only is Israel a home to all Jews who wish to come there; not only is Israel a place, where, because you are a brother or a sister, you are cared for; but it is also a place of great achievement. A place that is rising out of the desert—from naval bases to homes and cultural centers. A place that is becoming a great, great center of cultural and academic excellence. A place where Nobel prizes are awarded to authors and scientists; where innovation and creativity are applied to all sorts of problems; a place, in other words, where the Jewish genius flowers, as nowhere else in the world—another of the core values of that precious little place and another part of the greatness of Israel.

That winter, we couldn't work all that regularly because there was an unusual amount of rainfall, and in the hills, snow. Of course, I utilized the time to work on my study assignments which I took very seriously—my studies in Talmud, Bible and, of course, Hebrew. But it was during the same bad weather that I decided to visit a friend of mine and his wife whom I had heard had just arrived in Jerusalem. I took the bus to Jerusalem and waded through the storm to their one-room shanty. After dinner my host said, "You know who is here in Jerusalem? Howie Singer," a friend of ours who had just been ordained at the Seminary and whom I knew and liked very much. So, we slushed through the streets of Jerusalem and arrived at Howie's place. We knocked on the door and Howie answered it. I said, "Hello Howie," and I shall never forget what happened next. He did not acknowledge the greeting. He just stared at me and said, "Would you please say that again?" I obliged and then we entered the house. It turns out that Howie was the chief script writer for the new shortwave radio station that Israel had created in order to beam news of the new state to Jewish communities throughout the world. At that time there were three different language divisions. Yiddish, which would beam to Eastern Europe; Arabic beamed to Jews in Arab lands; and an English language section beamed to England and South Africa. Today, I believe, they broadcast in 21 different languages! It seems that the English Language Division was trying to find an announcer for the broadcasts which were scheduled to start in the spring. When I said "Hello Howie," he figured he had his man. Subsequently, I underwent several auditions and was eventually hired as the chief announcer for the station.

There were a few problems that had to be ironed out. One was my American rather than English accent. You will recall that this was the era of the "ugly American" and there was concern that British and South African communities would be put off by anything other than a British accent. The second problem was that, in those days, as an American citizen, I was not permitted to work for a foreign government under threat of losing my American citizenship. So I adopted the radio name of Bernard Jerome, mine and my brother's name, and kept my identity to myself.

With one of the problems ignored and the other solved, I embarked upon really one of the most exciting adventures of my life: Broadcasting live to far-flung Jewish communities thousands of miles away, who couldn't believe that there was a new country in the world called Israel, which had arisen like the Phoenix from the ashes of the Holocaust. I broadcast six days a week, at midnight, for 45 minutes—because it was three or four hours earlier in the west—in kind of a "variety show" consisting of music, interviews, speeches, skits, political commentary, and the like.

We even had a famous scholar teach Talmud on a regular basis. His name was Rav Assaf, and what a sight it was. I would be in the announcer's booth, and he in the studio, in the middle of the night with his Talmud propped up against the microphone teaching, with the aid of his "*gruben* finger," an unseen but attentive audience. My folks in Baltimore and my brother in Utica bought shortwave radio sets on a daily basis.

The job also gave me quite an opportunity to devote to my studies. I attended classes at the Hebrew University, taught by Martin Buber and Ernst Simon, among others, and made considerable headway on my assignments.

But the fan mail that we received from faraway places—little hamlets far off the beaten track—was not to be believed. The dominant theme was disbelief. How could it be? Is it possibly true that there was now an independent state called Israel? I'd end every broadcast with the Israel Philharmonic playing the *Hatikvah*, which never failed to bring tears to my eyes and, I presume, to the eyes of everyone listening.

So the fourth and final conclusion that I want to derive from my experience during that year in Israel, and which I feel is as relevant today as it was then, is the pride and the *nachas* that every Jew in the world, no matter where he lives, can take in the knowledge that after 2,000 years of statelessness and after the slaughter of a third of our people, we have accomplished something that no other people has ever accomplished—and that is the return to our homeland; the resurrection of our ancient language; and the reconstitution of ourselves as a free and independent state.

Well, I returned home to America in June of 1950 with $80 left of the original $85. I graduated the Seminary a year later, and came to B'nai Amoona shortly thereafter. I have been back to Israel perhaps 50 times in the last 60 years, but at least four of the principles and the greatness that Israel represents can be derived from that first experience, and continue to be in effect.

Those principles are perhaps somewhat more complicated today than they were then, but they are still operative, I believe, in our day and for the foreseeable future. Namely, that, One—Israel is the one place in the world where a Jew is welcome to come as to his own home. Two—Israel is the one place in the world where there exists a solemn obligation to care for and nurture people, especially Jews, who are in need. Three—Israel is the one place in the world where we see a state rising from the desert, where we see the flowering of Jewish cultural activity and Jewish genius to help realize our mission of establishing the kingdom of God on earth. And finally—Israel is the one place in the world which, despite its numerous problems, internal and external, will always be a source of wonder and pride to our people wherever they may be, and a rallying point for the Jewish heart and the Jewish soul. Long may Israel prosper and may God protect and defend her always.

Amen.

Now may I ask you to rise and join me in closing this "broadcast" by singing with me *Hatikvah*, Israel's National Anthem, the words of which are on the sheet in your Rosh Hashanah packet.

What I Learned in Retirement

I want to talk with you this morning about some of what I consider to be the religious insights that I have gained in retirement. Let me acknowledge right off that these insights may not be what one would call "new." But they are new to me. Harriet always tells me that it is the simple things that elude me. Perhaps what I have to say then is in that category. Perhaps I should have known these things a long time ago. But, for whatever reason, I have had to wait until recently to become fully aware of them. Interestingly, each of what I am calling "insights" derives from an actual experience, or set of experiences, that I have had since retirement. So, let me start, first, with a bit of background. Then I shall describe the experiences and what I have learned from them.

I retired on July 1, 1991, over ten years ago, after having served 40 years—first as Educational Director and then as Rabbi of Congregation B'nai Amoona, in St. Louis. Long before that date, which incidentally fell shortly after my 65th birthday, I had decided that, no matter what, I was going to retire at the end of that synagogue year and that I was going to leave St. Louis, difficult as that was going to be. My motivation for leaving was several-fold. First and foremost, I wanted to get out of the way of my successor. I didn't want to cramp his style, which happens often when a retiring Rabbi remains in the community, especially having served one congregation over a long period of time. Second, I wanted to try something new in my life. I felt that I had given the congregation and the Jewish community my best shot. So, being in passable health, I thought it might be fun to try my hand at some other kind of activity. The third motivation has to do with the fact that a number of important questions—questions about life and its meaning and its purpose, despite a lifelong immersion in Jewish religious study and Jewish communal activity—had not been answered to my satisfaction. I have always been captivated by nature and the outdoors—camping, motor homing, hiking and that sort of thing. I thought, therefore, that if I could retire to a rural, outdoor setting, the natural world might teach me some things about God and life's meaning that I had not been able to achieve until then.

So, when the time came, after a wonderful farewell weekend, Harriet and I took off for Idyllwild, which we had located and decided to move to some three years earlier. (How we found that particular place is a story in itself which I shall leave for another time). Now, one of the gifts that the congregation gave us as a going-away present was a 36-foot motorhome. Harriet drove it to Idyllwild, while I drove the biggest Ryder truck you could rent—filled with our worldly possessions. We had already, by then, decided that we were going to clear a virgin plot of land and that we were going to build us a home, with our own hands—from the ground up—on the plot. And this is what we did over a period of 18 months. Harriet largely designed the house, and another fellow and I built the house, calling in help as we needed it. During that time, we lived in the motorhome, which was parked in a corner of our lot. We had a phone, which was on a tree next to the motorhome, and all the amenities, by which I mean electricity, propane for cooking and heating and a septic tank for waste.

This brings me to the first set of experiences, and the first insight that I think I have achieved—the experience of working 10–12 hours a day with a hammer (or mostly with an automatic hammer called a nail gun) and a saw, and learning the meaning of, the beauty of, and the awe of, craftsmanship—an experience which has become, for me a moral, indeed a religious, value of surpassing importance.

All of my life, you see, I have revered people of the mind—scholars and intellectuals. These were the people who were my heroes, and I had the great privilege of studying with some of the best: William Foxwell Albright, perhaps the world's foremost archeologist, at Johns Hopkins University; Saul Lieberman, the foremost Talmudist of his time, at the JTS of America; Mordecai M. Kaplan and Abraham Joshua Heschel, two of the most influential Jewish philosophers of the 20th century, also at JTS; Gershorn Scholem, Martin Buber, and Ernest Simon, at the Hebrew University.

I have lived my whole life in awe of these people and others like them. But now, after building my own home and rubbing shoulders with all kinds of craftsmen—carpenters, plumbers, electricians, drywallers, insulators, concrete men, and gardeners—I have developed an entirely new perspective. I don't value the people of the mind any less. Rather, I have come to appreciate, to respect, like never before, anyone who does a task, any task, well. Especially people who work with their hands. People who master nature. People who fashion and create objects of use and/or beauty. In a word, craftsmen and craftswomen.

I used to subscribe to the somewhat patronizing distinction that so-called people of the mind would make between laborers, artisans and artists (and I remember uttering it once or twice from the pulpit). The statement, credited to Louis Nizer, (1902–1994) a famous attorney, which says: "Laborers work with their hands. Artisans work with their hands and their heads. Artists work with their hands, their heads and their hearts." Well friends, don't you believe it! Anyone who does a job well, anyone who puts out a quality piece of work—and there are more of these people in every field of endeavor than you can imagine—invests his entire self in that job. Including, obviously, his hands, his head and his heart. But also his eyes, his nose, his ears, his nerve endings and most of all, his *kishkes*—in order to produce, if indeed he does produce, a first-class job. The craftsmen I worked with and learned from had the ability to take a piece of raw material and to fashion from it something which is useful or beautiful, and often both. What a thrill to see a craftsman enter into a symbiotic relationship with his material, interact with it, love it, and agree to mold it and be molded by it. The result of which is an inner peace, a sense of harmony with the work, in which there is no leader and no follower, leading to an outcome which is in no way inferior to that which is produced by the mind professionals.

You know, I never really appreciated before the historical fact that many or most of the early rabbis—that is, the people who fashioned what we call Rabbinic Judaism which is the Judaism that all of us practice today—were laborers or craftsmen first, and then rabbis. Hillel, for example, was a wood cutter; a lumberjack. Shamai was a builder. Rabbi Joshua was a blacksmith. Rabbi Hanina was a shoemaker. Rabbi Huna was a water carrier. Rabbi

Abba was a tailor. While others were carpenters, tent makers, farmers and merchants. Doesn't it strike you as a little strange that in the classical, arguably the most creative period of Jewish history, the rabbinic profile was so vastly different from what it is today?

God forbid that I should criticize rabbis, some of whom are among my best friends. But maybe in the transition from those days to these, not only have we lost the appreciation of how most of the world occupies its time, but we have fashioned a Jewish culture—certainly in the Diaspora, if not in Israel—which is skewed in an overly mind-centered direction. I guess what I am trying to say is that all work, of whatever description, done well, not just those rarified jobs we usually think of when we use the word, deserves to be thought of as a "calling."

There are, you may be interested in knowing, a lot of different names for God in our tradition. God is called "king" and "judge" and "shepherd" and "father" and many other names. But do you know the very first name for God that is found in the Midrash? On page 1, in *Bereshit Rabba*, God is called *Aman*, which means, in Hebrew, craftsman or artisan. Why did the rabbis choose that word, *Aman*, to be the first name, the first attribute of God? Perhaps they wanted to teach us what they, themselves, evidentially knew very well. Namely, to create something, to do it right, to do it well, to do it with your whole self, in whatever field of endeavor, is a task that is worthy of the name "God."

Justice Oliver Wendell Holmes was once asked what he considered the best service that we can do for our country and for ourselves. He replied: "To see as far as one may to feel the great forces that are behind every detail, to hammer out as compact and solid a piece of work as one can, to try to make it first rate… and then to leave it unadvertised." As profound a religious truth as I know.

The second insight that I have gained during my retirement comes from the second set of experiences Harriet and I had. After the house was finished, or nearly finished, I received a call from the Cunard Steamship Company. Would I be interested in serving as the Jewish Chaplain aboard one of their cruise ships? Well, we considered the invitation for about 8 seconds, after which we answered with an enthusiastic "Yes!" The first cruise we took was to Spain, Morocco and the Canary Islands, over Hanukah. We enjoyed it very much. Apparently management was satisfied too, because soon we were invited for a cruise through the Panama Canal and Central America. Evidently, we were invited to join what is considered to be the plum of all cruising opportunities—the 3½-month World Cruise. Which just as the name says, takes you all the way around the world, with visits at some 30 to 35 ports of call.

The following year, we were invited on another around-the-world cruise, and the year after that, another, most of them aboard the flagship of the Holland-America Line, the SS *Rotterdam*. All in all, during a period of about five years, we circled the globe four times. We circled all of South America, with stops in Antarctica and many, many places that we had never heard of before. In sum, after the two years that we spent building the house, during the next five years we spent about a year and a half to two years sailing the world's oceans, visiting all of the continents and having the time of our lives!

Now, the first thing that struck me about this unique opportunity that Harriet and I had—what other poor Rabbi do you know who has been able to take his sweetheart around the world four times?—The first thing that struck me was the vastness of this world of ours. Even more so, the dizzying array of languages, cultures and religions which inhabit it—none of them Jewish! There is such a big, big world out there! It is filled not only with primitive, so-called native cultures, like the aborigines of Australia; it is filled with an almost endless diversity of proud, highly developed, often very sophisticated traditions of music and art and literature and dance and religion—every possible manifestation of high culture. None of which, I repeat, is Jewish! The people, none of whom are Jewish either, lead, for the most part, fulfilling, productive lives with high moral and ethical standards, in most cases; often, if the truth be told, within the context of a profoundly spiritual framework. This planet of ours is a virtual potpourri of non-Jewish cultures and civilizations that can hold their heads high in any forum. Let's face it—working in a synagogue, as I did all of my life, and being tied to the agenda of the Jewish community, one has a tendency to think that we Jews occupy center stage, if not of world culture, then at least of western culture. Well, that isn't true. We are a small fraction of the world population. We exert little influence over much of the world, in most areas of endeavor, including economics and politics. Few people around the world are aware of our distinctive religious culture and of our contributions to thought and science. What is perhaps most sobering, is that much of the world, including some fairly well educated people, have never even heard of us!

I had a kind of a foretaste of this discovery when we moved to Idyllwild. Most of our neighbors and friends are non-Jews. Of course there are Jews in Idyllwild. But they are not immediately evident, even though we have just started a new congregation called Har Shalom. But still, most of the people we come into contact with "on the hill" are non-Jews. And all I can say is that I have found these people to be substantial in every way, solid citizens with high values and serious commitments. Often charitable and generous. So that from the very start, I began to gain what was for me a new perspective on the relative position of Jews in the broader society. Yet, it was really not until the cruises and the dozens of countries that we visited along the way that this new perspective really crystallized. Let me tell you about it by means of an incident that occurred one day aboard ship as we were approaching Amoy on the coast of China.

It was my practice every day at sea to conduct a class, or really a discussion group, which I called "Ask the Rabbi." We dealt with any Jewish subject that was of interest to the 30–40 Jews and non-Jews who came on a regular basis. It was always my custom, a day or two before we would visit a port, to give an orientation to the port with particular emphasis on the Jewish community. I remember once we were approaching Amoy and I gave an introduction to the Jews in China. I started, as always, by quoting the relative population figures from my trusty *World Guide for the Jewish Traveler*. For China overall, it gave the population as 1 billion, 200 million people (I suppose it's more now). Then it gave the Jewish population. . . 5! I kid you not! Though there couldn't be a starker contrast, the figure is probably correct in terms of Jewish citizens of China. The former somewhat native community of Chinese Jews, which existed in Kaifeng at one time, disappeared about a generation ago. So over 1 billion, 200 million Chinese against five Jews is probably accurate. There was a man in the group by the name of Charlie Sigity, a non-Jew, who heard me quote these figures, though it was not until the next day that we heard what he did with them. It seems that soon after our class he had occasion to telephone a business associate of his in New York who happened to be Jewish. Armed with this new knowledge about the relative size of the Jewish community of China, he asked his friend, "Do you have any idea how many Jews there are in China?" The friend replied something to the effect of "*Ves ich fun tzoris*; I have no idea, but I'll say half a dozen, six." After which Charlie put him straight—"Really, five!" But when Charlie reported the conversation to us in class the next day, he ended by saying, "Aha, it's just as I suspected. You Jews are always exaggerating your numbers!"

Actually, Harriet and I were back in China recently, and there are a few more Jews than that in China today and even a few synagogues. But these Jews are not native Chinese. They are businessmen and women who work for large corporations, by and large; or, now, the several hundred Jewish families of Hong Kong who I guess are technically citizens of China. As well, of course, as the ubiquitous Israelis.

But that says it all, does it not? Five against 1 billion, 200 million, in the world's most populace nation! The same applies to most of the other countries in the Far East: Malaysia, Vietnam, Korea, Indonesia, Thailand and even India—no Jews! *Schon ugaret*, the Middle East—virtually no Jews; Egypt, Oman, Yemen, Saudi Arabia and all the rest! In all of Africa, there are hardly any Jews, including South Africa, which has been emptied out of about half of its Jews in the last ten years. The Jews of South America are very weak, with the possible exception of Argentina. As to Europe, believe me, Hitler did his work well. There are few viable Jewish communities, even there in what used to be the major centers of Jewish life. Obviously this realization was, by far, the most disheartening aspect of our travels. We sought out Jews wherever we went, and we found some. But once proud Jewish communities have, one by one, gone out of existence or soon will. I am thinking, for example, of Alexandria, Egypt, and of Cochin, India, once a flourishing Jewish community that now, at least a couple of years ago, numbered a total of 17 Jewish souls. There are, I suppose, a few bright spots; Australia, perhaps France; but not many. All of which leads to the incontrovertible fact that there are only two viable Jewish communities in the world today—America and Israel—for a total of about 13 or 14 million Jewish souls; a contrast with total world population not all that different from the 5 against the 1 billion, 2 million in China.

So where does all of that leave me? It leaves me with a double, but not contradictory, perception. On the one hand, in the face of the vastness of the world-wide human family, I feel, Jewishly, a degree of humility that I never felt before. But on the other hand, convinced as I am about the uniqueness and the preciousness of Jews and Judaism, I feel a renewed sense of obligation. An obligation to redouble our efforts in order to perpetuate our people and our way of life. The obligation to preserve and teach our profound views of life and values to anyone willing to listen. The fact is that we were always a small and seemingly insignificant people. That was as true 2,000 years ago and even more true 4,000 years ago, as it is today. Jeremiah quotes God as saying: (49:15) "For I will make you the least among nations"—which we have been. That did not prevent us from discovering what western civilization still regards as the ultimate purposes of human existence, setting western civilization on a moral and ethical course which it still follows, however imperfectly, and which still inspires the loyalty and admiration of vast numbers of people. The point is that the smaller the flame the greater the imperative to keep it burning; an imperative which rests squarely upon the shoulders of each and every one of us, here and in Israel, to live and to teach our way of life; not squandering or wasting one scintilla of our influence and our energy. Educating ourselves and our young, Jewishly. And reaching out to all who would join us. To the end that we may be, in the words of Isaiah (49:6; 60:3), "A light of nations, that God's salvation may reach the ends of the earth."

The second thing I learned in retirement, then, is that we are a very small people and that we have an awfully big job to do.

The third insight, like the first two, derives directly from a set of experiences I have had during the last ten years. That set of experiences, to put it bluntly, has been the experiences associated with growing old, of making the passage from my then-age, 65, to my present age of 75.

Let's face it—I am approaching the end of the journey and, without being morbid about it, the realization, at some point during the years since I retired, hits that, as the saying goes, "I ain't got long for this world." It's like my friend, Rabbi Leifman, said the other day, "Bernie, neither one of us is going to die young." And, of course, he's right. This realization results from all sorts of not very subtle hints. My CPA, for example, tells me that while I did not have to dip into my IRAs when I first retired, I have to do so now. It seems that Uncle Sam figures you can die any day now, and he wants his cut before you do. Your doctor, for example, tells you that you had better begin to take that new class of heart drugs called beta blockers because your heart is no longer beating with that youthful rhythm it once did. And while I am at it, the time has come to quit racquetball and tennis. "Walk instead," he tells me. The young cashier at the restaurant, when you ask for the senior discount says, "Oh, sir, I already took that off." Or, when it gets to be about 7 or 8 o'clock in the evening, I am not all that anxious to go out but am content to lie on the couch and doze with some insipid TV show for background chatter. Or, when you put the grandchildren to bed, instead of their wanting you to read a story, they say, "Saba, would you please tell us about the olden days?" Not quite to the point where the old timer says he never buys green bananas anymore, but still to the point where the signs are plentiful and unmistakable that time is passing—and that there is much more of it behind you than ahead of you.

I suppose that the first component of whatever wisdom I have garnered on the subject of what many are calling, "The Third Stage of Life" or "eldering" or "sagging" instead of aging, is the growing acceptance of my mortality. Here, too, it is not that I was unaware of the inevitability of human aging and ultimate death. Like, I once asked a doctor about a certain mortality rate, and he answered, rather thoughtfully, "Rabbi, it is still 100 percent." After all, how could I not be aware, when I officiated at as many funerals as I did, and tried to comfort as many mourners as I did? Yet, somehow, the awareness of our own mortality did not apply directly to me. Freud long ago wrote that people are incapable of imagining their own death. That we all go about our lives with the fact of our own finitude held at emotional bay, which was true of me until recently. Gradually, over the last ten years, that has changed. I am now fully aware that it will not be long until the final exam. A year more or a year less. Of course, like everyone, I hope it will be a year more. But the future, my future, is clearly in view. The greatest comfort, and perhaps the deepest insight on this subject, came to me after the house was built as a result, of all things, of a building error I made. Let me tell you about it.

On the main floor of our house in Idyllwild we have a Great Room where Harriet planned to have a couch, several lounge chairs, an entertainment wall, and so on. I was particularly interested in the placement of the couch. The reason is that I wanted to locate a skylight on the sloping roof just above the couch in such a way that when I would lie on the couch to read the morning paper—one of my favorite activities—I could look out the skylight to the beautiful conifer forest which goes up the side or our mountain. So, when we framed up the Great Room and it came time to locate the skylight at a particular spot on the roof, I was very careful. I lay down on the subfloor in the very place where the couch would sit. I looked up and sighted the exact spot, and then built the skylight at that spot in the roof. We then continued the building. We completed the roof. Put in electrical and plumbing and the drywall. Eventually, the house was finished. And we moved out of the motorhome into our new home, which soon sported a new couch placed exactly where Harriet said it would be.

I shall never forget that first morning. I got up early and went into town to buy my *LA Times*. Then I lay down on the couch; opened to the sports section—what else? I looked up at the skylight and... my heart sank! Right there, in the middle of the skylight, obscuring everything on either side was this gigantic dead tree! Not at all what I had intended. How could I have miscalculated so? I had no one to blame but myself. Every morning thereafter, I would get the paper, lie down on the couch, check the scores and then look up at this dead skeleton of a tree. All brown. No pine cones or pine needles. Filled with unsightly holes and crevices. Lopped off at the top. It happened to be the only such tree in the area and I managed to focus right-square on it. I tried to figure what I could do to rectify the situation. I couldn't very well go out and cut it down. It was on someone else's property. Harriet's plan for the layout of the room was not about to be changed. I had no recourse. I was going to have to look at that dead tree forever.

Several months passed by. One day, Harriet and I went on a hike up our mountain in the company of the local ranger. That is always a thrill. To hike with someone who knows flora and fauna and the ecology of the forest, and who willingly shares information. I shall never forget, in the middle of the hike, the ranger stopped next to a dead tree. Pointing to the tree, he asked the group if anyone knew what it was. "Sure," someone said. . . "It's a dead tree." "No," said the ranger, "It really isn't. It's what we call a 'snag.' You may think it is dead, but it is not."

"In fact," he went on, "there is, in nature, no such thing as 'dead.' This tree, at this stage of its life, performs very important functions. Because there is, in the forest, a whole class of creatures, flora and fauna that depend on snags for food and shelter. There are numerous insects and birds and critters that cannot make their nests or burrow in living trees because, either the bark is too hard to penetrate, or the living tree's sap is toxic to them, or whatever; but they can live in and off of snags! Snags become entire cities of living creatures," he said. "The bark, the wood, the crevices become home, providing shelter and food for a whole panoply of living things. If there were no such thing as snags, a whole class of flora and fauna could not exist. The entire ecology of the forest would be upset." "Then," he added, "Eventually, after a long time—nature is never in a hurry—the snag falls to earth. When it does, it begins to decompose. It becomes part of nature, inseparable from the rest of the soil. At that stage, it enables other living things to grow out of the forest floor."

The next morning I lay on my couch. I looked up, and for the first time saw not a dead tree but a snag, which suddenly had a beauty and a significance that I had not really been aware of before. Gradually, as the days passed, as each morning came and went, I came to realize that that snag taught a lesson—not just about forest ecology but about human ecology. It was a lesson not only about nature but about human nature; a lesson that I had to travel 2,000 miles to learn. A lesson that has comforted and sustained me every day since I heard it.

Yes, I am in the autumn of my life. And, yes, I shall die. But I shall not be "dead," as that term is generally understood. I shall be something like that snag. Providing shelter and nurture and nourishment, I hope, to those who come after me. First of all, there are our children and our grandchildren, for whom I hope that I have provided something beyond the genetic blue print that all of us pass on to our progeny. Second, there is the influence I hope that I have exerted to help fashion caring, concerned Jewish communities in St. Louis, and now in Bermuda Dunes. Third, there is our eternal never-to-be-cancelled membership in the Jewish people that will live as long as there is life on this planet. And, ultimately, there will be the final return to the earth from which we were fashioned to begin with.

What have I learned in retirement? I have learned that one of the greatest satisfactions available to a person is to hammer out a solid piece of work. Then to sit back, like a good craftsman should, and take pleasure in it.

Amen.

The Snag

Jews and the World

The five sermons in this section illustrate the difficulties that were faced and that are being faced in the search for peace and justice between Israel and its neighbors; the search for understanding and acceptance between Jews and the non-Jewish world; the search for human dignity and respect for all peoples.

Rabbi Lipnick pulls no punches in delivering his insights and clearheaded understanding of the world we Jews live in.

The First Yom Kippur following the Six-Day War

I know that I shall never be the same again. I don't think that you will ever be the same again. For that matter, I don't think that any Jew, in whom a Jewish heart still beats, however faintly, will ever be quite the same again.

The events of June 1967 constitute one of those high water marks in history—Jewish history and, perhaps, even world history—which changed things around. The Six Day War was not an "incident" of the past 4,000 years of our history. It was a major event—the kind of major event around which all other occurrences cluster, either as a prelude or as aftermath, the kind of major "moment" which puts its stamp upon history and assures that though things may return to normalcy, they can never be quite the same again.

No, not sufficient time has passed to afford us the kind of perspective we should want, even to understand fully, much less to react properly, to this moment. But, during this season, for the first time since June, all Jews are together in sanctuaries similar to this one all over the world. No Rabbi who lays claim to spiritual leadership dare dodge the high responsibility of reacting, however incomplete or insufficient his reaction must be.

The Six Day War brought about radical transformations in Jews in three related yet distant areas. The first pertains to the Jews' relationship to the non-Jewish world, particularly the Christian world. The second pertains to the place that the concept of *Klal Yisroel*, Jewish people hood, with its geographical center in Israel, now has in our lives. The third involves a judgment regarding the potential power of Jewry, here and abroad, when it is united into a single fellowship.

During the last number of years, the Dialog Movement has been growing in this country, inspired primarily by Christian clergy, but received quite warmly by most Rabbis and Jewish laymen. Contacts between Christians and Jews have become a regular part of the American landscape and many of these contacts were much more than social in nature. Ideas and differing views on many issues were exchanged. A high level of frankness and honesty characterized most, if not all, of these exchanges. I even participated in a dialog group sponsored by the National Conference of Christians and Jews.

As a result of these contacts—which have been more or less commonplace for the past 10 or 15 years—Jewish professional interfaith workers and many others began to feel that real understanding was in the process of being achieved, if it had not already been achieved.

During the third week of May and the first week of June of this year, our evaluation of the success of the Dialog Movement suffered a drastic revision. Many of us had occasion to approach the very Christians, particularly the Christian clergy, with whom "dialog" had been conducted over the years. We were afraid that Israel was about to be destroyed, and with it, another two million Jews. We had no reason to think otherwise, nor did they. But the experience that I had—an experience which was duplicated, like out of a mimeograph machine, in every other community in the United States— was that, almost to a man, the Christian Jerusalem, the effectiveness of the United Nations, the Christian pacifist conscience—was not about the lives of two million Jews. I am not quite sure exactly where, in the list of priorities, those two million lives stood. That they did not stand first was a very painful discovery.

Most of us have long since given up our trust in governments, whom we know act out of "self-interest"—but, our fellow religionists with whom we ate and talked and revealed our innermost feelings and who, so often to us had deplored their own silence when six million Jews were being killed in Europe—was it too much to expect them now? They failed to speak out when we most needed them. We hardly heard a peep out of them and that which we did hear was confused, complicated, equivocal and compromising.

Then the war broke. At that point one could discern a radical change in the thinking of the Christian clergy—which leads one to believe that conscience is often on the side of victory.

At that point there came a radical change in our thinking. Never again would it be quite the same with them. Not that any of us are withdrawing from

Dialog. It is important that we maintain relationships with our Christian neighbors whose failings may in fact, be a reflection of our own ineffectiveness in the Dialog. But, never again will we place the same naïve trust in them that we did. Never again would we allow ourselves to forget that Christian theologians are still debating not only the justice of Israel's cause, but the Jews' right to exist as Jews—which means your right and mine.

In the Catholic Journal, *America*, dated September 2, 1967, an honest writer makes the following admission: Christianity, he says, has misinterpreted Jewish presence to the point of almost annihilating the Jewish people, theologically and practically, in the plan of God—which, in plain talk, means that Christians see Jews and Judaism, not just Israel, as being superseded by Christianity, as being unnecessary and therefore, expendable.

Never again shall we allow ourselves to forget that, for all of the understanding and love that they may have for us, they understand us and love us only up to a point.

I am sure that I do not have to point out to you that our experience, *vis-à-vis* the non-Jewish community, was paralleled in Israel in a different way. Israel depended in 1956, after the Sinai Campaign, upon the U.N.—upon the assurances of the United States and others that a state of belligerency, not to speak of open hostility against her, would be ended. Yet, peaceable shipping through Suez was forbidden. Virulent, war-like incitement became the daily fare of the whole Arab world. Daily incursions into Israel by armed guerrillas took their toll of life and limb. Full- scale aggression was mounted against Israel.

When hostilities did break out, who, I ask you, stepped forward to help Israel? No one! I know that there are those who say that had things gone differently, the United States would have come to Israel's aid. But we will never know for sure and the fact is that Israel was alone and still is.

As I have said from this pulpit before, there are only two upon whom Jews can genuinely depend—God and ourselves! There has been, without question, a radical change as a result of the events of June, 1967 in the Jewish attitude towards the non-Jewish world, both here and in Israel.

There has been, too, a radical change in the sense of identity we Jews now have with all other Jews the world over, as well as with the geographical center of the Jewish people, Israel. It is no secret that our bond with other Jews, in other congregations, in other communities, in other countries, and in Israel, had somewhat weakened these past number of years. Not just on the part of those assimilated, weak-kneed Jews, who struggle for acceptance in the non-Jewish world and who see the bugaboo of dual-loyalty in every pro-Israel gesture made by the Jewish community. Even the good Jews—who fulfilled their obligations to Israel and the Jewish people with their annual contribution to the U.J.A.—even in them, the sense of *Klal Yisroel*, the sense of being part of a total world-wide Jewish people and the sense of obligation towards building our ancient homeland, was swiftly becoming not their concern but the concern of Rabbis, Jewish educators and other professional Jews, convenient banners trotted out dutifully for state functions.

Then came May and June of 1967 when we learned that Israel was in mortal danger. The American Jewish community rose in solid, undeviating support for their brothers in Israel. Pollsters estimated that 99% of all Jews in America supported the Israel position.

Not just in a moral sense. Hillel Foundations and Israeli Consulates throughout the country were overwhelmed by literally ten thousands of young people who wanted to go to Israel to take the places of their peers who had been mobilized for the army. It is told that when one high official of the Jewish Agency arrived at the front door of his office early in the morning on June 5th, a man jumped out followed by two younger men. He stepped up to the official and said, "I have no money to give but here are my two sons. Send them over, immediately!" During those days, this was no isolated incident. There are people in this very Sanctuary who reacted the same way. Some of their sons and daughters are still in Israel.

Not even in 1948 was the response so great. It was as though every Jew sensed that if Israel were destroyed no one of us would escape unscathed. We achieved a higher sense of solidarity with our Jewish brethren wherever they were, and a higher sense of commitment to our ancestral home than I can ever remember.

It is interesting that the very same process occurred in Israel itself. There too, many thoughtful leaders had become very much concerned about the sense of estrangement which Israeli young people felt towards Diaspora Jews. They even started a program in schools to counter the narrower "Israeli Identity." The Jews of Israel were losing, as their counterparts in this country, a sense of oneness with world Jewry.

Then came June 1967. I have it on good authority that it was not the Sinai Desert, with its oil, that was of concern to the Israelis; nor the West Bank which, from a military standpoint, is extremely important; not even the heights of Golan, in Syria, which to the people in the north of Israel is the difference between life and death. But Jerusalem. The Jewish, not the Israeli symbol! The symbol of Jewish history, Jewish solidarity and Jewish indestructibility. It was Jerusalem which made heroic men break down and cry like babies. It was Jerusalem which caused mothers to willingly enter the ranks of the bereaved—Jerusalem, the center of Jewish consciousness, past, present and future.

Almost as much as Jerusalem itself, the awareness of the unqualified support of American Jewry is what spurred Israel's soldiers on to victory. After the summer of 1967, not only we, but Israelis will never be the same either. They, and we, are walking in a dream, secure in the newly affirmed sense—the single, united, mutually dependent Jewish people.

The third radical change which has come about which convinces me that we shall never be the same again, relates to a realization of the potential power of the Jewish people acting in concert. Here, too, it is no secret that we Jews had been experiencing a growing sense of weakness and ineffectuality. It is exemplified by the Bettelheim-Hannah Arendt school of thought which psychoanalyzed the victims of the Holocaust and found out that they had not lifted a finger in their own defense. They had gone to their deaths not only as lambs to the slaughter, but as accomplices in a psychological, if not in a physical, sense. The Jews in Europe during the Holocaust, they said, were cowards.

On a completely different level in this country, we have been hearing that there is no such thing as a Jewish vote. The Jew votes individually. What we had thought of as the "Jewish Liberal Bloc" is really a figment of the imagination.

We had heard similar rumblings from Israel too. Young Israelis spiritually disowned their forbears of the Holocaust whom they considered cowards. At the same time, they themselves gave evidence of losing the pioneering spirit shown by their parents who had cleared the swamps and planted the deserts and founded the State. These young Israelis were abandoning the land in large numbers and flocking to the cities. Many were leaving Israel in search of material benefits in other countries. I myself, in 1955, predicted a serious, maybe an impossible, military confrontation with the Arabs in ten years, based partly on my negative evaluation of the young generation of Israelis. I wasn't at all sure that the youth I saw growing up in Israel then were capable of rising to the challenge posed by the Arabs and life in the Middle East. All of us, if we were honest, had serious questions about our power, about our strength, moral and physical, everywhere—in Europe, in Israel and here.

The extent of Israel's military victory of June, 1967, is as well known to you as it is to me. As someone wrote recently, that someday, 3,000 years hence, when our descendants read how the Israelis took on four armies, 20 times their number, and vanquished them in 60 hours, someone will get fancy with interpretations and claim the word "hour," in those times does not mean "hour," in our time, and the recorder of the saga wrote "his version," that no more need be said about the military victory—except maybe to remind you of the cartoon in which two little boys were playing Jews and Arabs. One was heard to complain, "He never lets me be a Jew!" This is a change!

As far as the victims of the Holocaust are concerned, suddenly our respect for them has soared, both here and in Israel. "Our soldiers and our population," wrote one Israeli after the war, "did not number two and a half million, because walking alongside us and in everybody's subconscious, were Hitler's six million martyred." Those people were far from cowards, many suddenly realized.

We experienced the same sense of strength in America. Take the financial picture. I am sure you realize that it is ingrained, in the Jewish soul that the

correct response to danger is to give money. This was certainly the immediate reaction to the Middle East crises but with one important difference—
much more money was given, by many more people, than ever before in
history. There are innumerable stories in every Jewish community which
describe not only the fantastic large-scale giving by people of means but
also, the literal sacrifice of their life's savings by people of modest means.
During the little more than two-week period which marked the height of the
crisis, well over a hundred million dollars was given, the bulk of it in cash.
In St. Louis, the amount approached two million. The drives did not begin
at the top as so many do. By the time the U.J.A. met to launch its campaign,
local campaigns were already well under way in dozens of communities.
Never again shall we underestimate our strength as a united people, here
or anywhere.

These are not only changes. They are radical transformations. Never again
shall we put inordinate faith in others. Never again shall we allow our sense
of *Klal Yisroel* and our love for Israel to wane. Never again will we underestimate the potential power of a united Jewish people.

Some of you may agree that these are transformations but not necessarily
for the better. In that case, we disagree. The fact of Jewish aloneness in the
world doesn't scare me. We are different my friends. Our standards are
different, our destiny is different and the world senses this difference even
if we forget it from time to time.

One of the most beautiful recent reminders was given by Elie Wiesel in
an address delivered shortly after the Six Day War. "Often it seems as if
the world considered our existence incompatible with its own. As if we
were—always—expendable. . . our friends are few. As for mankind, it is—at
best—neutral if not indifferent; it has learned little either in what concerns
us or in what concerns itself. . ."

We Jews have long been the conscience of the world, its alter ego by means
of which it tests itself and its truth; by means of which it punishes itself for
its failure to live up to truth. This is a very lonely and a dangerous position
to be in. Maybe though, it is better than theirs.

Our heightened sense of being Jewish is for the better, too, as is our greater
identification with the land of Israel. As to the former, we Jews—Reform,

Orthodox, Conservative, secular—should be closer. We should recognize our organizational loyalties as important but secondary. We should unite, whether on the Rabbinic or the lay level, in one solid fellowship.

With respect—our dedication to Israel—the whole matter has to be thought about very carefully. We should think in terms of much greater investment in Israel. Dr. Simon Greenberg has called for investing 25% of our capital in some Israeli economic enterprise or, at least, Israel Bonds. He has urged those who are in commerce and industry to give much more concerted thought as to how they can help build Israel's economic life. But, even more radically, we have to think in terms of greater immigration to Israel on the part of Western Jews. "*Aliyah,*" going to live in Israel, has to be high in our own thinking and in the thinking of the community. We must give serious thought to whether we, or any members of our family, might go to settle in Israel. We must think of new ways whereby the community will inspire greater visitation to Israel and permanent settlement of some of its members—becoming there a part of a great adventure; becoming part of the great mystery and nobility of the emerging future of this little country which will yet play a decisive role, not alone in the development of the Middle East, but of world civilization.

Finally, this new appreciation which we have of our own potential power, while it is dangerous, is pregnant with untold possibilities. Maybe we can solve the problem of Jewish education in this community. Maybe B'nai Amoona can establish summer educational facilities which will give our children the strength and the pride in their heritage that they deserve. Maybe we can establish a College of Jewish Studies to give our teachers the kind of background and inspiration they need to do the job that has to be done. Maybe we can make the Jewish Theological Seminary into a beacon of spiritual inspiration for the world. Maybe we can do all of those things which, once in a while, at home, or as I sit alone in my office early in the morning, after Minyan. Maybe we can do these things! Maybe we can.

Last evening, we began Yom Kippur with the Kol Nidre. As I was thinking about what has happened in Jewish life these past few months, it occurred to me that the Kol Nidre is the one prayer in the entire Prayer Book which applies. You see, the Kol Nidre was written in 7th-century Christian Spain in order to give Jews who had faltered in their allegiance—to their people, to their God and to themselves—a way of coming back. That is what the formula means. That the vows that we accepted in moments of weakness, to be like the Christian world in whose midst we live, are hereby rendered null and void. Our ancestors made mistakes and they were sorry.

We, too, have been guilty of similar weakness, if for different reasons. There is no better time to reverse the trend than on Yom Kippur, to proudly affirm our difference from others, to unqualifiedly renew our bond with our fellow Jews, and to take up our positions once more as the elect of the Almighty against whom no human onslaught will ever prevail.

In something less than six hours, we shall end this Yom Kippur service. If Kol Nidre was the first prayer we said, the last will be: "Next year in Jerusalem!" But, has it occurred to you that according to the calendar, Rosh Hashanah, which is the beginning of the New Year, was observed last week? Has it occurred to you that it is already NEXT YEAR?!?

Amen.

Peace with the Arabs

If all goes well, we leave for New York tomorrow, Monday, for Athens; and then, Thursday, on to Israel. Yes, it is that time of the year again. My wife and I are leading a group of 28 B'nai Amoona members on a three-week tour of Athens and Israel.

As last year, this is not a trip or a tour or a visit—it is a Pilgrimage, in the fullest sense of the term. Although some of the group have been to Israel before, none have been in the Old City of Jerusalem. None, I would wager to say, have prepared themselves for a Pilgrimage to Israel as intensely—one might even say, religiously—as for this one. We have met in orientation sessions a number of times; reviewing by lecture, by map study and by slides, the places we intend to visit. We have talked about the meaning behind the places and our hopes as to the Jewish transformation and elevation which should occur within each of us as a result of this Pilgrimage. We are primed, we are anxious; we anticipate a great, great experience.

You know that I have been to Israel before, a number of times, for which reason this Pilgrimage has, as you might expect, a little bit of a different coloration and purpose from that which can be identified with the group, as a whole.

I am going to take the liberty, therefore, of sharing some of my thoughts with you, as I prepare for my 5th *aliyah* to Israel, and my second since the June War. I find myself, this time, enveloped in one central overriding concern which can be conveyed in a single word: peace—peace between Israel and her Arab neighbors. We have seen, since Israel was proclaimed as a state, three devastating wars. Literally thousands of people have been killed, numerous lives ruined and untold quantities of property destroyed. Yet it would be the understatement of the year to assert that the problems, which caused the war, have been solved by the wars. If anything, the hatred and the animosity between Israel and the Arabs have increased in intensity. Numerous acts of violence occur daily along the borders and in the interior. Israel and the Arab countries are on a wartime footing, which is the rule in the Middle East now, rather than the exception. The Arabs are busy devising new means of violence and destruction and nobody would be the least bit surprised if, in the near future, major hostilities erupted again. The wars have solved nothing, unless they have bought 20 years of existence for Israel, which I don't at all minimize.

But as to putting basic problems to rest and assuring some kind of permanent stability, nothing has been solved. Peace seems more elusive today than ever. I find myself asking more and more whether or not we—by which I mean the Israelis and the Jews of the world—have done and are doing all that we might have done and all that we might yet do, on behalf of peace. My motivation, I hasten to add, does not derive so much from principle—although peace is a big principle in Judaism and with me—as much as from my concern for Israel's future and concern for the future of the Arab countries. Ben-Gurion was quoted as saying, just this past week:

"We have had three wars already. We won them, but he (referring to Nasser) could make a 4th war, a 5th war and, if he is defeated, a 6th war. But if only once he manages to defeat us, we will be finished. We are not going to destroy Egypt and all the Egyptians, but he can do it to us."

Actually, that is a very mild presentation of the situation. We once had an Arab speak to our post-graduate class, and he said basically the same thing as Ben-Gurion. Perhaps with the Arab penchant for exaggeration, he added, "We might lose a thousand wars, but we shall win the thousand and first."

I am slowly but surely arriving at the opinion—and out of concern for Israel and its future, out of concern for the Jewish people and its future, out of concern for the 2,000 years of struggle which led us to the great return and the next 2,000 which will be filled, I hope, with other great achievements on the part of our people—it is out of concern for these things that I reluctantly but inevitably arrive at the conclusion that we have got to do better.

The way I look at it, there are only two possible ways of relating to an enemy—one is to hurt him and the other is to help him. Neutrality I discount completely. I suppose, theoretically, neutrality is possible, but then, the person involved is not really an enemy. The word 'enemy' implies a dynamic relationship, in which people are thrown together. If you have an enemy living in India, he may be your enemy, but what difference does it make one way or the other? Enemy means that you have contact. If you will think about it, there are only two ways to relate to him—hurt him or help him. Let's look at each for a few moments.

Hurting an enemy seems both natural and effective. After all, he is your enemy. Hurt him and thereby render him less able to hurt you. But there is a problem with such an approach, short of killing the enemy. That is that nothing really gets solved by means of it. Hurting an enemy only hardens his determination to hurt you back. The history of feuds, reprisals and counter-reprisals and the whole philosophy of "tit for tat" are too well known to require review. If good begets good, so does evil beget evil. Judaism does perhaps permit hurting an enemy in self-defense. But only in a case in which the assailant not just has a knife, but has it posed about to strike. After all, your life, which is about to be forfeited, is no less valuable than his. But what about a preventative approach to self-defense, in which if you don't get him eventually he will get you? Here it isn't quite so clear.

You may remember the encounter between Saul and David, as described in the First Book of Samuel. Saul had been pursuing David in an effort to kill his rival. David was hiding in a cave. The story continues:

"And Saul went into the cave. Now, David and his men were sitting in the innermost part of the cave, and the men of David said to him, "Here is the day of which the Lord said to you, 'Behold I will give your enemy into your hand and you shall do to him as it shall seem good to you.' Then David arose and stealthily cut off the skirt of Saul's robe." In other words, David could have killed or wounded his mortal enemy but didn't—he only cut off the end of his robe.

Upon which the Midrash, in the name of Samuel ben Nachmani, comments that at that moment David's evil urge appeared and said, "If you fell into his hand, he would have no mercy for you and would kill you, and from the Torah it is permissible to kill him for he is a pursuer." Accordingly, David leaped and swore twice, "By God, I won't kill him." In other words, the tradition hesitates to permit us to hurt our enemy in all but a clear-cut case of self-defense, where the danger is immediate and patent.

The other alternative, of course, is helping an enemy. "When you encounter your enemy's ox or ass wandering, you must take it back to him. When you see the ass of your enemy prostrate under its burden and would refrain from raising it, you must nevertheless raise it with him." Two very, very unusual verses containing the germ of a very, very, important idea. The operative phrase in each verse, is "your enemy," in the first, and, "the person who hates you," in the second. Here the Torah does not advise neutrality towards an enemy. It doesn't advise hurting him either. It advises helping him!

The reason is made in a Midrash on this verse which reads as follows: "When your enemy sees that you came and you helped him, he will say to himself, 'I thought that he was my enemy, God forbid. If he was my enemy, he would not have helped me. But if he is my friend, I am his enemy in vain. I will go and pacify him.' He went to him and made peace. Accordingly, the Torah says, 'And all her paths are peace.'" In other words, you help an enemy for the purpose of turning that enemy's heart around, to empty from it the hatred and animosity which reside there and to make him into a friend.

Now, you may think that this insight is not applicable to the Arab-Israel situation. That this is a case simply of the Arabs plotting the destruction of Israel and that they have to be stopped—however and by whatever means necessary. First of all, few complicated situations are that simple and second, and most important, hurting the enemy through warfare doesn't do the job. We have to be willing, as Jews and as Israelis, to help our enemies, the Arabs, much more effectively than we have in the past.

Take the case of the Arab refugees. I know that the refugee roles are inflated, that the host countries have made not the slightest effort to integrate them into their own economies, and that the Arab refugees are a political football in the hands of the Arabs. Still in all, the refugees are two million souls—Arab souls, it is true, but souls who are suffering the deprivation of their homes and lands. Israel may not have driven them out, yet Israel cannot wash her hands of their plight.

I don't believe we have done enough. New and more imaginative ways of helping Arab refugees and of turning their hatred into friendship must be explored. Would it be a bad idea for the American Jewish community to raise U.J.A. funds for them? Maybe $50 million spent in this way would be more effective than $50 million spent on Phantoms. One big argument would be removed from the Arab's arsenal of big arguments, and the refugees would be helped in the bargain.

Take another area: Cooperation with the big powers and Israel's insistence on face-to-face talks with the Arab countries. Certainly, many of the Arab leaders are out of their minds and might well violate any agreement made on their behalf by the big powers. Yet, I wonder if they would honor agreements that they made many more honestly. I feel that the efforts of the big powers have to be welcomed and that Israel should engage in all of these conversations, holding a very big olive branch and not a stick, in its right hand.

One of the biggest problems is the so-called "occupied territories." Here too, many have taken an extreme position. As far as I am concerned, it is all negotiable, and when you accuse me of being willing to give up Jerusalem, I want you to know that Jerusalem is dearer to me than any other place in the world. But, not even Jerusalem is dearer to me than peace, and one could go on and on as to what we could do that we haven't done to demonstrate to the world and to the Arabs our willingness to help. This does not make the Arabs less our enemies. It is because they are our enemies that we have to demonstrate such willingness. "When you encounter your enemy's ox or ass wandering, bring it back to him. . . when you see his animal lying prostrate under a burden, help him raise it." How much more so when it is the man himself who lies prostrate? The Arabs lie prostrate all right, under many burdens—ignorance, squalor, hatred and a self-seeking, medieval, almost feudal leadership. As Jews, we have got to help lift those burdens.

Even as I say all of this, I am well aware that I don't live under the gun like the kids in the Hulla Valley or the tractor drivers in the Jordan Valley. As I say all of this, I am well aware that such a high-sounding approach is meaningless unless it is met with some response from the other side, and that it does take two to make peace. I am reminded of the old Chinese proverb: "I am the bread and thou art the eater. Can there be peace between us?" Still in all, we haven't gone as far as we can go. We must make it abundantly clear to the Arabs, to the rest of the world, and, most of all to ourselves, that we are prepared to do anything, except die, and to pay anything, except blood, and to make any concession necessary, in order to achieve peace.

These are my thoughts and my major concerns as we prepare to depart for Israel. I am not alone in these concerns. There are other voices, including no less a person than Ben-Gurion's, that are being raised in a similar vein. It will be my purpose while in Israel to talk to them, to encourage them and to explore ways and means of aiding them.

All of you be well. I hope to see you in about three weeks. During this time, may Israel, and may the world, take another step or two closer to peace. For it is my firm belief, in the words of the prayer: "that He who makes peace in His high places will yet grant peace unto us and unto all Israel," And let us say, Amen.

David Ben-Gurion

May 2, 1987

Monday is 5th of Iyar, Independence Day, the 39th anniversary of the founding of the State of Israel. This year, Israel Independence Day highlights the role of David Ben-Gurion in the history of Israel. In St. Louis, for example, our annual walk is entitled "Walk Through Israel—in the Footsteps of Ben-Gurion." Now the reason for the emphasis upon Ben-Gurion is that 1986–1987 was observed as the centennial of Ben-Gurion's birth. He was born in the year 1886.

Monday is the culmination of the Year of Commemoration. What I thought I would do today, in honor of Israel Independence Day, is to tell you about three encounters that I had with Mr. Ben-Gurion and what, on reflection, those encounters tell us, both about the man himself and about the state which he did so much to fashion.

The first incident goes back to the 1930s. I must have been 11 or 12 years old when it happened. I had been, from the age of about 9 or 10, a member of a Young Judea Youth Club. In any event, an important Zionist meeting was being held in Washington, D.C., which was only about 40 miles from my home in Baltimore, and my father took me to the meeting. If I am not mistaken it was in the Mayflower Hotel.

What a thrill! I was able to see and hear all of the famous Zionist personalities that I had heard so much about in Young Judea. I remember that Dad and I were walking through the lobby, and there in a corner—I can see it in my mind's eye like it happened yesterday—I saw David Ben-Gurion sitting on a bench—alone. There was no question as to who it was because Ben-Gurion was always recognizable with his big mane of flowing white hair. I was a bit of a *chutzapadic* in those days (and maybe I still am), but I walked up to Ben-Gurion, and I introduced myself to him in Hebrew! I was very proud of the fact that I was learning to speak Hebrew, and I remember thinking to myself that if I would speak Hebrew with Mr. Ben-Gurion, it would be one of the high-water marks of my life; and it was! He responded to me, also in Hebrew. We had a short conversation. I remember introducing my father to him. And that was the total encounter. . . a very proud moment for me.

Now, this simple incident occurring as it did in the 30s in Washington, D.C. is suggestive of the role that Mr. Ben-Gurion occupied in the pre-state days, in fashioning the Zionist movement and in the respect he commanded within the whole Jewish world. He was certainly one of the main architects of the movement which brought the state into existence.

Born in Russian Poland, he founded a Zionist youth organization in Poland. At the age of 20, he moved to what was Palestine, going to work in the orange groves and in the wine cellars. He worked as a watchman. He worked as a farmhand, and he also set about the task of organizing the Zionist movement in Palestine itself. His conception of the emerging state was a socialist labor conception. That is, he was of the opinion that a major revolution in Jewish life was needed. That Jews had lived an abnormal existence in the Diaspora as urban shopkeepers and *luftmenschen*. That our people, first and foremost, had to change its attitude toward labor, including menial labor, if it was to succeed in creating a state.

He was not a strict Marxist. His main point of difference was that instead of one class, the working class, fighting another class, the upper class which is orthodox Marxist thinking, the whole Jewish people should become the working class. His slogan for Labor Zionism was "From class to becoming the nation as a whole." What Ben-Gurion wanted was a socialist society which would be distinguished by land-owning Jews, like everybody else, and by equality—Socialist equality.

One of the main instruments that he created to try to accomplish this goal was a kind of Jewish labor union in Israel, but it was quite different from what we know as a labor union. Its purpose was to foster settlement of Jews on the land and to become an economic and political body which would help to bring about a cooperative workers' society.

In 1915, Ben-Gurion was exiled by the Turks. He spent some time in Salonica and finally ended up in New York, where he worked to organize the Zionist movement in this country.

In 1917, he married his wonderful Paula, who was his nurse and wife until her death in 1968. I remember her very well. She used to hover over him like a mother hen. It was probably one of the great matches of modern history.

In 1918, he organized the Jewish Legion, which, in World War I, joined the Allies in its fight against Germany. He became Chairman of the Jewish agency and a prolific journalist and speaker.

Through the 30s, which is when I met him, and the 40s, he was involved in creating the structures, attending the meetings, speaking at the conferences, appearing before national and international bodies—including during World War II when the Nazi persecution of our people brought the realization of the need for a Jewish state to the attention of the whole civilized world. He was one of the main architects, so called, of illegal immigration to Palestine, and he became the head of the pre-state defense effort. It was only natural that when, on the 5th *Iyar*, 1948, the state came into existence—largely at his insistence—he was chosen to be its first Prime Minister and Defense Minister. Shortly thereafter it was he who declared Jerusalem as the eternal capital of the Jewish people. David Ben-Gurion—one of the major architects, one the major creators of the movement beginning in the late 1800s and culminating in 1948—which brought the State of Israel into existence.

The second incident that I want to tell you about involves a little place called Sde Boker which is a *kibbutz* in the Negev desert. From 1948 to 1953, Ben-Gurion, as Prime Minister and Defense Minister, was active in establishing the main institutions of the new state. For example, it was he who created the Israel Defense Force. It was he who created a military force which became, not only the defender of the State, but one of the legendary military forces of all history.

At the beginning of the State, it was he who introduced free education in an effort to wield the diversified elements of Israel into one nation. He placed the advancement of science and research as a central factor in the development of the country and of the people. But, by December 1953, Ben-Gurion felt as though he needed a rest from the tensions of high office, (as well as from all the years that preceded his prime ministership), and he resigned from the Government.

When he resigned he decided to go live in this small *kibbutz* called Sde Boker, which is where I saw him next. I shall never forget the few days that we spent together in that *kibbutz*. First of all, you have to picture its setting. The *kibbutz* is fairly far south of Beersheba in what was, certainly then in 1953, a desolate, arid section of the country. I remember arriving by hitch in the back of a truck where there was a tractor which was not properly tied down. So that on the rough road, I had to dodge the tractor as it slid around the truck bed. But thank God I arrived safely and came into this *kibbutz*. The total number of people in the *kibbutz* at that time was 28, of whom Ben-Gurion was one. It occupied just a small area with a little eating hall in the center and a few bunks, like a little camp.

His house was perhaps a little bit nicer than the others because he had his library there. But believe me, any cabin on the Meramec River is far nicer, and the whole thing was surrounded by a barbed wire fence.

The 28 of us, I remember, had dinner together in this little mess hall. One plate, one fork, and I don't think that there was a spoon. There were a few fresh vegetables, but hardly anything to eat. A very, very, modest, meager meal.

Then we spent the evening visiting and playing chess, and I will never forget that night because as I lay on my bunk in a little 2 x 4 room the field mice were playing on the floor without interruption the whole night. I remember being concerned that they would climb onto the bunk, so what I did was sleep on a table all night with the hope that the mice, or the rats, whatever they were, would not climb up the legs.

The next day I was not terribly rested, but rested enough, I suppose, to be able to pitch hay with Mr. Ben-Gurion in the sheepfold. It was his job in this little *kibbutz* to take care of the sheep, and that is where he lived.

Where he lived, and why he lived there, tells a great deal about what kind of a person he was and the kind of an Israel he wanted to see. If the first part of his life was devoted to creating the Zionist structure, this part of his life was devoted to trying to communicate to the people of Israel certain ideals that were necessary, from his point of view, to make the state the kind of place it should be. Chief among those ideals, beyond the normalcy and equality that I spoke of earlier; I guess one can describe most succinctly by the term "pioneering." He wanted the people of Israel to be pioneers, to be willing to work themselves, to go into the desert areas, to develop those areas, not to depend upon Arab Labor; to develop themselves and the land from the ground up without dependence upon others and the largess of other nations. He saw his stay in Sde Boker as the great symbol of that conviction. Now this is not to say that he was not concerned about the development of the mind and the intellect. On the contrary, he was, in addition to a sheep herder, throughout his life one of the great intellects of the Jewish world. His study included the Bible, Greek Philosophy, Buddhism, the philosophy of Spinoza and many, many other subjects on which he was a significant authority.

The third incident occurred in February 1955, when Ben-Gurion was called back into the service of the government as Minister of Defense. At that time I was working for the Israel radio station, and I covered Ben-Gurion's return from Sde Boker to the Knesset. I shall never forget the incident. There was a large crowd gathered at the doorway of the Knesset (which at that time was a different place from where it is today) and Ben-Gurion arrived for the purpose of resuming his involvement in the Israel government. I remember the car in which he arrived. It was an old Plymouth, a brown, khaki-colored Plymouth. Out stepped Ben-Gurion greeted by soldiers standing at attention, Ministers dressed to the hilt, and a pretty good-sized throng of Jerusalemites. He got out of the car dressed in an open khaki shirt with khaki pants and old dusty shoes, like he had just come from the Negev, which is indeed where he had just come from.

He entered the Knesset and took up the reins of leadership again.

What always impressed me about this incident was the modesty that the man demonstrated. It reminds me of a story that they tell about Ben-Gurion: In those days when the Russian ambassador came to Israel to present his credentials to Ben-Gurion, Ben-Gurion was told that he had to be in formal attire. That is, a morning coat with an ascot and a top hat, which he did. But immediately after the ceremony he had a meeting of the labor party in some hall in Jerusalem that he had to rush to, and he didn't have time to change his clothes. So when he got up on the podium to begin the meeting and he was dressed so out of character to what was his normal dress, he started out by saying, "Ladies and gentlemen, you will have to forgive me for coming in my working clothes!"

In any event, what this return by Ben-Gurion to the government in 1955 symbolized to me was his modesty and his willingness to do what had to be done personally on behalf of the cause to which he was dedicated—the cause of the Jewish people and the cause of the State of Israel.

From that moment on, and I suppose even earlier, every utterance of Ben-Gurion, in speeches, in written communications or whatever, emphasized the need for Jews personally to put themselves on the line in terms of identification with Israel and the job that Israel needed to do. Whenever you would talk with him he would make the point that there was no such thing as a Zionist who did not come to live in Israel. As a matter of fact, he advised the dissolution of the whole Zionist organization outside of Israel. And he wanted to see the ingathering of all Jews from wherever to the state. Whenever he met a group of Americans or a group of whomever, his first and last question in the conversation would be "Why don't you come here and live? Why don't you make *aliyah*?"

Frankly, I don't know if I can identify totally with that point of view. At one time in my life I thought that I would go to Israel to live. I suppose that if I had another lifetime I would make good on that intent. But there can be no doubt that Israel came into existence in the first place, and will continue to exist, because people are willing to leave whatever commitments they have and place the welfare of the Jewish people and the welfare of the state ahead of those commitments—as Ben-Gurion demonstrated at that time and as he indeed demonstrated throughout his life.

David Ben-Gurion will certainly go down in Jewish history as one of the great, great figures of all time. It is hard to know whether the state would have come into existence had it not been for his talents and his dedication. We do know that he was extremely, extremely important in the process and we know something else too, and that is that many of the characteristics of the state and many of its most endearing and beautiful qualities came, of course, through many sources. But one of the most significant of those sources was David Ben-Gurion. Not a shul-going Jew, by any means, but really one of the greatest figures in the history of our people.

So, congratulations to the State of Israel on its 39th birthday! May it go from strength to strength. May it have peace and happiness within its borders and may those who helped to bring the third Jewish commonwealth into existence, among whom Ben-Gurion is one of the most eminent, be remembered fondly and with the great gratitude that each and every one of us feel. A sentiment which I invite you to join me in saying, Amen.

Yom HaShoah—Holocaust Remembrance Day in Poland

April 13, 1988

The decision of the St. Louis Center for Holocaust Studies to make music the central pillar of tonight's Yom HaShoah observance is very, very wise. In order to tell you why I think so, let me hark back to my visit to Poland several months ago and to the experience I had in visiting the death camps there. I visited Majdanek, Sobibór, Auschwitz, Birkenau, Buno and Treblinka. Naturally, I reacted to those visits with deep emotion and with somewhat muddled and confused perceptions. In such an atmosphere, a person's wires get crossed. It is frightening, touching, grisly, and disturbing—all at the same time.

As I visited the barracks, the work places and the ovens, as I walked the grounds of these various factories of death, one of the realizations that came upon me was the smallness, the insignificance of the physical sites in relation to the enormity of the crimes that were perpetrated there. Four million Jews killed were in Poland and most of them were killed in these little areas, these small, on the face of it, insignificant establishments. So that realization that forced itself upon me, as I walked and looked, was how could so much evil be committed in so short a time and in such small places by so few people?

In Sobibór, for example, only 60 German soldiers and 300 Ukrainians succeeded in killing one-quarter of a million people and disposing of their bodies. The truth is that the enormity of the crimes of the Holocaust can only be understood, can be felt best, by means of art. The function of art is to take reality—a slice of life—extrapolate it and magnify it to point out its importance, its significance and its influence.

Thus it is that the reality, the full dimension of the Holocaust, can be understood fully through art—literature, painting and perhaps music above all. The organizers of this program, therefore, are to be commended for knowing the unique power that music has to inform and to transform, to teach and to touch the soul, and for helping us to appreciate thereby the tragedy and the surpassing importance of what happened during the Holocaust.

Actually, there is a historical precedent for this approach which I myself participated in during that same trip to Poland. For those of you who may not know, relations between Poland and Israel are becoming much warmer of late. There has been a resumption of diplomatic relations. There are now cultural exchanges between the two countries and a good deal of tourism, particularly on the part of Israelis to Poland.

The week that I was in Poland was the week that the Israel Philharmonic made its first and thus far, only appearance in Eastern Europe. It was my great pleasure to be with Zubin Mehta, the Musical Director of the Israel Philharmonic; Itzak Perlman, the violin virtuoso; and 119 members of the orchestra itself. (We stayed at the same hotel in Warsaw). I met these people Erev Shabbat, just after they returned from Auschwitz, on the eve of the concert in Warsaw they were to give the next night. You have to understand that these musicians were Israelis. Some of whom had themselves lived in Poland before the war and a number of whom were children of survivors. If my visits caused me vertigo, imagine what their visits did to them!

In any event, I attended their concert Saturday night in the Warsaw Concert Hall, followed by a reception for the diplomatic corps given by the head of the Israeli legation. It was there that I learned of a tribute that the Israel Philharmonic had decided to offer to the memory of the Warsaw Ghetto, its martyred inhabitants and its brave fighters. The tribute would occur Sunday morning, the next day, prior to leaving for a concert in Budapest. And here it was 11 or 11:30 Saturday night, following a great, triumphant concert that they and Perlman had just given.

Investigation by Mr. Mehta had revealed that there was a formerly Jewish-owned theater in the old Warsaw Ghetto in which a Jewish symphony orchestra, walled in from the outside world, performed from 1940—1942, prior to their being sent to the death camps. The theater is now called *Kino Femina*, which loosely translated means Girly Cinema. It is a small, seedy place but one of the few buildings of the ghetto left standing, and possibly the only authentic spot that could be associated with the ghetto orchestra. The members of the Philharmonic, therefore, decided that in tribute to the heroes of the ghetto, it would go to that theater that night and play music—for each other, for a few of the survivors who were still alive and for those of us Rabbis who had happened upon the event.

I can't begin to describe that midnight concert to you. We had to walk down a flight of stairs, which was painfully negotiated by Perlman who was on crutches. A Marilyn Monroe picture was playing, and I guess all totaled there were about 150 people.

Mr. Mehta gave an introduction and then there were four performances; two solos, one on the French horn by two children of survivors, and both of whom played original pieces composed for the occasion. This was followed by a rendition by the Jerusalem String Quartet, and the evening was capped off with a recital by Perlman with a tour-de-force performance of a Bach solo piece on the violin.

It was now about one in the morning and the evening closed with the singing of *Hatikva* and *Ani Ma'amin,* the song of faith which the Jews of Warsaw had sung on their way to the death camps. Very few words were uttered that evening but much great music was played and heard and sung.

When we left that little theater, when we left Poland the next day—the Israelis to Budapest and the rest of us to the United States—we knew that the Jews of Warsaw, the heroes of the ghetto, had been memorialized and honored to the best of our ability to honor—because of, and through, the medium of music.

May that same medium have a similar effect upon us this evening, and may the memory of our coreligionists who died for the sanctification of God's name in the Holocaust be for a constant benediction and blessing always.

Amen.

The Yahrzeit of the Attacks of September 11

2004 (5765) - Rosh Hashanah I

This past weekend, we observed the third *yahrzeit* of the terrorist attack on the World Trade Center and the Pentagon. I use the word "yahrzeit" advisedly, because whatever else 9/11 was, it was the day on which almost 3,000 innocent people lost their lives. September 11, therefore, is and will always be a big, a very big, *yahrzeit*. In addition, 9/11 was the day on which America lost its innocence and was catapulted into a global war against the demonic forces of Muslim extremism—joining the little state of Israel which has been engaged in this same struggle for well over 50 years, and joining, if truth be told, the entire western world which faces a challenge perhaps unprecedented in the whole history of our civilization.

I take the liberty of dealing with this subject today, the first day of Rosh Hashanah, because I am deeply worried by what I see and because I frankly don't know when I'll get another chance to share these concerns with you. What I have decided to do today, therefore, is two things. First, I want to share with you my best read on what I feel the nature of the threat is, and the second thing I want to do is share my assessment of the State of Israel's specific involvement.

It is my opinion that America, known to much of the Muslim world as the "Big Satan," and Israel, known to that same world as the "Little Satan," against its will is involved at this time in a full-blown culture *kampf*, a war of civilizations. We in the west confront, I believe, nothing less than the concerted effort by the radical, fundamentalist fringe of Islam to conquer the world, including the western world, for Islam.

I hasten to point out that this is not the agenda of all the 1.3 to 1.5 billion Muslims who inhabit the globe. There are many Muslims who are tolerant and decent and have no thought whatsoever of imposing their religion on the rest of us. Yet there is a significant fringe for which this is the number one item on their agenda.

A Muslim scholar recently sought to soothe our concerns by pointing out that this radical fringe represents no more than 3 to 5 percent of all Muslims. A scant comfort this is when you stop and think that 3 to 5 percent is something in the neighborhood of 39- to 65-Million individuals sworn to our conversion or destruction, and are willing to pay any price in order to achieve it.

Islam has serious, endemic problems. It is not, for example, contrary to what we have been told, an inherently peaceful religion. The word Islam, we have been told, is related to the Hebrew word "Shalom" and means "peace." This is not true. The word Islam means, "submission," which is a very different matter. Because the main purpose of Islam, especially in its more militant form, is to obtain everyone's submission to *Allah* and his representatives. Islam tends, therefore, to be an imperialistic religion much more so than present-day Christianity and certainly more so than Judaism.

The Koran describes the inevitable enmity between Muslims and non-Muslims in the strongest of terms. These commands cannot be explained away or softened by modern theological interpretation. Because, unfortunately, there is very little such science in Islam today, unlike Christianity which, since the Reformation and Counter Reformation, has continually updated itself and adapted to changing conditions. And unlike Judaism, which has experienced what is called the *haskalah*, the enlightenment, Islam remains a religion sunk in the Dark Ages. The Koran is still taught in most schools as the immutable word of God. Every teaching of which is literally true. Islam believes in theocratic states, ruled by Islamic law, called *Sharia*. Moreover, Koranic teaching that the faith can be, and in suitable circumstances must be, imposed by force has never been ignored.

The history of Islam has essentially been a story of conquests and re-conquests. The seventh-century breakout of Islam from Arabia was followed by the rapid conquest of North Africa, the invasion and conquest of Spain, and the thrust into France that carried the crescent all the way to the gates of Paris. This period became known in the Muslim world as the First Great Jihad. It took the Christian world half a millennium of re-conquest to expel the Muslims from Western Europe, which occurred at the end of the 15th century at the Battle of Granada in Spain.

The Second Great Jihad came with the Ottoman Turks and the downfall of Constantinople. At first the Muslims were successful but eventually were pushed back in to the Middle East, where they watched the gradual ascendancy of Christian Europe as the world's leader in technology, exploration and colonization—engendering and adding to the feelings of humiliation and degradation which was fast becoming a chief characteristic of Muslim society.

Today, according to them, we are entering upon the Third Great Jihad in which the Muslim fight with the western world, while no less determined than the previous two Jihads, takes several different forms.

One is demographic. The number of Muslims settling in Europe, for example, is beyond computation because most of them are illegals. But they are getting into Spain and Italy in such large numbers and have such large families that, should present trends continue, both of these traditionally Catholic countries will become majority Muslim during this century. It is predicted that in only twenty years, Holland, too, will be predominantly Muslim. As to the situation here in the United States, which incidentally is regarded by them with some justification as the successor to and inheritor of European/Western civilization, we too are not immune to the inroads of this demographic attack. I don't know if you know, but, last Friday in Chicago, 30,000 Muslims attended their annual gathering sponsored by the Islamic Society of North America, in order to plan how to become more effective and more influential in the United States. Thirty thousand people, mind you!

Beyond the demographics, the more activist fringe of the Muslim world, from what I can tell, seems to be devoted to a three-pronged, overriding strategy. First is to get the United States out of the Middle East, like what happened in Southeast Asia when the United States was driven out of Vietnam. The second part of the strategy is to take control of the oil wealth of Muslim countries which represents, incidentally, about 75 percent of known oil reserves, and to use that wealth to advance their program. The third part of the strategy, and it pains me to say the next sentence but I have to say it, is to develop nuclear weapons or other weapons of mass destruction in order to destroy Israel. If you think I exaggerate this third point, let me tell you that in an address at Tehran University on December 14, 2001, Ali Akbar Hashemi Rafsanjani, the former president of Iran, boasted that Israel's possession of nuclear weapons would be useless when the world of Islam came to possess nuclear weapons. He said, "The use of a nuclear bomb in Israel will leave nothing on the ground, whereas it will only damage the world of Islam." Rafsanjani, in other words, indicated his willingness to sacrifice millions of his coreligionists in order to obliterate Israel.

This Third Jihad, like the first two, is after nothing less than world domination in which one will have to accept Islam or death. It is true that some of the more moderate strains of Islam do accept infidels, which the rest of us are, but relegate them to the status of "*dhimmis*." That is second-class citizens who have no inalienable rights; who cannot own property; who cannot build houses higher than Muslim houses; who are subject to the *jizya*, which is a poll tax; who are required to wear distinctive clothing; who are banned from owning or bearing arms or owning horses; and our wives and children may be enslaved for particular offenses. If you think I am making up the latter point, all I have to do is remind you of our good friend, the radical Shiite cleric, Muqtada al-Sadr, who told worshipers during a sermon on Friday, May 7, 2004, that anyone capturing a female British soldier is permitted to keep her as a slave.

The worst is that there seems to be no real internal opposition to this extremism. To the best of my knowledge the response of virtually every so-called moderate Muslim leader to the threat posed by the fundamentalists has been to accede to, or to tacitly accept, this extreme interpretation of Islam and to further the Islamization of all social, cultural and political institutions in their own countries. Religious scholars of the main Islamic party in Jordan have forbidden any Islamic cooperation in the anti-terror effort. One of the leading Islamic clerics in the Gaza Strip recently told thousands of worshipers during services that the United States was responsible for causing the severe frustration that led the World Trade Center terrorists to do what they did, and a leader of Russia's Muslims—in between blowing up schools—said that it was, "Zionist Special Services that carried out the September 11 terror attack on America." Now, friends, all religions, including Judaism, have their "nuts" that say and do nutty things. But we don't hear the Pope or chief Rabbi of Israel or the Archbishop of Canterbury or the Dalai Lama saying things like this. The point is that the present political leaders of Islamic countries, and their highest religious officials, stand in mosques, hold the Koran in their hands and exhort their people to hate others and fight holy wars against them.

To the best of my knowledge, not one Islamic cleric in any Muslim country anywhere in the world has ever issued a *fatwa*, a religious edict, against suicide bombing or any suicide bomber, against terrorism or any terrorist. Not one Islamic cleric in any Islamic country anywhere in the world has issued a *fatwa*, for that matter, against Osama Bin Laden. They did issue a *fatwa* against Salman Rushdie for writing a book. In the name of Islam, they called for him to be killed for writing it. Not a single Muslim cleric, of course, has condemned one, just one, of any of the thousands of terrorists' attacks that have been perpetrated against Israel.

It is no accident either that among all the Muslim countries in the Middle East, not a single one is a democracy. Islam is a tool of repression and deprivation and brutality. Islamic countries have governments which, with the assistance of religious leaders, treat their own people, especially their women, in abominable ways: depriving them of minimal human rights; not letting them speak freely; and not letting them have any say as to who governs them, robbing them of their essential humanity.

As to any kind of a separation between church and state or between mosque and state, forget it. With globalization and democracy sweeping the globe and making the lives of so many people so much better, the Middle East is the one and only corner of the world in which the tide of democracy has not taken hold at all, in even one Islamic place. Every single Muslim country in the Middle East is run by leaders who are either crazy or corrupt or both. Someone recently did a count of active conflicts in progress around the world today. Of the thirty that were documented, twenty-eight involved Muslims against non-Muslims, Jews, Christians, Hindus, Buddhists, whatever. Somebody also reckoned that fully two-thirds of political prisoners are held in Muslim countries and that they also, those same countries, carry out about 80 percent of the executions performed in the world today. In a word, western civilization—that's us—faces a threat unparalleled in history. A threat, in my humble opinion, which is potentially lethal to all we hold dear; nothing less than a war which some have already begun to call World War III, between the western world and the push towards imperial, absolutist Islamic domination.

Now, as usual, like the proverbial canary in the mineshaft, it is the little Jewish people who were the first to feel the extremism—long before 9/11. And true to form, like the Nazis, who singled out the Jews as blocking their path to world domination. Like the communists, who similarly saw the Jews as the main stumbling block to their dreams of world domination. So the Muslim extremists have singled out the Jews, particularly the Jews of Israel, as the main obstacle to what they see as their effort at world domination.

It was Dennis Prager who pointed out that the Muslim terrorist threat is even worse than the Nazi threat, in at least two respects. First, while both Nazis and Arab Muslim anti-Semitism had closed societies and fed their people a steady diet of horrific lies about Jews, Nazis tried to hide their murder of Jews from the German public. They did not have the confidence that enough Germans would support the murder of Jewish men, women and children. So they tried to keep what they were doing somewhat secret. Arab, Muslim, and anti-Semites seem to have no such problem. Those who kill Jews are public celebrities. They become role models for the youngest of their children. The Palestine University in Nablus, for example, puts on exhibitions, celebrating, mind you, each of the suicide bombings that occur in Israel. I remember some time ago there was an exhibition there which consisted of a replica of the Sbarro restaurant in Jerusalem which was bombed—complete with Hebrew inscriptions and with replicas of human body parts and pizza slices strewn about. Pictures published on the Internet show Palestinians waiting in line to see that exhibit.

The second, even more frightening, aspect of Arab-Muslim-Jew hatred, which makes them more dangerous even than the Nazis, is that they do not value their own lives. Whereas of course, the Nazis did. The point is that no libel against the Jews is too awful or too incredible for the Arab world. The father of Mohammed Atta, the suspected ringleader of the September 11th attacks, told *Newsweek* that his son was kidnapped by Israelis, and that it was Israelis posing as Arab Muslims who actually attacked America. He could say this and millions of Muslims believe it, as well as the notion that no Jews died in the World Trade Center because they were alerted in advance. You may recall, too, that the wife of Yasser Arafat told then first lady Hillary Clinton that Israel was poisoning Palestine water supplies and that Jews were deliberately spreading AIDS in the Arab world.

Imagine five-million Israeli Jews, thirteen-million Jews worldwide, occupying one-tenth of one percent of the land mass of the Middle East, and an even smaller percentage of population are what stand in the way of the realization of the extremist agenda. Which, I repeat, is to Islamize all non-Muslim countries of Asia and Africa, with Europe not far behind, and eventually to confront the whole West, America included, with a choice of accepting Islam or death. Among Muslim extremists there has long been a saying, "After Saturday comes Sunday," which means that after they finish off the Jews, they will do the same to the Christians.

Now, as you may or may not know, Harriet and I spent a number of weeks recently in Israel working for the IDF, the Israel Defense Forces, in a program called Sar-El, as did several other B'nai Amoona members. We lived among the people, walked the streets, rode the buses, and shared ever so briefly their fears and their uncertainties. And also doing a little work which I hope was a small contribution to the Israel war effort and perhaps even to their general well-being. It would be dishonest for me to claim that the homicide bombers, the more than 5,000 separate acts of terror that Israel has endured in the last several years resulting in the death of close to 1,000 Israelis and the maiming of thousands more as well as the economic pressures, are not having a serious effect on Israeli society. Indeed they are.

People are tense and, yes, afraid. You get on a bus and reflexively scrutinize the people there. Is there a bomber among them? You take a walk, reach the corner, and question whether you should turn left or right, knowing that potentially that decision is the most important decision of your life. Or, if you were a resident rather than a visitor like we were, every single day you question whether today is the day you should call in sick. Or even more important, is this the day you should send your child to school or keep him at home? Tourism has all but dried up. Investment has all but ended. Numerous businesses have been seriously affected. But this I tell you, without a moment's hesitation, and that is that Israel and Israelis have great depth and much hidden strength. There is no power on this earth, with the possible exception of the United States, which can bring Israel to its knees. Ultimately the terrorists' attacks will strengthen Israel's resolve, because most Israelis realize that this isn't a way of Palestinian desperation but part of a long pattern of Palestinian self-destructiveness and part of their Third Great Jihad.

The day before I left Israel two trips ago, the bombing at the Frank Sinatra Building at the Hebrew University occurred. I recall how disturbed and put off I was, not just by the incident itself but by the images I saw on TV, of Palestinians dancing in the street of Gaza, celebrating the deaths and mutilations. They were images which seared themselves into my brain and which I carry with me to this very day. A few days after returning home, I received a letter from a colleague, Rabbi Danny Gordis, who wrote shortly after that very same Hebrew University incident. I want to read part of his letter to you so that you can contrast his response to the TV images of those dancing Palestinians. I think that the contrast puts this whole subject into bold and accurate perspective. Danny wrote as follows:

We were at a bris today. It was a particularly moving morning because so many of the people who were gathered to welcome this new baby were friends of the Hebrew University students who were killed last week. The move from mourning to celebration was not easy but it was a welcome change of pace nevertheless. There is a point in the bris, he continues, where the baby starts to cry. It has nothing to do with pain because it occurs before the mohel actually does anything. Usually it is when the baby's diaper is taken off as the baby doesn't like being cold. And typically the mohel will make a little joke at this point in order to put people at ease. Today the mohel did not make a joke and the baby just cried, not loud and not long, but he cried. It did not much matter because most of the adults in the room were crying too. We were crying because of what happened last week, and because of what happened last month, and because of what happened last year and the year before that, and frankly because of what's probably going to happen next year too. We stood there with tears in our eyes and without a joke to ease the pain because the phrase that is uttered at a bris, "Blessed art Thou, O Lord Our God, Ruler of the Universe, who has

*commanded us to bring this child into the Covenant of Abraham, our Father,"
is no laughing matter in Israel. It is no joke to be part of the Covenant here. It
makes you a target. It gives you enemies.*

*But then, at another point in the bris, it is customary for those gathered to say
together, "Just as this child has entered the Covenant, so may he enter a life
of Torah, of marriage and good deeds." What a simple prayer that is. It is our
prayer that this child should live as part of a sacred tradition. That he raise a
family and that he do good deeds. That he become, in other words, a mensch.
There is nothing that is much more important than that, at least to us.*

Well, friends, that was Danny's and his friends' reaction to the Hebrew
University bombing which, in a nutshell, is to me what this whole Third
World War, or Third Jihad, is all about. On the one hand glorifying a culture
of vilification, of repression, of violence, and of dancing in the streets in
the face of death, against a culture which ushers a newborn into a life of
learning, of raising a family, and practicing good deeds. Friends, as Jews, let
us draw strength from this knowledge; from the simple realization that we
are always on the front line in the fight against death and barbarity. That as
Jews, we are always the vanguard in the war against repression and brutality.

As such, we again find ourselves the primary targets of those intent on
returning civilization to the Dark Ages. As history has repeatedly proven,
what begins as a threat to the Jews ends with a threat to all civilization, and
that by clinging to a semblance of normal life and refusing to be terrorized,
we are fighting a fight whose implications extend far beyond Israel and our
little people. Whether or not it is universally recognized, it is we who are
holding the line for us all. Israel and the little Jewish people are holding the
line for our collective future as well as for our own—in a war upon whose
outcome may well depend the entire future of western civilization. May 5765
see the beginning of the triumph of that future. May God give strength to
His people and bless His people and all mankind with peace. A sentiment
which I invite you to join me in saying, Amen.

Rabbi and Educator

Rabbi Lipnick's mentor, when he was a young student, was Dr. Louis Kaplan, a highly respected educator, teacher and administrator in Baltimore where Bernie, as he was known, grew up. He was so impressed with Dr. Kaplan that his ambition was to go into education as a career. Nevertheless, he followed his older brother, Jerome, who was a profound influence and mentor, into the rabbinate. When he came to B'nai Amoona, he did not seek to be its assistant rabbi; he became its education director.

The six sermons collected here all deal with his love of being a teacher and an educator. As an educator he saw the drawbacks of formal classroom teaching of young Jewish children. He saw the substantial benefits of informal education such as Jewish camping and youth groups. He created the *Vov* class experience where B'nai Amoona 8th graders spent the summer in Israel with families that had children their age; he started summer day camps at B'nai Amoona; and a preschool. He brought the USY (United Synagogue Youth) program to St. Louis in order to provide Jewish teens with Jewish social experiences and informal learning opportunities. He found time to lead tours to Israel for adults and families, another highly effective form of informal education.

You will find in these sermons the challenges that have to be met, by every Jewish educator, that emanate from the American culture—from assimilation, from narcissism, and from consumerism. One answer, Rabbi Lipnick believed, besides informal programs which had their limits, could be a Jewish day school, where the children, from an early age, learned the values, the skills and the essential rituals of the truly Jewish way of life. True to this belief, he pulled together the necessary community resources and started a Jewish day school. In the last sermon in this section (given in 1991), Rabbi Lipnick wonders out loud just how good an educator and Rabbi he was. He says to the congregation: "In a word, the success of my Rabbinate at B'nai Amoona and the success of our whole religious enterprise is literally in your hands."

His words are as true today as they were in 1991.

Honoring our Teachers

Seventh Day of Passover, April 17, 1960

The period between Pesach and Shavuot, called *Sefirat HaOmer*, or the "counting of the Omer," traditionally is devoted to remembering and honoring the Jewish teacher. Recalling the heroism of Rabbi Akiba and his twenty-four thousand students who lost their lives fighting the Romans, this period of time was set aside as a remembrance of the importance of the teacher in Jewish life. The observance culminates in the scholars' holiday on Lag BaOmer—the 33rd day of the Omer. Today is the 6th day of the Omer, and I can think of nothing more fitting than that I should devote my sermon today to the Jewish teacher. To his role in Jewish life, to the difficulties he faces, as well as to some of the solutions to these difficulties that we may be able to suggest. I offer these words in a spirit of great reverence and deep respect, in accordance with the statement in the *Pirkei Avot*, "Let your reverence for your teacher be as sacred to you as your reverence for Heaven."

Let me start by telling you a true story, which occurred about 2000 years ago and which is reported in the Jerusalem Talmud. It seems that there was a delegation of three of the greatest rabbis of the age, who went on a mission to inspect the state of education throughout Palestine to ascertain whether or not there were sufficient educational facilities available. They came to a particular community where there were no teachers. Meeting the illustrious delegation, of course, were the heads of the community. When reception ceremonies had ended, the rabbis said to their hosts, "Bring us the guardians of your community."

They immediately sent out and called in the military guard who were presented to the rabbis as the guardians of the community.

"No," the rabbis exclaimed, "these are not the guardians of the community. They are, rather, its destroyers."

The people were amazed. They sheepishly asked, "Who, then, are the guardians of the community?" And the rabbis answered, simply and directly, "Teachers are the guardians of the community!"

In so saying, the rabbis made their point—for that community and for every Jewish community since. It is our teachers, who, from time immemorial, have protected authentic Jewish values. It is our teachers that taught Jews the values of Judaism so that individual Jews might perfect themselves intellectually and spiritually; perfect themselves so the Jewish community might become a holy community. It is our teachers that guarded and zealously preserved the integrity of the Jewish community. It is the teachers who preserved our sense of identification.

Possibly no other people in all the world has regarded teachers with greater esteem and respect, historically, than we Jews. And with good reason. Yet, I feel that it is a mistake to laud, as we so often do, only the great teachers of our past. *Sefirah* should remind us of today's teachers, whose contributions are as significant as those of our past teachers, in terms of the challenges facing Jewish life in America. Recognition of our teachers' contributions should not be postponed until some future generation.

There is probably no more dedicated group in Jewish life today than our teachers. Teachers are hard at work trying to perform the task of making Judaism part of the daily life of every Jewish person. Teaching that Judaism is not a peripheral activity of the Jew, but teaching us to regard Judaism as the very core of our individual and corporate existence. Teaching that Jewish History is not an exercise in chronology but helping us to appreciate the long, proud record of the Jews' search for God and truth, and helping us to accept our sacred obligation to continue that search.

Teaching that the Hebrew language is not an archaeological curio; rather, helping to reinstate that language as the medium both for understanding and deepening our Jewish insights.

Teaching that Zion is not the far-away locale of our "former" glories, but the scene of present and future creative achievements, as well.

No group fulfills a more important role in the survival and improvement of Jewish life than do our teachers. However, at perhaps no other time in Jewish history has the Jewish teacher faced more formidable opposition from those who would seek to destroy Jewish education in America today. There are at least three major ones on attack present in Jewish life today.

The first is the negative influence of the general environment in which we live. In America, to an alarming extent, business psychology measures significant work in terms of profit and efficiency. Only activity which leads to financial profit is deemed worthwhile. Jewish study, whose goal is to improve society, transform people, and preserve a religion is often deprecated. Oscar Hendin shows how strongly this attitude is portrayed on our mass media. "In *Our Miss Brooks*," he points out, "is pictured a female, eager to be married but unsuccessful, and therefore condemned to remain in the classroom. Her male counterpart is the ineffectual, humbling Mr. Peepers. Such people, incapable of the real work of the world, deserve no more than amused tolerance."

You know, sometimes it is even difficult to convince people that teachers work, altogether. "He who can, does; he who cannot, teaches." How many times have we heard this quip which is more than a quip? Of course, nothing could be further from the truth. The teacher works harder, possibly, than anyone! Don't allow yourself to be fooled by the "small number of hours" that a teacher spends in the classroom. The teacher's output of energy—not to speak of accomplishment—cannot be measured in the amount of time he spends actually teaching his class. The teacher spends time preparing. He spends time broadening his knowledge. He spends time talking to parents. He spends time marking papers. He spends time thinking and worrying as he faces one of the most difficult challenges that a person can ever face— building minds and touching hearts. If you have any doubts, try it sometime!

It was Jacques Barzun who said, "The pace, the concentration, the output of energy in office work are child's play compared with handling a class; and the smaller the class, the harder the work. Tutoring a single person—as someone has said—makes you understand what a dynamo feels like when it is discharging into a non-conductor" (*Teacher in America*, p. 27).

It is not easy to be a teacher, and it is doubly not easy to be a teacher in America, where the teacher is too often regarded as a non-productive, almost necessary evil. It is triply not easy to be a Jewish teacher in America whose goal is not to produce riches of the pocket but rather riches of the spirit.

If the pressure of the general environment makes the work of the Jewish teacher difficult, so do the warped values of the Jewish community. The "would-be" protectors of the good name of the Jew, the professional Jewish public relations people, are considered much more important than our teachers, judging by the rewards they receive and the position they occupy in the community.

Would that half the amount of money spent on combating anti-Semitism were spent on Jewish education. Would that half the feverish social, political and communal activity, conducted on a national and local level by tens of Jewish agencies, were devoted to the cause of Jewish education. We Jews are confused. Who are the status figures in our society? Men of wealth, perhaps? Men who are highly regarded by the non-Jewish? And perhaps men of social standing? Whoever these status figures are, they do not include the Jewish teachers.

The third of the destroyers is to be found in the Jewish home, and takes the form of indifference towards positive Jewish causes, particularly Jewish education. Many parents, remembering their own Jewish educational experiences with revulsion, cannot appreciate the values to be derived from that education. They permit Jewish education to be discarded, like a worn coat, when the child reaches age 13 or 15. They recognize little responsibility to create an atmosphere of receptiveness for what the child is learning in school. Jewish parents, having little conception of their own need to study, have ceased to regard themselves as "students" of Jewish culture. The result of such indifference is lack of regard for the teacher and his goals. Harry Golden, in *Only in America*, says, "I think it would be better if we went back to the old system, when the teacher sent for a parent and he stood in the hallway, with his hat in his hand, waiting to be interviewed and maybe a little scared about the whole thing, too."

Negative influence in the American environment, confused values on the part of the Jewish community, and indifference on the part of the Jewish home—these are the destroyers of the community. These are the obstacles encountered by the Jewish teacher, and they are most formidable. Is it any wonder that our real defenders are fighting what appears to them to be a thankless and hopeless battle? Zevi Scharfstein, one of the old master Jewish educators in America, recently published a book on the occasion of his seventy-fifth birthday, called *The Path of Life for Teachers*. Writing in Hebrew, Scharfstein presents a reckoning of his sixty-odd years of experience in Jewish education. As I read his words, written, incidentally, in magnificent Hebrew prose, my heart bled. One could detect, between the lines and in incident after incident, the defeat, the worry, the heartache, the failure which characterizes his estimate of his life's work. In one passage in particular, he says, "The teacher has come to see himself as doing pointless work—work which seems to be without purpose, without hope, without the pleasure of creation. The taste and the pleasure of teaching have been stolen from him."

This is a serious condition. Jewish teachers have come to feel that they have been left out and left behind by the Jewish community, and they are not far from wrong! We must restore them again to their traditional role as defenders of the community. We must join them in the fight against the destroyers. We must not become easy prey to these destroyers which threaten from within and without.

There must be major changes in all three areas that I have mentioned. Jewish parents must make their homes an extension of the religious school curriculum, rather than vice-versa. Adult education, administered by qualified, first-rate personnel, must be made to flourish again. As a result, the ability to read a Hebrew word and recite a *Haftorah* will not define the success of Jewish education. Parents will be satisfied with nothing less than complete involvement in Judaic religion and culture for themselves and their children. Parents must put aside recollections of their own experiences—theirs was a different age! The "*Heder*" has given way to the modern educational institution. The rebirth of the State of Israel has changed matters immeasurably, as Jews have gradually achieved a truer image of themselves than ever before.

Major change in the Jewish home must be accompanied by a serious attempt to adjust the values of the entire Jewish community. The Jewish community should recognize teachers as being among the highest status members of our people, not the lowest. One of the saddest of all sights is the way in which a teacher typically becomes retired. After many years of sparsely attended PTA meetings, thankless back-breaking and mind-shattering labor, an "affair" is held. A small gift is presented and the teacher smiles a faint but knowing smile. A lifetime of effort and this is the thanks of the community. Teachers must be paid salaries and awarded tenure commensurate with the high position they occupy.

It may interest you to know that two years ago, the average income of the 17 professions was 63 percent above the average teacher's salary—and Religious School teachers fare still worse! Their guidance should be sought on community issues. They should be encouraged to take an active part, especially in congregational life. I know that teachers should get satisfaction out of their work, and they do. But satisfaction is not the entire story. Our own estimate of the value of what we do is influenced, to a great extent, by the value others place on our work. The Jewish community divulges its sense of values through the people it chooses to honor. Whom, I ask you, does the Jewish community delight to honor, by and large?

Just as the indifference of the Jewish home must be dispelled; just as the confused values of the Jewish community must straightened out—so too the negative influence of the American environment must be challenged. We Jews must reiterate, forever and a day, the belief that business success is not the goal of life—that success in living a good and a worthwhile life is the goal. We must stress those elements of America which are valuable and which enhance, rather than detract, from Jewish education. Personality development and its importance, a great achievement of American education, should be thought of as having as much significance as the mastery of the text. Positive attitudes and the value of concomitant learning should be regarded as important as learning what the book says. Albert Einstein said, "Education is that which remains when one has forgotten everything he learned in school." In America, our goal must be to rear Jewish personalities with humanity at heart. At no time in Jewish history was the general environment more sympathetic and propitious to the accomplishment of this task than here in America. Here, democracy is a working concept, applicable to every facet of life, capable of making Jewish education even more effective and worthwhile than it ever was.

Yes, Jewish teachers have to be restored again to their position of defender. I realize that teachers have to merit this high station and earn it. Yet, I feel that they never can, really, until we join them in fighting the destroyers. United, we join them in countering the negative aspects of our environment, the warped values of the Jewish community, and the indifference of the Jewish home.

There is more we can do. A friend of mine's dearest recollection of school occurred when he was in the sixth grade. His teacher came into class with tears in her eyes. She explained the reason: "I just met a former student," she said, "and, after 25 years, he remembered me." How often do we remember our teachers? Especially our Hebrew School teachers and our Sunday School teachers, who are the defenders of everything we hold dear? We are in gratitude bound to them. We must come forward to encourage and to assist them, at every turn. I, personally, am very proud of the fact that the PTA this year devoted its dinner meeting to honoring four of our teachers who have served our Religious School ten years or more. However, I cannot hide my disappointment in the fact that only 100 members of our congregation were with us that evening to pay our teachers the respect and honor due them.

We at B'nai Amoona have made a start, but we have a long way to go. I suppose that even more important than honoring and respecting our teachers—and this, even teachers would admit—is honoring and respecting the ideals for which they stand. We must reenact their devotion to Judaism. We must echo their dedication to permanent Jewish values. We must emulate their efforts to bring about a resurgence of Jewish life in our time. In such a fashion, will we join our teachers as defenders of the Jewish community, laboring together with them, to become learned of the Lord.

Amen.

Undying Music

Rosh Hashanah 1962

For the first time in 45 years, the B'nai Amoona pulpit is without Rabbi Halpern. Every single one of us, from the moment we entered the sanctuary this morning, was painfully aware of this fact—we need no reminder. Our sense of loss is very great as we contemplate now, with perhaps even more awareness than last April, that the Rabbi of B'nai Amoona for two generations, our friend and spiritual mentor, Rabbi Halpern, is no longer with us. The pain of his passing, which may have dulled somewhat over the past 5½ months, shoots forth again as we begin these awesome High Holy Days.

Yet in a sense, Rabbi Halpern's presence is felt even more profoundly now than when he occupied this pulpit. The influence of our parents and forebears continues long beyond their earthly sojourn—at these moments when we least expect it, we feel their gentle urging. Thus it is with Rabbi Halpern. His teachings are revived and his influence is felt at many different times. This is just such a time, and we all feel it!

Music, as you well know, occupies an important place in the High Holiday Service. The *nusach* of the High Holidays is unique and engaging. The *Chazan* is at his best and always he is assisted, even in congregations which do not have choirs all year long, by the finest choir that can be prepared. Still, if the truth be known, the beauty of the service is not dependent solely, or even principally, upon these voices which delight our ears and speak to our hearts. There are other voices abroad in the sanctuary. The musical chords produced by these voices are just as audible, and no less important, than mine or than those of the *Chazan* and choir. Those voices comprise what George Eliot called, *The Choir Invisible*. Let me read the first part of the poem to you and I believe you will understand what I mean:

O May I join the choir invisible
Of those immortal dead who live again

In minds made better by their presence: live
In pulses stirred to generosity,
In deeds of daring rectitude, in scorn
For miserable aims that end with self
In thoughts sublime that pierce the night like stars. . .

Yes, joined to our earthly voices are the voices of the great "choir invisible," composed of all the great teachers of our people, extending from Abraham, of the Ur of Chaldees, to Abraham Halpern, of B'nai Amoona. Joined to our voices are those of the immortal dead who live again in minds made better by their presence. They live in pulses stirred to generosity. They live in deeds of daring rectitude that we perform. They live to the extent that we, their descendants, scorn miserable aims that end with self. They live in thoughts sublime that pierce the night like stars.

Let us now identify, one by one, the voices of this vast "choir invisible" which sing to us of our spiritual legacy. Such identification will provide us with infinitely more than a lesson in Jewish history. Such identification will provide us with even more than an accompaniment to our own spiritual cravings. Their song and their voices, as they reverberate through these halls and as they fill these portals, will provide us, personally and as a congregation, with the score by which we shall create our own undying music. Our own triumphant symphony of living Judaism in this, our generation.

The first voice in *The Choir Invisible* is that of our father, Abraham, of whom Isaiah says, in God's name: "For when Abraham was but one, I called him and blessed him." It was Abraham who was the first to raise his voice above the dissonant pagan vulgarity of his day and proclaim once and forever, the "world redeeming truth of the One God of Justice and Mercy."

Abraham was the pioneer of ethical monotheism. Undazzled by the heathen splendor of Babylonia, he forsook home and family and devoted his life to spreading the truth of the One God who is both sternly just and warmly merciful. The world has not been the same since, nor have we, his descendants, been the same. Abraham calls upon mankind to imbibe the knowledge that what we do has broad and ultimate significance. We are not subjects of a capricious, soul-less pantheon of pagan deities to whom justice is a mockery, and pity an admission of weakness. Nor are we specks of worthless dust, cast about by the four winds in an endless, meaningless swirl called "life." No, we are children of a just and merciful God who binds both Himself and us to the twin duties of righteousness and compassion. Abraham never doubted that the wicked cities of Sodom and Gomorrah were deserving of punishment for their crimes, by a God who demanded and exacted just behavior on the part of His children. But, by the same token, he never doubted, for one moment, that if there were a modicum of righteousness to be found in those cities, God would indeed spare them.

Nay, Abraham challenges God, in a statement which rings forth through the ages, with the same great sublimity as when it was first spoken: "Shall not the Judge of all the earth do justly?" For the first time in history, the real question was asked, and Abraham came away with the answer.

Yes, God is bound by justice and so are His children. Yes, God is obligated to pity, and so are His children. It is Abraham's voice that we hear rising, in volume, on this sacred occasion as we give ear to *The Choir Invisible*.

The second voice we discern in *The Choir Invisible* is that of Abraham's son, Isaac, whose message comprises the Torah reading on the second day of Rosh Hashanah. Abraham taught faith in the One God of justice and mercy; Isaac taught the need for sacrifice on behalf of that faith. The story of the binding of Isaac is familiar to us all. God told Abraham to take his son, his only son, whom he loved, and to bring him as a burnt offering to the Lord. Abraham obeyed and prepared to do as the Lord had bidden him. Abraham and Isaac ascended the mountain, and the sacrifice was readied. Then, suddenly, God stayed the hand of Abraham, saying, "Lay not thine hand upon the lad, for now I know that thou fearest God, since thou hast not kept back thy son, thine only one, from me."

It is Abraham who has long been glorified for his complete devotion to God. But, to me, deserving of equal praise, if not higher praise, is Isaac. Tradition tells that at the time of the binding, Isaac was no child—he was 25 years old. Furthermore, Isaac knew why he was going up to the mountain. He asked his father and his father told him. Still, Isaac did not falter. He willingly submitted to an ordeal which, in his mind, would result in his death.

Throughout Jewish history, the remembrance of this event never left our people. It served as the classic example of the Jew's willingness to offer to the Lord our dearest possessions, unto life itself, if need be. Too many times, in our history, the example of the courage of Isaac and his father gave Jews the courage to say "No" to their persecutors and to face the dread corollary of their resoluteness—*Kiddush HaShem*; the sanctification of God's name; martyrdom.

In this time and in this place in America, Jews do not face the terrible alternatives placed before our Fathers. Nonetheless, the example of their willingness to sacrifice spurs us to the knowledge that, if the faith of Abraham is to persist, if this high religious ideal is to endure, we must be prepared to sacrifice on its behalf, unto life itself. The example of Isaac's willingness to sacrifice for our faith is the second strain which reaches our ears in *The Choir Invisible*.

As we continue to attune our ears to *The Choir Invisible*, we distinguish still another voice, powerful and commanding—the voice of Moses, our teacher. Faith in a God of justice and mercy is the foundation; willingness to sacrifice is the unconditional acceptance of that foundation. But to Moses was left the method, the program in life, built upon the foundation of belief. It was Moses who ascended Sinai and snatched from heaven that very program, in the form of the Torah. He presented his divine treasure to the Jewish people. In so doing, he set before us, clearly and forthrightly, the translation of belief and commitment into a program of living and feeling and acting, and he bade us follow it.

Have you ever wondered about the fact that Moses, the great liberator of Israel, was the very one who tied the bond of service between God and Israel? This is no contradiction. Man deserves and needs freedom—and let no man enslave another. Yet, by the same token, if man does not harness his freedom to divine goals, that freedom soon degenerates into abysmal emptiness, into "miserable aims that end with self."

"Let my people go", said Moses. For what purpose? He anticipates: "that they may serve Me!" The whole of the Torah, as it was transmitted by Moses and interpreted over the ages by his spiritual descendants, does not come to our ears as we harken to *The Choir Invisible*, now. It is too vast—it requires a lifetime of study in order to master a fraction of its beauties and its insights. Yet, the crucial place of Torah as our guide to just relationships with our fellowmen, its crucial place as a blueprint of our duties to the Divine, these do reach our ears as we hear the voice of Moses sing to us from *The Choir Invisible*.

We have identified the voices of Abraham and Isaac and Moses as part of *The Choir Invisible*, but there are others.

There is, for example, the voice of Isaiah, representative of all the prophets of our people, who took the faith of Israel and its Torah and made both speak to the crucial issues of their day. Judaism was not to be an esoteric faith reserved exclusively for the intimate confines of the home or the synagogue. Judaism had to be related to the larger whole. It had to become the instrument by means of which Jews reacted to the burning political and social problems of society.

Isaiah, for example, foresaw the time when the faith of Abraham, and the Law coming forth from Zion, would bring about an era of peace and trust among peoples. "Nation shall not lift up sword against nation, neither shall they learn war anymore."

Judaism, if it was to mean anything, had to mean a better life for Jews and for all the peoples of the earth. The voice of Isaiah and the other prophets, whether on the subject of war and peace or on the subject of just weights, or on the subject of honesty in government, shot out like sparks from an anvil. These sparks seared the wrongdoers of their day. They destroyed, once and for all, any notion that there is no connection between religion and the marketplace. Those sparks continue to shoot forth from the prophets and their writings, and they light in us the determination to make Judaism relevant to the social issues of our day. They urge us to use our faith to remove suffering, to fight immorality, wherever it may be found. It urges us to bring society yet a little closer to that glorious "end of days" when "the mountain of the Lord's house shall be established as the top of the mountains." The voice of Isaiah is clearly discernable in the great "choir invisible."

Finally, the voice of our Abraham is clearly recognized—Abraham E. Halpern, of B'nai Amoona. To say that Rabbi Halpern spoke of these same things to us is unnecessary. He was the director of the "choir invisible" for two generations. He modulated and harmonized the voices of Abraham and Isaac and Moses and Isaiah, and many others, as they sang their message to us.

In 1948, Rabbi Halpern pointed out that "Abraham disturbed the concepts of his day when he dared to argue with God about the cities of Sodom and Gomorrah." He echoed Isaac's contribution in 1955, when he said that the Jew had to "surrender his whole being unconditionally to God." He reiterated the message of Moses when he spoke of Moses' "determined indignation" against Egypt, and he referred to the Torah of Moses as the very life of the Jew. Finally, of Isaiah and the prophets, he said, "They carried the torch forward and they turned on ruler and prince, on king and the man in the street, and demanded that they walk in justice and humbleness before God." "Religion," he continued, "must always offer pronouncements on the great social problems that confront mankind because, too often, organized religion has been too timid to arise, as did our prophets of old, to demand of all men that they live in accord with the laws of social justice." Now, Rabbi Halpern has himself become part of the great "choir invisible," which sings to us; which sings to us of faith in a God of justice and mercy; of the willingness to sacrifice for that faith; of freedom and Torah; of peace and social justice. He may not be here physically, but his voice and his message, together with those of his fellow choir singers, fill this hall and our hearts full of undying music.

Many people, since Rabbi Halpern's passing, have asked me about B'nai Amoona's program for the future. Men cannot live in the past, only. This, I believe, we all realize. As late as 1960, Rabbi Halpern told us that "we cannot afford to rest on the laurels of the past," that we must not allow "our rich assets to remain unproductive." The past, and particularly that glorious segment of it, lived and practiced at B'nai Amoona these two generations, urges our search to vaster issues. The future at B'nai Amoona will see a passionate seeking after the God of Abraham. It will be a future in which men and women will be urged to greater sacrifice on behalf of our honored faith. It will be a future dedicated to Torah and to the study of Torah. It will be a future after the tradition of the prophets, in which all the social issues of our day will be measured and evaluated by the yardstick of a divine morality.

We shall sing loudly and clearly, and we shall sing in harmony with the great "choir invisible."

So, to live is to bring supreme glory to our forebears. So, to behave is to heap supreme honor upon the memory of Rabbi Halpern. It is to such living and to such behaving that I summon you on this occasion. I summon you to one other act of pious devotion in Rabbi Halpern's memory, which in many ways, is just as crucial as what I have said.

The B'nai Amoona Board of Trustees has created the Rabbi Abraham E. Halpern Educational Foundation, whose purpose it is to encourage young people to devote their lives to God and to Judaism. The future of our faith is no stronger than its leadership. The future of Judaism is no stronger than our ability to create leaders who can both sing the undying music of the ages and who can lead our people in that song.

The Rabbi Halpern Educational Foundation will seek a significant sum of money—$100,000—which will be guarded in perpetuity in Rabbi Halpern's memory. The income of it will be used to encourage young men to enter the Rabbinate and Cantorial service. To encourage young men and women to enter the Jewish teaching field. To encourage young people, generally, to embark upon a career of service in Jewish life.

Can you think of a more fitting and lasting memorial? This is a memorial which will endure as long as there are Jews to whom the perpetuation of Judaism is dear. This is a memorial which will endure so long as there are young people who can be induced to listen to *The Choir Invisible*, and to record its music upon the souls of their generation. May this be forever!

You will be approached for a contribution immediately after the holiday. I ask you to remember that it is not the success of the drive which hangs in the balance. Nor is it merely the future of our people and our faith which hangs in the balance. It is the future of Rabbi Halpern's song which hangs in the balance.

Rabbi Moshe Avigdor Amiel once pointed out an apparent contradiction with respect to Rosh Hashanah. "On the one hand, this holiday is called," he said, "'the day of remembrance.'" "On the other hand, it is called 'The Day of Remembrance' and suggests to us the old, the past, that which is no more. The New Year suggests to us the future, newness, that which is yet to be."

Perhaps never before in the history of B'nai Amoona have these two characterizations of Rosh Hashanah been more appropriate. Today, we remember. Today, we look ahead, and in so doing, we cement a bond between ourselves and the past which will result in a glorious future, such as perhaps we never dreamed. A future in which the just and merciful God will reign supreme; A future in which Judaism, guided by well-informed, dedicated youthful leadership, will flourish; A future in which our world will find the road to peace and mutual trust; A future in which each of us, in the words of the final portion of the poem, will "...*be to other souls the cup of strength in some great agony, enkindle generous ardor, feed pure love, beget the smiles that have no cruelty...*" So shall we, in our own good time, join *The Choir Invisible, whose undying music is the gladness of the world.*

Amen.

The Choir Invisible
George Eliot (1819–80)

O May I join the choir invisible
Of those immortal dead who live again
In minds made better by their presence: live
In pulses stirr'd to generosity,
In deeds of daring rectitude, in scorn
For miserable aims that end with self,
In thoughts sublime that pierce the night like stars,
And with their mild persistence urge man's search
To vaster issues.
So to live is heaven:
To make undying music in the world,
Breathing as beauteous order that controls
With growing sway the growing life of man.
So we inherit that sweet purity
For which we struggled, fail'd, and agoniz'd
With widening retrospect that bred despair.

Rebellious flesh that would not be subdued,
A vicious parent shaming still its child,
Poor anxious penitence, is quick dissolv'd;
Its discords, quench'd by meeting harmonies,
Die in the large and charitable air.
And all our rarer, better, truer self,
That sobb'd religiously in yearning song,
That watch'd to ease the burthen of the world,
Laboriously tracing what must be,
And what may yet be better—saw within
A worthier image for the sanctuary,
And shap'd it forth before the multitude,
Divinely human, raising worship so
To higher reverence more mix'd with love—
That better self shall live till human Time
Shall fold its eyelids, and the human sky
Be gather'd like a scroll within the tomb Unread forever.
This is life to come,
Which martyr'd men have made more glorious
For us who strive to follow. May I reach
That purest heaven, be to other souls
The cup of strength in some great agony,
Enkindle generous ardor, feed pure love,
Beget the smiles that have no cruelty,
Be the sweet presence of a good diffus'd,
And in diffusion ever more intense!
So shall I join the choir invisible
Whose music is the gladness of the world.

My Dreams for B'nai Amoona Shortly After Becoming Rabbi

December 7, 1963

To Dream! To dream is to engage in one of the most beautiful and one of the most important of all the arts. Unfortunately, dreaming is an art which is swiftly being lost in our society, in our time. The reasons are hard to come by. One of the reasons that dreaming is a fast-disappearing art is that most of our lives are lived on the plane of activity, on the plane of response to immediate stimuli. Most of our movement is in the realm of the momentary, the expedient.

Such dreaming as we may do is limited, unfortunately, to the hours we spend asleep. It hasn't always been this way; nor was it this way, particularly, in Jewish history. In today's *sedra*, we read the wonderful and moving story of one of the greatest dreams that the world has ever known; and by far, the greatest dreamer of Jewish history. We read the story of Joseph—Joseph the dreamer. Joseph was just a lad, one brother among 12. But that he was different from his brothers was clear right from the very start, for Joseph dared to dream! He dared to dream dreams of greatness and achievement, for himself, and for his people. He dreamed of an inexorable Hand pushing him and his people to heights of achievement and success. This rude shepherd boy dared to dream than an unseen Power was driving him and his family into a position where, one day, they would become a source of life and sustenance to each other and to the then-known world.

Joseph dreamed, yes, and through his dreams excited the enmity of those around him. His dreams came true; gloriously so. Indeed, but for his dreams and their eventual realization, we Jews would not be here today. Nor could all of the subsequent dreaming of Jewish history have occurred.

During these past several months, I have had some time on my hands. During this period, for some reason or other, the immediate, the momentary and the expedient ceased to have the same importance as formerly. These things did not seem quite as urgent as in the normal work-a-day week. During this period, I like to think my perspective widened, as I too, dared to dream dreams!

Today, as we recall the great dreamer, Joseph, I ask you to share with me some of the dreams that I have dreamed.

First of all, let me start by saying that the crises facing our people today are no less severe than those that faced Joseph in his day. I am arriving swiftly at the realization that the Jewish people stand, at this moment, upon the threshold of very difficult times; upon the threshold of great and serious challenges which, if not successfully met, could spell—God forbid—the end both of our people, and of our faith.

This awareness is brought into focus as we look at the falling Jewish birth rate in this country. This awareness is brought into focus as we see the growing problem of intermarriage throughout America. We become aware of the crying dearth of rabbinic and other Jewish leadership. We recall the precarious position of our coreligionists in Israel and as we see the enervation of Jewish life in the Soviet Union. We are in the midst of great crises in the life of our people and our faith. Somehow, I feel that there is an inexorable Hand which has been placed upon the shoulder of Congregation B'nai Amoona, and upon myself, to become a source of life and sustenance—for ourselves, for our people, and, indeed, for our entire community.

The time has come for us to dream together the kind of dreams which will enable us to answer the demand of that Hand which I sense. If you, and if I, do not dream such dreams, I ask you who will? Therefore, I say to you what Joseph said to his brothers: "Hear, now, I pray you, this dream which I have dreamed." Yes, members of B'nai Amoona, hear, now, I pray you, the dream which I have dreamed.

The first part of the dream centers about the word 'commitment'. I dream that, one day, membership in this congregation will mean personal Jewish commitment on the part of each and every person who has the high honor of being affiliated with B'nai Amoona.

Secondly, we will submit ourselves to the elevating regimen of Jewish observance. *Kashrut*, for instance, will not be something for only the rabbi to observe, but will become the personal obligation of each and every member of this religious community. Prayer, for example, will not be an exercise engaged in on a regular basis by mourners only, but will be the constant outpouring of the grateful or troubled souls of each of our members.

And the Shabbat! The Shabbat will not be honored by our people more in the breach than in the observance. The Shabbat will become a day of deepening our commitment, a day which will be set apart for the spiritual and intellectual regeneration of our people. The Shabbat will be a happy time in our homes, as will the other festivals; occasions when parents and children will gather in conviviality and in love, and drink deeply from the cup of Jewish joy.

And something else about the Shabbat: We have, by general standards, a fine group of worshippers on the Shabbat. But I dream of a time when all of our members, the great majority of whom are not to be found in the Synagogue from one year to the next, will stream into these sacred halls in order to cement their bond, on at least a weekly basis, with our great and emerging tradition.

I dream of a day, too, when the obligation of Torah study will be assumed by each and every one of our adults. Our leadership will set the example for the entire membership, who then follow them into the study courses, the lecture halls and the library. There will come a time when we shall have to find additional instructors and create a new and refurbished library, as well as new classrooms and new courses. There will come a time when the level of our courses will have to be elevated far beyond the elementary level. I dream, in other words, of a time when each and every member of this congregation will accept upon himself the commitment of loyalty to God and devotion to Torah.

I have dreams concerning the whole relationship of our people to congregational life. That relationship will be more than a financial one. It will be a relationship in which all of our talented people, in every walk of life, will not be content to be part of that great amorphous mass which is neither known nor recognized. These people will step forward and offer their abilities and their talents and their substance, freely and willingly. They will help the congregation to improve and to flourish as never before in its history.

That will be a time when we shall have to create new committees and new forums in order to accommodate the inspired thinking of so many of our people, whose thinking is heard so seldom now. I do have a dream for B'nai Amoona and for its members!

My dreams for our members are in no way separated from my dreams for our youth. I dream of a time when we shall have incorporated into our educational program the most effective methods and materials of instruction which will be presented by the finest possible faculty of instructors. This so that all of our children will be filled with authentic knowledge of our faith, and will be filled with pride in the privilege they have to perpetuate that faith.

I dream, too, of increased standards in our Religious School; where every child will become a student in our Hebrew School; where none of them will entertain the idea of quitting before their graduation from at least our elementary department. I dream of a Hebrew nursery school being conducted in this building, each and every morning of the week. When that project succeeds, I dream of starting a Foundation School which will offer the first three years of Jewish and general education on these premises—five days a week for those families who desire it.

I dream of a camp operated all year round by B'nai Amoona, not far from St. Louis. A camp where children and adults can spend weekends or longer, summer and winter, living and learning and singing and creating in a completely Jewish environment.

I dream of an expansion and intensification of our high school department, where many more students than presently decide to continue their education beyond the elementary level.

I dream of a time when Camp Ramah will be peopled by dozens of our children who will live and breathe Hebrew and Jewish experience for two months in the summer. I dream, also, of an expansion and deepening of our youth program—L.T.F., U.S.Y., U.S.I., and U.S.J., through which hundreds of our children will socialize and learn under the guidance of well-trained and well-equipped youth leaders.

I dream of a time when, every year, there will be at least one—or dare I dream of two—of our youngsters who will decide that their life's work shall be in the area of Jewish service, whether in the Rabbinate, the Cantorate, or teaching. I do dream of these things!

I know that these dreams cannot stop at the doors of B'nai Amoona. For none of this can happen unless we have a responsive community in which to live—a sympathetic community here and nationally. Thus it is that I dream of a day when we shall see, in St. Louis, a Hebrew teachers college and a teachers training school, in which qualified young people will receive the skills and the inspiration required to teach our youth and our adults, and from which they can come back to B'nai Amoona and receive from us the respect and the kind of salaries worthy of their function.

I dream of the leadership of B'nai Amoona fanning out into the community, taking active, crucial roles in many of the important causes that every community must sponsor. I dream, too, that our relationship with the Conservative Movement will become ever closer through greater participation of our people in congregational meetings and conventions. Not just one or two attending a convention, but dozens who will desire to learn and to grow and to expand their horizons, and then to pay back, into B'nai Amoona, what they have learned.

Finally, I have the dream that all of this will happen in a world where men and nations will come to realize the folly of war and greed; that all of this will occur in a world of peace and tranquility and tolerance, which, by our efforts will have had no small part in bringing about.

Yes, indeed, I have dreams! Dreams which God has allowed me to dream with you—dreams which life and circumstances have bidden us dream together.

I am not unmindful of the gaping distance between dreams and their realization. Boards and committees will have to meet to put skin and bones upon these dreams, not to speak of the funds which will be required for many of them. God willing, we shall get to that stage. Someone once said that "A man's dreams are an index to his greatness." The very same applies to a congregation's greatness; a congregation's dreams. B'nai Amoona's dreams are an index to its greatness!

I feel that B'nai Amoona is great! In so much so that there is no doubt in my mind that we shall respond to that inexorable Hand and become a source of life and sustenance—to each other; to St. Louis Jewry; to Conservative Jewry nationally; and to mankind at large. Is this immodest? I don't mean it to be. Let us not make the mistake of confusing modesty with timidity. B'nai Amoona has a great obligation and the kind of future in which timidity must be replaced by tenacity. For it is my conviction that our redemption, and, indeed, the redemption of the Jewish people, literally depends upon it.

Joseph was a great and courageous dreamer. Yet when the Chief Butler and the Chief Baker brought their dreams to him, Joseph asked, "Do not interpretations belong to God?" However, we can ask it a different way, "Do not the realizations of our dreams, in the final analysis belong to God?" The answer clearly, for Joseph and for us, is "Yes!" The realization of our dreams are indeed in the hands of God. But in the words of Rabbi Tarphon, "It may not be your duty to complete the task and to realize all of our dreams, but we are not free to desist from the effort."

May our efforts, in the days ahead, be crowned with great and abiding success.

Amen.

The Rationale of the *Vov* Class

September 20, 1971 - Rosh Hashanah 5732

Rabbis usually deliver sermons on Rosh Hashanah, and I have been no exception. But this year, today, I don't want to deliver a sermon. I merely want to visit with you and talk with you. I want to talk about a lot of things which are close to my heart and I hope close to yours.

As you know, since the High Holidays last year, I have been away (sort of) on what I have been fond of calling a "partial sabbatical," with emphasis on the word "partial." It is rather interesting and perhaps even paradoxical that during this period of relative separation, I don't think that I have ever felt closer, either to you, or to the rock from which we were hewn. This last year was a year of surpassing significance, and hopefully growth, for me. So, settle back now (for this may take a while—sermons, you see, can be timed, but not visits!—as I tell you a little bit about what happened this past year, and the possible implications for the congregation, for Jewish education generally, and for me, personally.

Where did it all start? I guess it started about 30 years ago, when Dr. Louis L. Kaplan, Director of the Board of Jewish Education of Baltimore, my teacher and friend, called me in one day and said, "Bernie, I want you to teach at the Isaac Davidson Hebrew School." Now, I want you to know that that was a very big moment in my life. I had just turned all of sixteen and, until the year before, I had been a student in that same Isaac Davidson Hebrew School. How could I go and teach among the venerable faculty who were my teachers? Those were the days, friends, when faculty was venerated. Even Hebrew School faculty. I, at sixteen, was to be one of them? But Doc said, "You'll do it, and you'll do a good job." It was at that moment that a lifelong love affair between Jewish education and me began.

Approximately ten years passed by—years spent at Johns Hopkins University and at the Seminary—years of involvement in one or another aspect of Jewish study and Jewish education. Then, I came to B'nai Amoona, not as Rabbi Halpern's assistant, if you remember, but as Educational Director. Those were wonderful years, years of labor and love, and of some accomplishments: We succeeded in building, or helping to build, some positive relationships between our students and Jewishness; we produced our share of rabbis; and had what was generally acknowledged to be a rather effective educational program, certainly for St. Louis. But, even then I remember, especially as I pursued graduate studies at Washington University, a gnawing inside of me, the realization that, despite our so-called successes, we really weren't doing the job. We really were not making it; the kids were not really learning a great deal. Even worse, their commitment to Jewishness was really not very deep.

Not our fault, probably. The pressure of this environment, the lure of other lifestyles, the pull of other causes, whether social or personal, had the effect of dampening, if not deadening, the effectiveness of the educational program which we were conducting. Even the successes, one suspected, should be credited more to the influence of the home or to a camping experience or to a particular individual teacher's charisma, much more than to anything that we were doing.

Mind you, I am not here talking about the slogans of that era, like "Vanishing Jew," or the others that became popular around that time. I am talking about my own experience. When our kids would come back to be married—those who did come back—and I would ask them about their relationship to Judaism, about the effect upon them of our educational endeavors. The simple fact is that with many, even most, we hadn't made it. I know that there were exceptions. I know that not in every case was the experience negative—in some cases it was very positive. But, being Jewish—certainly with respect to the forms of Jewish identification—was, by and large, far from our kids. Incidentally, I couldn't blame this on anybody else. They had been my students and they were the products of my best efforts—nobody else's!

Rabbi Halpern died and you invited me to become your rabbi. Those years, '61, '62, '63, until about '66, the religious establishments of the country, B'nai Amoona among them, were riding the crest of popularity and success. It was standing-room only around here on Shabbat, and the Membership

Committee had no anxieties. I was busy delivering sermons, officiating at weddings and funerals, attending Bar Mitzvah parties, and raising a sometimes-neglected family of my own. Others assumed the burden of our educational structure: Good people—sincere and serious people—like Rabbi Asher, Mr. Molad, Rabbi Sobel, and more recently, Rabbi Switkin. I became less and less directly involved in the school.

I remember that some of you criticized me, during that period, for not showing enough interest in the school. I want you to know that of all the criticism I have ever received in my life—and I have had my share, deservedly—I think that one hurt the most. But you learn to live with that criticism. In any event, and through no fault of any of those fine people I just mentioned, it was obvious that the situation, the first glimmerings of which I had seen ten years earlier, was now even more critical. The general community was becoming less and less Jewish. Every step forward seemed to be accompanied by two steps backward. Yet, again paradoxically, after becoming Rabbi, the very detachment that I had from the day-to-day operation of the school enabled me to think, perhaps more deeply than I ever had, about possible alternatives to Religious School as we know it. And this I did. Driven as I was by the conviction that unless alternatives to the present forms were found, and found quickly, yet another generation, or two, or three, would be lost. History is not in the habit of giving you many more opportunities than that.

After several abortive attempts, I lit upon an idea, arrived at by thinking through the elements of the most successful Jewish educational enterprise that I knew: Jewish summer camping. Based upon the example of Jewish camps, I extracted four principles, four working hypotheses, which I felt would have to guide whatever alternative could be conceptualized.

The first of these hypotheses I came to call a "change of venue," that is, the need to dissociate the alternative, whatever it would be, from the past. To put it bluntly, I felt that our kids had had a belly full of conventional Jewish education within these walls and would be utterly turned off to anything which resembled it, even remotely. It had to be new and preferably separated, spatially, from the building.

The second principle was democratic education. Following the philosophy of the great progressive educator, John Dewey,—who, as far as I am concerned, is as Jewish in his approach to people and to education as any Jew I have ever met or read,—I felt that students would have to come before text. Also, those human problems would have to be given at least equal weight to the forms of our faith, important though they are.

Third, a total-living situation, not a formal classroom atmosphere, but experiencing Judaism in a natural, life-embracing encounter.

And the fourth of the working hypotheses—nature. You know, I am one of those camping devotees. There is something about trees and grass and flowers which I love and need. I think Judaism has a great deal to say about nature, and I felt that if it were applied to Jewish education, it would have a salutary effect.

Well, the rest begins to be history, and rather well documented history, at that. We chose the Hebrew School *Vov* Class, the post-Bar Mitzvah group, comprising of students who had just completed their 13th birthdays, for the simple reason that, with them, there wasn't anything to lose. Most kids quit intensive Jewish education anyhow after Bar Mitzvah, nationally; 98 percent in St. Louis. We knew that even if the experiment failed, it wouldn't be too serious. It turns out that the choice of this age group was a decision of importance. It so happens that thirteen is the beginning of adolescence. In the life of the developing human being, ages thirteen and up are the most crucial, critical and determinative of all. If the period following birth is critical to life—and it is—these years, which are like a rebirth, are just as critical. It is precisely at this time, after Bar Mitzvah, that they are lost to Jewish education. Even though, we chose the *Vov* Class because we felt we had nothing to lose. The Bible says that God takes care of simpletons: so we set up the *Vov* Class program.

Instead of conventional Hebrew School classes, the group took nine weekends, monthly, away from B'nai Amoona, most often in a natural setting. Interchange between teachers and students was highly informal. And, being over a Shabbat, there was, as the working hypothesis specified, a total Jewish living situation. In addition, the group met on Wednesday afternoons and on Sunday mornings, ostensibly for the purpose of preparing for the upcoming monthly weekend. Obbie Price, past president of the congregation, and a young assistant named Ronnie Wolfson, undertook to head up the program.

It was a good year that first year. There were problems, but not so many that Mr. Price and Ron Wolfson and I did not suspect that maybe we were on to something. Surely it deserved to be tried again, and it was tried again the following year. This time it was headed by Ron and his wife, Susie.

Meanwhile, I personally was preparing to enter the picture much more actively. I requested a sabbatical from the congregation. I also requested readmission to the Graduate Institute of Education, at Washington University, with the intention of completing my requirements for the Doctor of Philosophy degree by means of a dissertation in some way connected with the *Vov* Class. Both the sabbatical and permission to do the dissertation were granted. What I ended up doing was becoming a non-participant observer at all or most of the sessions of the *Vov* Class. I recorded what was happening and tried to understand it, both during the sessions and later, as I poured over my notes, in endless hours of analysis and contemplation.

Actually, Ronnie and the class were not terribly clear, at the beginning, especially as to what it was they were trying to accomplish in the *Vov* Class. Nobody had bothered to write out a curriculum. We had decided to let the experience write its own curriculum, within certain guidelines and within a certain framework, of course. Each weekend had a theme. Wednesdays, we tried to teach a little Hebrew. In general, subjects—Jewish and general—were dealt with as they came up. Everybody was groping for what the whole thing was about. Ronnie himself had many misgivings. Parents wanted to know what their kids were learning and, meanwhile, I sat, stony-faced and silent, infusing the drama and the beauty and the perplexity of it all. How do you educate kids, in this day and age, to Jewish consciousness and involvement?

But then, things began to happen in the class. Although I think I can tell you what happened, I am not quite sure I can tell you why, even though I have just completed a book on the subject. But gradually, as the class lived together day after day, and particularly weekend after weekend; gradually, as the Shabbat, and the lighting of the candles, and the *Kiddush* began to be second nature; gradually, as this very gifted teacher began and continued to love his charges; gradually, as the kids began to understand each other and to share the depths of their yearnings and their needs and their pain; gradually, as they began to hurt each other and see specifically Jewish insights for the repair of their own and their classmates' hurt; gradually, as the need to interpret to parents what was happening began to be apparent, as things began to happen—the purpose of the class slowly but unmistakably emerged.

It was suggested, first by one of the students and picked up by the teacher, and it was finally articulated in what, one day, may become a very significant phrase in the history of Jewish education: "Learning to live together Jewishly." That was the purpose of the *Vov* Class. Yes, that was what the *Vov* Class was doing, with reliance upon those four principles: Leaving this building; being treated with respect and with love; living in an all-embracing Jewish environment, if only for a few brief weekends. We had taken a disjointed aggregate of individuals and had welded them into a single, functioning, integrated, natural, family-like, life-enhancing community, within a Jewish setting. They had been learning to live together Jewishly.

As I watched this process and thought about it and wrote hundreds of pages on it and read hundreds of books related to various aspects of it, it gradually dawned upon me that this is the missing link. This is what had been lacking all along in our Jewish educational programs. This is the step which had been not only neglected, but this happens to be the step without which Jewish education is pointless and meaningless.

Well, do I have to tell you what has happened in the last 25 years? You know it probably better than I. As the year drew to a close, many things happened, only two of which I would like to single out.

First of all, a significant number of the kids demanded a continuation of the program into the *Zayin* year. At the beginning it was nine who wanted to continue. Then eleven and, now, as of this moment, each and every one of the fifteen kids in the group has returned! Fifteen out of fifteen of these young people voluntarily returned to continue their Jewish education!

The second thing that happened is that they decided that they want to go to Israel as a group, not just to deepen their knowledge of Hebrew and Bible and other cognitive subjects which now have meaning for them, but as a community. They want to reach out for contact with other and larger Jewish communities, of which there is no finer example in the world today than the Jewish community of Israel.

You know, people, when you stop and think about it, it is so simple; it is so basic; it is really so obvious. We have to supply the community, first! It seems that everybody in the world knows the meaning of that word "community" and its operation in human life, except we who are in Jewish education!

I don't know if the implications of the *Vov* Class and what it did are obvious to you. Let me spell out a few of them.

One is that at B'nai Amoona we are going to have to begin to talk about creating small Jewish communities within total-living situations to replace our Religious School, as we now know it. We are talking about a gigantic enterprise. We are talking about an enterprise which requires more thought and planning and dedication than we have ever given to Jewish education, and we are talking about an enterprise which will cost more money than we ever dreamed would have to be spent on Jewish education. We are also talking about an enterprise which will require the concerted effort of every single member of this congregation, and beyond. Even then, I am not 100 percent sure that we are big enough, or dedicated enough, to make the kind of personal and financial investment required of such an innovative approach to Jewish education in this congregation. But, folks, we are going to try! I am convinced, and I hope to convince you as time goes on, that nothing less stands a chance of perpetuating the Jewishness of this congregation, and perhaps of American Jewry itself, in the years ahead.

As far as the personal implications are concerned, I want you to know, friends, that I see this as my personal challenge, as your rabbi, in the future. Rabbis can and do emphasize one or another aspect of the broad rabbinic field—either sermons, or pastoral work, or administration, or scholarship— and all of them no doubt are important. But mine, from here on in, is going to be Jewish education and, specifically, the approach which we have been pioneering in the *Vov* Class.

I was studying the *Machzor* the other day and I looked again at the Torah reading for Rosh Hashanah. It deals with Mother Sarah's pregnancy, and the birth, and later the trial of Isaac. This is a curious thing if you stop and think about it. After all, Rosh Hashanah, the whole High Holiday season, is a very personal occasion. One would expect a personal theme, perhaps God's first revelation to Abraham, or Moses' communion with the God-head on

Mt. Sinai. But no, the rabbis didn't choose these. They chose as their theme for these holidays what is, after all, the Jewish people's first experience in Jewish education: How Abraham and Sarah, as parents, faced for the first time in Jewish history, the task of communicating their new faith to the next generation; how to imbue in Isaac the consciousness of his Jewishness and the desire to perpetuate it.

This has been the central problem of the High Holy Days and of the Jewish people ever since. For, like Abraham and Sarah, we too are giving birth to children, and we have to find a path whereby they can become Jews; whereby they can reach the kind of commitment represented in the *Akedah*, when Isaac resolved to forge the next, that is, the first, link in the chain. I can do no better than to give utterance to the prayer that we may be granted the strength and the wisdom to be able to forge ours, the most recent link. So that when the story is finally written, we, too, may be seen as worthy of the written; we, too, may be seen as worthy of the blessing God spoke at that time to Isaac and to his parents: "In My name have I sworn," saith the Lord, "because thou hast done this thing. . . I will surely bless thee and I will multiply thy children like the stars of the heaven, and like the sand upon the shore of the sea; and thy children shall inherit the gate of their enemies; and in thy seed shall all the nations of the earth be blessed."

Amen.

A note from two former *Vov* class students:
The Nir Galim *program has had an enduring and meaningful impact on both of us as well as on many of our peers. We developed relationships with our Israeli families while living with them in an Orthodox Moshav, working in the fields with our Israeli brothers and sisters, and traveling the country in depth. This unique experience provided lifelong memories and an everlasting connection with Israel, our* Chevrah *and Rabbi Lipnick (z"l). What incredible insight this beloved visionary provided for so many young teens. May his memory be for a blessing.*

Debbie Goldberg Dalin
Maxine Goldman Weil
Members of the 1975 *Vov* Class

The Decision to Charge a Tuition Fee for Religious School

January 26, 1980 - Parashah Bo

B'nai Amoona, like all institutions and like all of us individually, is presently involved in what might be called a fiscal re-evaluation. The inflationary spiral and the financial crunch have caused us to think very deeply about B'nai Amoona's program—which parts, in the interest of economy, can be jettisoned; which can be altered; how, in general, we may re-order our priorities and our programs in order to stay afloat financially. A variety of suggestions have been put forward. But there is one suggestion in particular which seems to be receiving considerable support of late, and it is about it that I want to talk with you today.

I refer to the suggestion that, to make ends meet, B'nai Amoona can no longer afford the luxury of providing Jewish education for children at no cost to the family, beyond membership dues. The time has come, says this suggestion, for us to charge a small tuition for attendance at Religious School. Not the full cost of educating the children—this would be out of the question —but at least a nominal fee; something to help to ease the financial burden which weighs so heavily upon the congregation. Those who put forward the suggestion hasten to point out that in cases of real need, a way will be found so that families who are unable to pay the fee, whatever it is, will not be denied Jewish education for their children. Every B'nai Amoona child who wants an education will get it.

Now on the face of it, this suggestion has a good deal to commend it. Look at the arithmetic. Family membership dues are about $450. In addition to everything else, that figure entitles a family to send its children to the Central Agency for Jewish Education afternoon Hebrew School. The cost per child to the congregation, of that afternoon Hebrew School, is $265 per year, and the cost is going up next year. One does not have to be a financial wizard to know that if there are, let's say two children or three or four in a family, the cost to the congregation far exceeds the amount that is paid in dues by that family. Nor does this take into account the cost of the Sunday School, which the congregation also pays for, and all the other many privileges and services which are available to a family by virtue of its membership in B'nai Amoona.

It is like the old story that is told about the pants store. The proprietor advertised two pairs of pants that cost him $10 apiece, for $15. (In other words, he lost $5 on every two pairs of pants.) So they came to him and said, "How can you possibly do it?" "How can you stay in business at that rate?" To which he answered, "Volume!" It makes sense, say the protagonists of this point of view, to charge a nominal tuition fee for Jewish education. In order to help cut the growing and very worrisome deficit that the congregation has to contend with.

I am opposed to this suggestion. I consider it a dangerous break with B'nai Amoona tradition and a serious breach of Jewish principle, and I would seriously hope that such a fee can be avoided. Let me start out by saying that I in no way impugn the motives of those who are for the idea. They certainly have the interest of the congregation at heart and are no less devoted to Jewish education than any of us. Still, I think it would be a grave error.

To the best of my knowledge, from the very start at B'nai Amoona, from the very beginning of the history of this congregation, the Jewish education of children has been regarded as the obligation, and the privilege, of the entire B'nai Amoona family. That is, the Jewish education of members' children was never seen as the sole responsibility of their parents. The theory was that B'nai Amoona is a community. Its children don't belong just to their biological parents. The children belong to us all. If not in every sense, then certainly in terms of their Jewish education. This idea was not original with B'nai Amoona. We Jews, in Talmudic times, that is close to 2,000 years ago, legislated the concept of communal responsibility for education. Rather than individual responsibility, every community of a certain size had to engage teachers and conduct a school at a time when the people of Asia and Europe were still running around with loin cloths. It is a concept which was later adopted by all of western society and is practiced to this very day. In University City, Ladue, Clayton, or Parkway, the entire community pays an education tax, and everyone, whether they have children in school or not, is required to pay the tax. The concept is that maybe once you did have kids in school. Or one day you will have kids in school, or even if you never have kids in school, the total community has the obligation of conducting an educational program. Once again, because the kids belong to the total community—if not biologically, then culturally. A person pays according to his means and, I repeat, there is no such thing as deducting taxes because you don't have kids, or avoiding participation in some other way. Some observers have gone so far as to say that this concept of public education is what made possible this great experiment of America. Without it we could not have had a ghost of a chance of forming a cohesive society in this land.

Well, the very same concept has always applied to B'nai Amoona, and still should be, I think.

Support for this concept, I feel, is found in today's *sedra*. The *sedra* starts out by describing the eighth plague, which were locusts. It appears as though Pharaoh, by now, is beginning to weaken. After all, this is the eighth plague. So Pharaoh calls Moses to him and suggests that perhaps they can "negotiate" the release of the Jewish people. Moses and Aaron were brought again unto Pharaoh and he said unto them "Alright, go serve the Lord, your God: but who are they that shall go?" Moses answers: "We will go with our young and with our old." Now consider Moses' answer for a moment. On the face of it, Moses should not have answered that way. Strangely, he put the youngsters before the oldsters. He should have said 'with our old and our young we will go;' not 'with our young' first, and then 'our old.'

Jewish culture, at that time, was not a youth culture. Kids did not come first. Elders did, as is indicated by many, many passages in Scripture. Why then, here in his answer to Pharaoh, did Moses put children first? As I studied the passage this week in the light of this problem that the congregation is facing, the answer suddenly occurred to me. The plagues, you see, and this conversation between Pharaoh and Moses and Aaron, followed directly on the heels of the decimation, the annihilation of Jewish young people. You remember that the final straw which forced God's hand, as it were, which caused the plagues, was Pharaoh's decision to kill off Jewish children. A decision that was probably all too successfully carried into practice. One Midrash says that the reason that the first plague was the Nile turning into blood was that the Nile was already red with the blood of Jewish babies that had been killed in it. It is for that reason that when the Exodus was about to occur, Moses adopted the priority that he did. The kids, the few that were left, were precious. The survivors were very, very dear! Not just to Moses, and not even just to the people who lived at that time. But to all future generations of Jews. Because the simple fact is that the whole future of the Jewish enterprise which was about to get under way, at that moment, depended upon them, upon the kids. Therefore they were mentioned first!

Friends, it seems to me that we face a similar situation today. It should be well known to you by now that the Jewish community faces a situation of less than zero population growth. We are not reproducing ourselves, and legend is the number of Jewish young people being lost through assimilation and intermarriage. There are no Jewish kids any more, or certainly very few. In our own School, it wasn't long ago that we had over 700, and now the figure hovers around 300. What is true of B'nai Amoona is true of every other congregation in the country.

Now is not the time to tax families with kids. Especially for the purpose of Jewish education. Just the opposite! If the Jewish community had any sense, it would subsidize families with kids and would subsidize their Jewish education. Congregations would give them a reduction in dues. After all, the parents have to feed and clothe children and send them to college. To tax them in addition for Jewish education, in any kind of special way, would seem to me to be precisely the wrong course to follow. We must encourage Jewish parents to have kids and to give them Jewish educations—not discourage them! The simple truth, you see, is that today, precisely like at the time of the Exodus, every child is precious. And the whole future of our congregation, of our people—not only in terms of the immediate future but the long-term future of our people—depends upon them. At this particular junction of history they have got to come first.

Now obviously, the money has to come from some place. But my contention is that it should come from the total B'nai Amoona family, equally. I know our President is considering ways and means of giving those members who have the financial wherewithal the privilege of providing Jewish education for all the children of B'nai Amoona. How? By having them pay dues in excess of the minimum. I hope that many of you will be hearing from him soon and that you will do voluntarily what the Jewish community has done for two-thousand years, and what B'nai Amoona has done for one-hundred years. That is, participate, to the extent that we are able, in providing Jewish education for all the children of this congregation.

I think that B'nai Amoona is kind of a special place. But frankly, even after all these years, I am unable to say with real precision what it is precisely that makes us special. As I think about this subject now, it occurs to me that perhaps it is, at least in part, this policy and this principle that we have honored, lo these many years—namely, the acceptance of total congregational responsibility for Judaism—that makes us special, and different. I am proud of the fact that we are one of the few congregations in the country which accepts in theory and in practice this concept. How ironic it would be, in this "Year of the Jewish Family," to abandon it. Let us therefore, all of us, put our collective shoulders to the wheel and declare to the Pharaohs of the world—and not least of all to ourselves—that we shall go forward with our young and also with our old.

Amen.

We All Write a Book of Our Lives

1990 - Rosh Hashanah II

The rabbis say that when Adam sinned and was punished by God with mortality, that is, with ultimate death, he pleaded with God. Adam said, "God, how terrible this is!" "I don't mind being held responsible for the death of the wicked, but I will be accused of being responsible for the death of the righteous, too." "Don't worry, Adam," replied God, "I'm going to have every person write an account of his own life and he will seal it with his own hand." Indeed, it is not Adam, and it is not God, it is we, each and every one of us, who is the author of the book of his life. It is we who have written it and it is we who are writing it.

Every day that we live, its pages record what we do and how we do it. True, the Torah pictures God as poring over a Book of Remembrances, on the basis of which He seals our fate for the coming year. But you should know that the book is not one which God, or anybody else, wrote for us. It is the one that we have written ourselves and with our own hand. It is that book that God studies, compassionately to be sure, eager always to see evidence of *Teshuva*, repentance; of *Tefillah*, prayer; and of *Tzedakah*, good deeds, on our part. All with which will allow Him to mitigate the decree. But the book is ours! And the seal of every person's hand is upon it.

If you reflect for a moment on this image of a book, which is so closely associated with Rosh Hashanah, and if you compare it with what we know about how most books fare nowadays, you might be downright depressed. It is said that only one in ten thousand books becomes a Best Seller, and that only one in fifty thousand books is remembered past ten years. Tax laws are such that a publisher can't possibly keep books around in the hope that they will be appreciated in the future. If books are not instantly successful they are remaindered or shredded to clear the shelves for the next batch.

It is no wonder that many young people see the books of their lives in much the same way. A good income and a promising future are not enough. They feel that they must be millionaires by the age of 30, or that they, too, will suffer the human equivalent of being remaindered or shredded. This also may explain the business people who won't invest a company's profits in the future, simply because it might not look good on the current quarterly report. Instead, they sell off the assets of a fine company for high quarterly profits and then, on the basis of that apparent success, they try to move on to another job and another similar shenanigan. It may help to explain, too, why so many people end up writing books that, in my opinion, are really non-books. Even those books that do make it to the Best Seller list, very few of them have any substance to speak of. In many cases they are How-To books, or lists of one kind of trivia or another. Sometimes they are ghostwritten accounts of the sexual or other exploits of one or another well-known person. In like-fashion, so many people today are authoring non-books of their personal lives. Moving from one task to another, their lives are mostly records of "How-To"—how to survive from one day to the next; or how to pass the time in this "trivial pursuit" or another.

My friends, Judaism would have each one of us write a different kind of an account, altogether. One so different that I don't think I should even use the word "book" to refer to it. I think I should rather use a Hebrew word which is so much more appropriate for the kind of document that I am referring to. The word is "*sefer*," in the singular, and "*sefarim,*" in the plural. Not "book," but "*sefer.*" If you want to know what the difference is between a book and a *sefer*, you have to spend a moment thinking about the quintessential *sefer*—the *Sefer* Torah. It is "the book," par excellence. Or, to use the Greek term, the Bible.

In contrast to the books of little substance which surround us on all sides, the *Sefer* Torah sets out, to the best of our people's ability, to understand the theme and the purpose of all of human existence. It contends, for example, that the world had a beginning. That it just didn't spring into existence. But that it was created by God as the stage for the great human drama in which we, you and I, are the main characters. According to the reckoning of the ancients, the world was created and the drama begun exactly 5,751 years ago, yesterday. The beginning, says the *Sefer* Torah, was essentially good but as a result of human willfulness and disobedience, things got all messed up. God then called Abraham and his descendants to live the kind of lives and to create the kind of society which would return creation to its pristine beauty and goodness. God commanded us, the progeny of Abraham, through the study of the *Sefer* Torah and by living the life prescribed in the *Sefer* Torah, to help bring the world into a glorious future, known as the end of days. Or the Messianic Era. At which time we, or those who come after us, will see the establishment of the Divine Kingdom of justice and truth on earth. "When the Lord shall be one and His name one."

Now to the extent that, personally and as a people, we write accounts in consonance with these ideals, we author true *sefarim*. Books that may not be distinguished by their design or by the beauty of their covers. Since when did any intelligent person ever judge a book by its cover? They are, however, distinguished by a unique and beautiful cosmic theme. They are written in a vocabulary which includes words such as compassion, *Tzedakah*, Shabbat, kosher, loyalty, sensitivity, faith; and most of all these *sefarim* tell the stories of ordinary people, like you and me, leading decent, honest and courageous lives—Jewish lives, helping to advance society in the direction of the Messianic Era. People, by our lights and by the lights of our tradition, are true heroes. That, incidentally, is why a *Sefer* Torah, and all *sefarim* written in its spirit, are considered holy by our tradition. In fact, *sefarim* are the only holy objects in Judaism, which is the reason that they are treated with respect and deference and indeed love.

Frankly, I don't know how many of these *sefarim* will make the current Best Seller list. But I am not sure that it is all that important one way or the other. Rabbi Wolfe Kelman, who died just a few months ago, was once displaying his brother's newly published *sefer* to a friend. The friend remarked, "Well, it is an impressive scholarly work. But I suspect it is not going to be a Best Seller." It so happened that Rabbi Louis Finkelstein, the former Chancellor for the Jewish Theological Seminary of America, was passing by and heard the comment. So he said, "You know my definition of a Best Seller?" He pointed out that it is a famous *halachic* compendium on the liturgy written in the 13th century by an Italian Talmudist named Zedekiah Ben Abraham

Anav. "The book sold 200 copies each year in the 13th century. In the 14th and 15th century it also sold 200 copies a year. This century and in the next century and in the 23rd century it will continue to sell 200 copies a year. That is my idea of a Jewish Best Seller!"

What a beautiful thought! Imagine a book that is so valued and so respected that it sells 200 copies every year for the past seven or eight hundred years, and is expected to do the same for the next seven or eight hundred years! Which, in effect, is my and Judaism's wish for each and every one of us, for next year and for all the years thereafter—that we shall write *sefarim* out of our lives. Their quality will testify from now until the end of time that we helped to move the world a few steps closer to the blessed future of which we dream.

It seems to me that the same task that confronts each of us as individuals confronts all of us as members of this congregation. Just as we are authors of our own individual accounts, so we are all coauthors of a volume which has been in process for over a century. We may well call this volume *B'nai Amoona for All Generations,* which, as you may recall, is the title of the congregation's centennial book which was written in honor of B'nai Amoona's 100th anniversary about 10 years ago. By and large, B'nai Amoona has written a quality document during these past 110 years. It has written a fascinating story of a group of Jews who, for generations for the most part, have remained faithful to the traditions of our people and who, at the same time, have been responsive to the needs of the hour. Overall, a document which, I believe, is fully worthy of being called a *"sefer."*

But the collective B'nai Amoona *sefer* is far from finished. One current chapter is about to end as I complete, on July 1, 1991, my 40th year of service to the congregation— m11 as Educational Director and 29 as Rabbi—following which Harriet and I will be moving to California. But there are other chapters of the B'nai Amoona *sefer* still to be written. Good chapters! Chapters which will be in accord with the proud history of B'nai Amoona and, at the same time, serve to move it forward. Ultimately in the direction of that blessed future which lies ahead, and towards which every authentic *sefer* aspires.

You know, this is a truly wonderful time in the congregation's history. All the elements are present to enable B'nai Amoona to write a real classic *sefer*—absolutely as good as, or better than, what has been written until now. For example, we sit on 33 beautiful acres with magnificent facilities. As nice as you will find anywhere in the country and, God willing, these facilities will be paid for, in full, by the time I leave. Our leadership has committed itself to burn the mortgage at my farewell next June—and to continue the construction of the Ted and Sis Fischer Chapel/Pavilion as well. Even more important than our facilities is our programs, particularly our educational programs. A decade ago I predicted that this site would become the center of traditional Jewish education in St. Louis, and indeed it has! Five schools meet in our building, and two summer day camps. This is not to speak of a wonderful youth program, a fine music program overseen by our Hazzan, an adult education program, excellent auxiliaries, including the Women's League, the Men's Club, the Couples Club, the United Synagogue Youth, and many *havurot*. You would have to look far and wide before you'll find a better shul than this.

Yet, we all know that formidable challenges lie ahead. The single, biggest one, in my opinion, is the maintenance of the Shabbat morning service on the same high level of beauty and participation that it has enjoyed throughout our history. The Shabbat morning service, as I have stated many times from this pulpit, is the central pillar of our synagogue program. It is where the B'nai Amoona family comes together regularly. Sharing its joys and sorrows. Communing with God. Raising its voices in prayer and thanksgiving. It has long been my conviction that among all the ritual acts available to us, the Shabbat is the single most important, and the one which, in addition to the great personal enrichment that it provides, stands the best chance of keeping us and our children Jews and this congregation strong. Like our theme of several years ago, "Friday night at home and Saturday morning in Shul"—when we recapture, as individuals and as members of B'nai Amoona, on a weekly basis, the unique relationship with God and the Jewish people that is available to us.

There are serious challenges that are present in the area of Jewish education. It is getting harder and harder to impart authentic Jewish values to our children. As to adults, ignorance of Judaism is rife. *Kashrut* is on the wane. Home observance of holidays needs much work. In the area of the Jewish family, I don't have to catalogue for you the problems that we face. There is a 50 percent divorce rate out there, and an almost like-figure for mixed marriages. Singles of various ages, widows and widowers have received scant attention in our program. Single-parent families and alternate lifestyles present tremendous challenges for the future. The same is true in the area of older adults. Are we doing all that we should be doing on behalf of our aging population which is growing proportionately day by day? Of course, there is always the need to maintain and update our facilities as solutions are found to the challenges in these areas, and in others, which there is simply no way of anticipating now.

As you know, each Rosh Hashanah, it is my custom to establish a theme for the ensuing year, and I hereby declare the theme for 5751 to be "B'nai Amoona in the Year 2000." Its purpose is to encourage us, during the course of this year, to think about and to outline the kind of *sefer* that B'nai Amoona should write in the next decade: How B'nai Amoona can take the record of its first 110 years and continue writing a record; which—because it will be in touch with authentic Jewish values and purposes; which, because it will help to advance our individual as well as our society's goals in the direction of the millennium, literally and figuratively—will be a *sefer* in the truest sense.

Some months ago, the President appointed a Future Planning Commit- tee. The committee has been working very hard. It divided itself into four subcommittees: one on Education; one on Family and Youth; a third on Older Adults; and the fourth on Facilities and Grounds. Each of them is staffed by a member of our synagogue staff, with professional assistance. The committee has prepared a questionnaire which will be in the mail to you, I hope next week. I want to ask you to please take the time to answer the questionnaire—one response per family. And to do so quickly. While it may seem long, it is designed so that it can be answered quickly. Don't be put off by its apparent length. The purpose is to have you tell our leadership and me what should be the theme and the content of the succeeding chapters of B'nai Amoona's *sefer*. We shall take your responses and conduct, during the course of the coming year, several town meetings. On the one hand, like all memory, it deals with the past as well it should. But at the same time, Rosh Hashanah requires a different sort of memory. Not only memory of the past, but memory of the future, as well.

As individuals and as members of B'nai Amoona, Rosh Hashanah asks us to remember the future. This memory of past and future, combined in the same breath as it were, is like the name of the holiday itself. Rosh, meaning "the beginning," and Hashanah, meaning "the year." Rosh Hashanah—the beginning of the year. Now the word "*shanah*" has two meanings embedded in it. In its simple form, it means "to do over again." In other words to repeat the past. But in the intensive form, the same root in Hebrew means "to change." Not to repeat, but to change and to improve, and this is my hope and prayer for B'nai Amoona as it approaches the year 2000.

That, while it never forgets the past and those of us who may have had a hand in shaping it, at the same time it will remember its future and make that future an ever more glorious, an ever more authentic, and an ever more beautiful *sefer*. Hopefully, that when God Himself looks upon us, He will remember us and inscribe us in the *sefer* of life, blessing, sustenance and peace—during 5751, during the next decade and during all the years thereafter.

Amen.

Goodbye, Farewell and Amen

June 8, 1991 - Shelach

Editor's Note: This was Rabbi's main address at his farewell weekend—so not so much a sermon as a speech.

You know, there is certain symmetry to life. Just as the salmon return to their place of birth, people return, almost inevitably, to their origins. I feel the same self-consciousness and nervousness today as when I delivered my first sermon from this pulpit—actually the one at Washington and Trinity, almost 40 years ago. While I know that one should never thank anyone for coming to shul, I do want to express, on behalf of Harriet and myself, our deep gratitude for the extra effort that all of you made to be here today, particularly those who are from out of town. Our children: Jayme, Mark and Emily; Tammy, Alan and Marisa. Our in-towners, Becca and Joshua; Mark and Nancy and Michael. And Dr. Jesse and Corinne—who, are actually between towns. Would that Daniel could have been here with us today. We welcome our sister, Joan, and her husband, Rabbi Kass Abelson, Past President of the Rabbinical Assembly. Their children and grandchildren: Robbie, Barbara; Jacob and Benjamin. Mimsie and her daughter, Ariella. As well as Jonathan and Susie and Daniella. Welcome, too, to sister, Len Saulson, and her husband, Dr. Stan and to people who may not be blood relatives to us, but are like family: Rabbi Morton Liefman, Vice President of the Jewish Theological Seminary of America, and Dean of the Cantorial Institute; Rabbi Jack and Sue Riemer; Rabbi Irwin Kula; Marvin and Sharon Walts; Moe and Harriet Brown; Lou and Lisa Hellman; and of course, Rabbi and Mrs. Eric Cytryn, Sarah and Jacob. As well as many others who have come from such distances to share this weekend with us. Harriet and I are deeply appreciative.

An introduction to what I want to say today was suggested to me by something I heard Rabbi Simon Greenberg, Vice Chancellor of the Seminary, say recently. Dr. Greenberg was honored at the latest convention of the

Rabbinical Assembly, for reaching the age of 90. It was Harriet's and my pleasure to be on hand to hear the many good things which were said about this venerable Rabbi and particularly to hear what he had to say. I can tell you that he delivered one of the most beautiful and moving addresses that I have ever heard. He posed the question as to how he was able to post such a record of productive longevity. He answered the question by saying that very early on he rejected the philosophy of life which states that all is vanity. That instead he attached himself to a verse from the Psalms from which all of his blessings, including his active longevity, stemmed. The verse, from Psalms 119:30 states, "The path of faith, 'amoona', have I chosen." "The path of *amoona* I chose." Suddenly it hit me! Like the Psalmist himself and like Dr. Greenberg, I too, chose that path, with one slight addition. Not the path of "*amoona*" did I choose, but the path of B'nai Amoona. Indeed, like them, from that choice made four decades ago, not all, but many, many of the blessings which are mine, stem.

With apologies to my colleagues who are present, I state publicly and without fear of contradiction, that no Rabbi ever had a better congregation than I have had. B'nai Amoona is a true, holy congregation. Heir to a long and honored tradition of over 100 years. Having been served by dedicated *Klei Kodesh*, headed by my predecessor, Rabbi Abraham E. Halpern. Incorporating in its membership, past and present, some of the finest *Baal Abatim* to be found any place. This is a unique and wonderful congregation. This pulpit has always been a free pulpit. I know of not one single instance in all of these years of an official attempt at intimidation. Oh, there may have been some individual tries along those lines. Never did they represent the congregation or its officers. B'nai Amoona has had, and God willing, will continue to have, a pulpit where the Rabbi can speak the tradition and his own mind without fear.

The congregation has also been wonderfully responsive to rabbinic ministrations in numerous other ways. It committed its resources most generously, to many of the physical and programmatic projects that we worked on together. It responded consistently to the needs of the Conservative movement and to the needs of society at large. Also, it has made serious effort to learn Torah, to practice Judaism, in form as well as in spirit. I repeat, this is a true, holy congregation. What an honor it has been for me to serve the cause of God, Israel and Torah within its walls. You know, come to think of it, I made only one serious career decision in my life. It was to come to B'nai Amoona. First as Educational Director and then to stay on as Rabbi and, like with Dr. Greenberg, many of the blessings that have been mine, rabbinically and otherwise, flowed directly from that decision. I humbly thank you and those who preceded you. Who, though they are no longer here in body, are very much in my mind and heart at this moment.

Now as you can guess, this time of transition that I am undergoing is a time of serious reflection and soul searching for me. Not unlike the soul searching which occurs in the transition between the old and the new year. Around Rosh Hashanah and Yom Kippur. Well, it was another of my teachers, Rabbi Mordecai M. Kaplan, while I was a student at the Seminary, who provided me with the yardstick for the soul search. He made a statement—really he leveled a challenge—which I heard then and have never forgotten; in fact, a challenge which has haunted me these past 40 years.

Dr. Kaplan once said that the duty of a Rabbi is to keep his congregation from becoming worse Jews than they were when he became their spiritual leader. The point that Dr. Kaplan was making, I think, was that the American environment is constantly conspiring to make Jews in this country less Jewish. American society—and no one knew more about American society and its influence on Jews than Dr. Kaplan—American society, by its very nature, makes it extremely difficult for traditional Judaism to hold its own. For Jews to participate fully in American life and at the same time to maintain ties with Jewish culture and Jewish values in an authentic way. So this was his challenge to his students, among whom I was included. You, my congregation, should be no worse Jews now, as I leave, than when I began. Honesty dictates that I face squarely that challenge. How indeed did I make out? Did I pass the test or did I fail it?

Well, I suppose, in order to get an accurate answer I have to come up with some kind of criterion for what means a better or a worse Jew. It occurs to me that I could try something relatively simple, like measuring observance. That is, I could devise some kind of a scale regarding ritual observance then and now and try to tabulate whether B'nai Amoona is made up of Jews now who are more or less observant than the members were 40 years ago. But even as I suggest this, it occurs to me that observance is far from the whole story. High moral and ethical behavior is at least as important as observance, and maybe that is what ought to be measured in order to determine whether the congregation is made up of better Jews now, than then. Is our ethical level, our moral standards, higher or lower today than they were two generations ago, if that is what 40 years represent?

Then again, maybe the criterion ought to be Talmud Torah—that is time spent in the study of Torah. Or perhaps the knowledge of Torah which, certainly from a traditional standpoint, is one of the main pursuits of the Jew. The tradition says, "The study of Torah is equivalent to all the Mitzvot." Or it could be that the criterion should be what is sometimes called spirituality, a relationship with God which is really not fully covered either by observance or moral behavior or Torah study. And here, too, I wonder. Are B'nai Amoona members more God-conscious, more in touch, than they were 40 years ago? Or less?

Perhaps the standard ought to be *Tikkun Olam*. You know that it is our obligation as Jews to help repair the world through programs of social welfare, charitable endeavors and the like. So that the question is "Do B'nai Amoona members exhibit more social consciousness now, than then?" As individuals and as a congregation, do we give more charity now than did our forebears? Friends, I want you to know that if I take my teacher's admonition seriously—and I do—these are tough questions that I have to face. . . now!

Without attempting a definitive and detailed response on each of these points—which would take us much farther afield than we can go today—I think you will agree that we are not far and away better than our forebears. We may even be behind, certainly in some of the areas which I mentioned, and maybe in more than some. Now I know that excuses are available to me. The loss of Jewish community over which I certainly had little control. The advent of television and the decline in respect for books, including Torah. The elevation of materialism and hedonism as the purpose of life. Most of which I really could not have affected one way or the other. Yet that was the essence of Dr. Kaplan's challenge! That is why he leveled that challenge to begin with, because he knew that these formidable obstacles would be working against us—me—from the very first day on.

Well, the truth is that I was not good enough to do the job that needed to be done. True, the environment has worked against us and numerous other factors have intervened. But I did not, despite the kind words which have been said and will be said about me this weekend, I did not measure up. I know that I was short, for example, in piety. It may sound a bit strange to say, but I never excelled, even to my own satisfaction, in prayer and devotion. I was inadequate, as well, in the area of scholarship. I never knew enough. Either the time was lacking or brainpower was lacking. I never commanded the knowledge and the insight that I wanted, that I needed, to do the job which needed doing.

And these are only two of the obvious lacks. I'll stop here, not because there aren't others, but because it might prove embarrassing to continue. But, the upshot is, you can believe me, that during these days of farewell, I wonder very deeply whether, if I had had more ability, I would not have to fudge as I am certainly doing, on a response to Dr. Kaplan's test—because there would be a clear, present and obvious awareness that, according to any measure of Jewishness, this congregation is superior to what it was 40 years ago. But I am afraid that that refuge is not available to me!

Then again, and on deeper reflection, maybe I am selling, not myself short so much, as you, the members of B'nai Amoona. If I have learned anything as an educator—and that, after all is what I started out to be at B'nai Amoona and have been ever since—if I have learned anything as an educator it is that you never know. A word here, an idea there, and tomorrow it is all different. Where a person is now may not be where he will be a week or a month or a year from now. If we haven't made it yet, that doesn't mean that we are not going to make it. If we haven't achieved the goal thus far, in no way does that mean that the goal will not be achieved ever. We are becoming people—in more senses than one, and the same can be true of a congregation.

A long and bright future beckons ahead for B'nai Amoona. And maybe some of the words that we spoke to each other, some of the experiences that we shared with each other, maybe some of the seeds that we planted together, will take root and grow and blossom and yield fruit and propel this congregation forward in all of the areas that I mentioned: Observance, Torah, morality, spirituality, and the repair of the world. Far ahead of where it is now. And far ahead of where it has been. The fact is that whatever the quality of past rabbinic leadership—my own included—it is really up to you. The final determination is yours to make. *In a word, the success of my Rabbinate at B'nai Amoona and the success of our whole religious enterprise is literally in your hands.* And you know what I think? I think that with the great Rabbi that you have coming, Rabbi Eric Cytryn, with the Hazzan and the fine staff that will support them, that with the wonderful officers you have, the beautiful physical facilities that you have, you can do it and that you will do it and perhaps make up for some of my and our past inadequacies. I have no doubt that this congregation has the potential of helping all of its members become better Jews in every way. Not at all inferior to those who made up the congregation 40 years ago. I chose the way of B'nai Amoona. I have never been sorry and, God willing, I will never be sorry.

You know, friends, it is my custom to relate whatever I say on Shabbos to the *sedra*. This is the classical Jewish approach to sermons and it is the approach that I have followed all of these years. Today will not be an exception. The name of today's *sedra* is *Shelach Lecha* which freely translated means "get going." So—the time has come for Harriet and me to get going. Which we shall do as of July 1st. But you should know that we do so with gratitude to God. With thanksgiving to our families. For their love and for all of the sacrifices that they have made through the years. With deep feeling for you. For all the many blessings which are ours. We will stay in touch, obviously, and we hope to be back from time to time. In the meanwhile, we wish you God speed, health and happiness, with much respect and love. Shalom, shalom, farewell and God bless.

Amen.

The Struggle For Civil Rights: USA and USSR

The United States was in turmoil. Martin Luther King, Jr. had penned the open letter from Birmingham City Jail on April 16, 1963, after he disobeyed a blanket injunction against demonstrations in that city. Attorney General Robert Kennedy sent 400 Federal Marshals into Montgomery to restore order in areas that were torn by racial violence. Medgar Evers was gunned down in his driveway in Jackson, Mississippi, on June 12, 1963. The March on Washington for Jobs and Freedom occurred on August 28, 1963. A little less than a month had gone by when the Rosh Hashanah sermon of 1963 was delivered. The Civil Rights Act would be passed by Congress in 1965.

After the Six-Day War in 1967, the USSR cut diplomatic relations with Israel. Those Jews living in the USSR who wanted the freedom to live as Jews, and had declared their desire to immigrate to Israel, were denied the right to leave, were terminated from their jobs and lost many citizenship rights. They were called "Refuseniks." This policy continued for several years, causing severe economic and emotional suffering for thousands of Refuseniks.

The three sermons in this section highlight Rabbi Lipnick's deep concern for the struggle for civil and human rights at home and abroad which, characteristically, motivated him to take direct action.

The March on Washington

September 19, 1963 - Rosh Hashanah

Editor's Note: In 1963, referring to a "Negro" was as correct as using "African American" is today.

The High Holy Days began, for me, three weeks ago.

Exactly three weeks ago, August 28, 1963, I participated in the March on Washington for Jobs and Freedom—as moving, as inspiring and as intensely a religious experience as I have ever witnessed. A quarter of a million fine people, Negroes and whites, professional men and housewives, ministers and laymen, Rabbis and educators, labor leaders and legislators, government officials and just plain, ordinary people. A quarter of a million strong—gathered in Washington that day—to daven!

What is davening? Davening is the pouring out of one's heart before the Creator of us all. Davening is recounting past sins and making, repentance. Davening is rehearsing Divine goals and setting a program of action for attaining those goals. Davening is prayer, deeply sincere, utterly consuming prayer. In Washington that day, I, and a quarter of a million other people, davened! Let me tell you about it.

I made the trip as the Social Action Chairman of the St. Louis Rabbinical Association, in the company of two other Rabbis, the Executive Director of the Metropolitan Church Federation, the editor of the St. Louis Catholic Review, and dozens of other leading citizens of this community. The predictions of large crowds and clogged transportation facilities bore no resemblance to the facts. We arrived the evening before and, apart from a chance meeting with the Reverend Martin Luther King and a small crowd in the lobby of the Statler Hilton, it was not apparent that anything out of the ordinary was about to occur.

Even the next morning, as we drove to Capitol Hill for visits with Senators Symington and Long and Representative Curtis, there was no hint anywhere of what was about to transpire. The Washington Monument grounds, where the marchers were supposed to gather, were practically deserted as we passed it. The great white marble of the government buildings, separated by long, stately thoroughfares, seemed to bespeak an almost stoic unconcern with the whole affair. Oh there were a few M.P.s and policemen at intersections but Capitol Hill and Washington had an air almost of nonchalance on that lovely, cool August morning.

The Senators and the Congressman greeted us warmly, and eagerly sought our views concerning President Johnson's Civil Rights Bill, to be passed in 1964, which the March was designed to foster. We spoke of our conviction that the whole Civil Rights issue was a moral issue that cut across all political considerations and which demanded solution immediately. We said that the bill represented a minimum program and that it deserved the widest possible support. Each of the lawmakers pledged his support even though Senator Symington reminded us of his long-standing policy never to commit himself, in advance, on any specific legislation.

After the more than two hours of interviews, we went to the Washington Monument, and there it was—that immense sea of people! Where had they come from between 9:30 and 12:00? The 1,514 buses, 21 special trains, 10 regular trains, planes, autos, on foot—it was as though some giant magician had waved his wand and, presto, there were a quarter of a million people come together to demonstrate the need for freedom and equal educational and job opportunities for all citizens! The March to the Lincoln Memorial, about a mile away, had already begun, and we fell in behind the teeming throng.

Slightly ahead was the great proud banner of the national organization of Conservative Synagogues, the United Synagogue of America, which endorsed the March and the Civil Rights Bill, as did scores of other national and local Jewish organizations. It was one of those banners that stretched almost the width of the street. One side of the banner was held by Rabbi Max Routtenberg, of Rockville Center, New York, and the other side by the wonderful Dr. Professor Simon Greenberg, Vice Chancellor of the Jewish Theological Seminary of America. I relieved him and shared his mitzvah for a block or two.

Behind us in the line was a group of marchers from New York, chanting and singing beautifully together:

"We shall overcome,
We shall overcome,
Someday,
Deep in my heart, I do believe,
The Lord will set us free."

And thus, we plied our path—slowly, quietly, almost serenely. We soon stood in the shadow of the Great Emancipator, Abraham Lincoln, at whose shrine the program was to be conducted.

The first hint I had that this March was more than a March came to me as I observed the people around me. I was struck almost immediately by the way the people were dressed. Now, everyone knew that this was going to be a long, hot day, in the 80s. Intelligence dictated that old clothes, or at least sport clothes, be worn. But strangely enough, jackets and ties were the order of the day. Fine dresses, rather than casual clothes, were worn by the women. I know I wore my best suit that day, and so, I think, did everybody else. These people had not come to relax, and certainly they had not come to fight—they had come to daven! They had come to a religious service. They were not loud. They were not boisterous. The mood of the crowd—and you can feel the mood of a crowd—was reverence; genuine, honest, sincere, gentle reverence.

Now, you know that in large crowds there is jostling; it can't be avoided. But in this large crowd, if you pushed, you said "Pardon me." Or, if you were pushed, you said, "I hope you are all right!" This crowd didn't come to push. They came to daven. What was true of the March was even truer of the program. There was prayer that day. The speakers, Jew and gentile alike, delivered sermons rather than speeches, replete with Biblical texts and homiletical twists. There was a *Chazan* named Mahalia Jackson. "*Mahalya*" means "praise God," and she did just that! Her voice rose in great swells of emotion and entreaty as she sang and, at moments, seemingly caved:

"Stand by me, Lord,
Stand by me, Lord,
Lord, if You leave me,
Stand by me, Lord."

We Jews daven that way during this season. "Cast me not off from Thee, O Lord, and do not, I pray Thee, remove Thy Holy Spirit from me."

The congregation—yes, it was a congregation—at what appears to have been pre-planned intervals throughout the long five hours of standing, responded with "Hallelujah," "Praise the Lord," "Amen," and "Truth, Truth, Truth!" The sermon of Reverend King then provided the fitting and climactic benediction to that day's proceedings:

"I have a dream. . . I have a dream that one day on the red hills of Georgia, the sons of former slaves and the sons of former slave-owners will be able to sit down together at the table of brotherhood.

I have a dream that one day even the state of Mississippi, a state sweltering with the heat of injustice, sweltering with the heat of oppression, will be transformed into an oasis of freedom and justice.

I have a dream that my four little children will one day live in a nation where they will not be judged by the color of their skin, but by the content of their character. I have a dream."

I looked around. In front of me stood an Episcopal minister crying like a child. My brother, Rabbi Jerome Lipnick whom I met by chance at the March, caught it all in one word when he whispered, *"meshuga.* This is *meshuga!"*

Then they dispersed, the quarter of a million who had come back to Abraham Lincoln to reaffirm their faith in the promise that had been made 100 years ago—the promise that equality and freedom would be extended to every man, woman and child of this land, irrespective of the color of their skin. As the buses moved onto the main arteries of Washington in fuming cadence, the whole Negro population of Washington stood on the sidewalks in silent approval, waving goodbye to those who had come. Despite the tiredness and fatigue of those in the buses—many of whom had not slept for three days—the gentle waving was returned. The sight of that waving filled all of us with the knowledge that our davening that day had been good—good for us; good for Washington; good for Jews and Christians, for Negroes and white men; good for America.

I must confess to you that as I reflect upon the circumstances of my trip to Washington, I realize that those circumstances were far from pleasant. I did go, and I am as pleased as I can be that I did. But when I left my home and family that day, I left with anything but a carefree heart. The day before I was to leave I received a letter in the mail, which, after much thought and reflection, I have decided to share with you. It is addressed to Rabbi Bernard Lipnick, 21 Princeton Place, University City, Missouri. And, it reads as follows:

"We are warning you. A nigger is a murderer, rapist, killer, a savage and a descended from cannibals.

Rabbi Lipnick, you better stay out of this racial trouble for the good of yourself and family, the Jewish population, and to stop the rising hatred of the Jews in this county.

Why take chances on your life, job and the safety of your family?"

It was signed *"A group of members from the B'nai Amoona."*

I read the letter, and I read it again. It is written in pen. Printed letters; a few spelling errors. Intentional? maybe not. Undoubtedly a crank! But then I got to thinking, and I re-read it, especially the last paragraph, "Why take chances on your life, job and the safety of your family?" This paragraph can be taken several ways. Was this a threat? The safety of my family! I was about to leave town! Ours is a big, old house. A crank? Maybe; then again, maybe not!

I decided to take the letter to the police. They pointed out that the sender, or senders, had been extremely careful. A fingerprint test revealed that the paper had been meticulously wiped clean. They also offered the opinion that the letter had been written, probably by someone in the congregation, who objected to my going. Until that moment, the thought that someone in the B'nai Amoona family could have written the letter had never occurred to me. "Impossible!" I told the police. "My members write me, their Rabbi, such a letter? Impossible!" The police were ready to grant my point, although they continued to feel that the signature was authentic. I didn't accept their theory then, nor do I now. I can't picture members of B'nai Amoona sending me such a letter. But, should I go in the face of what appeared to be a threat against my wife and children, or not?

We decided that my plans would remain unchanged, although, of course, certain security precautions for my family had to be taken, and were taken. During the entire time that I was away, I thought about the letter and its contents. I turned its words over and over in my mind. Suddenly, it occurred to me that that letter writer had actually done me a very great service. If I had had any doubts about the wisdom of participating in the March, or if I had had any indecision about the need for such a demonstration, the letter and its contents removed all doubts and all indecision. Without realizing it, the author or authors of that letter, had put down in black and white, clearly for me to see and to see again, what the Civil Rights Movement has to fight and why there was a need for the March on Washington. What had been in me, until that point, a somewhat vague sympathy for the Civil Rights Movement, became when the letter arrived, a flaming passion against the evils of discrimination and bigotry visited upon the Negro. I would have you share this same passion with me on this, one of the holiest of Jewish days.

Nor can I think of a more effective way to achieve this goal than to have you join me in exposing the falsehood and the bigotry contained in the document that I just read to you. Really analyzing the contents of that letter will serve to remove any question you might have about the need for a crash effort now on the part of each of us, both to right an ancient wrong and to give concrete expression to our religious and democratic ideals.

The letter has three paragraphs. First, "A nigger is a murderer, rapist, killer, a savage and a descended from cannibals." In this sentence, my writer reveals what has forever been the first sin, and possibly the worst of all the sins, bigotry. It is not that the word "nigger" is used. "Sheenie," "kike," and "dago," are the same kind of words, and they really are not so bad. The first and worst sin of the bigot is stripping from each individual Negro his individuality. The bigot considers each Negro to be part of one big, faceless, amorphous group. Negroes are not individuals; they are members of a group of non-differentiated parts, called "niggers." The Negro is not permitted any individuality of his own, a personality of his own, his own individual wants and needs, dreams and hopes. He is just one of the "nigger group," without distinctiveness and without name. I remember a Negro once told me that until he was a teenager, he thought that whites weren't supposed to call Negroes by their given names—just by the one name, "boy." "Come here, boy." "Do this, boy." "Do that, boy." Unfortunately, this is the point of view of many of us, although seldom are we as direct and open as my letter writer. All Negroes are part of one big, look-alike group.

Perhaps this is the explanation of how otherwise decent people can deny Negroes jobs and voting privileges and public accommodations, as well as a home in our neighborhoods. Perhaps this is how it becomes possible to beat Negroes and to bomb their homes. After all, it isn't an individual who cries out in pain and in anguish—which we couldn't stand—it is only one of 'that group.' With this attitude, it is also understandable why we fear Negroes. Some are rapists and some are murderers. It seems to follow that each is a rapist and a murderer.

Against this first sin of bigotry, Judaism and Americanism are patently clear. Among the first words on the subject were written in the Creation story, the anniversary of which we celebrate today, Rosh Hashanah: "And God created man in His image." Notice, it says "man." One man—not two and not three. Certainly not black and not white.—Just "man," one man. If these were the first words on the subject, among the most recent were those of the American creed—*We hold these truths to be self-evident, that all men are created equal*—not groups; but, men, individual men, black and white. I met individual Negroes, on the March, people as fine and as good as any white person would hope to be: doctors, professors, writers and professionals of various descriptions. They formed a group, but, it was a group whose cohesion was not that of color. It was a group that was held together by an ideal and a dream. That is why I, and tens of thousands of other whites, could be part of the group.

Some Negroes are bad, but doesn't the very same apply to all groups? Let every Negro by judged on his own individual merits. That is all that is demanded of us, by our Faith and by America. That is all that every intelligent civil righter seeks.

Our letter writer continues: "Rabbi Lipnick, you better stay out of this racial trouble for the good of yourself and family: the Jewish population, and to stop the rising hatred of the Jews in this country." This constitutes the second sin of bigotry: "divide and conquer." Who better than the Jew, should know that the persecution of one group inevitably results in the persecution of all? Not as the letter says but just the opposite—The most effective way to increase hatred for every group is to allow hatred for one to go unchecked; conversely, the best way to uproot hatred for every group is to excise it, wherever it may be found.

Jews should be, and many are, at the forefront of the Civil Rights Movement. However, many are the other Jews who have outfitted their consciences with convenient forgetting devices. It has been but two generations since Jews were the objects of scorn and derision. Dare we stand idly by while others are afflicted by exactly the same kind of scorn? As usual, Dr. Abraham Joshua Heschel, echoing our Tradition, puts it brilliantly: "How many disasters do we have to go through in order to realize that all of humanity has a stake in the liberty of one person; whenever one person is offended, we are all hurt. What begins as inequality of some, inevitably ends as inequality of all."

Never before, in history, has there been a clearer demonstration of this truth than the Washington March. We were all there; Puerto Ricans, Mayflower Americans, Jews, Minnesota Swedes, whites and blacks. We were all there, because we are all fighting the same fight.

The third paragraph of the letter constitutes the third sin of the bigots: "Why take chances on your life, job and the safety of your family?" Having classed all Negroes together into one big, faceless group, and having attempted to separate me, as a Jew, from my obligation to help Negroes gain equality, the writer resorts to force, or at least to the threat of force. To this inevitable and logical conclusion of bigotry, the Washington March was the most effective and eloquent answer that America has ever seen. Thank God for leaders like Martin Luther King and Amos Ryce of St. Louis who, in the Tradition of Gandhi and others, are replying to force by means of passive resistance. These leaders gathered a quarter of a million people together, a quarter of a million people, who did not come to Washington to fight, but who came to daven. Perhaps a few will die in the course of this struggle, maybe even a few Rabbis. But, the tide of freedom for the Negro—in the South and in the North, in the East and in the West—cannot be reversed and cannot be contained much longer. Force and intimidation never really work, no matter who uses it or where.

I must say a word about some of the excesses resorted to by some in the Negro community. Every movement, however fine, has its excesses. The Civil Rights Movement is no exception. Force and the disregard of law, such as we saw at the Jefferson Bank, are absolutely to be deplored and are deplored by responsible Negro leadership. Don't let us make the mistake of allowing these isolated occurrences to remove from us the obligation to redress excesses. Force is the third sin of the bigots and those who adopt their methods.

The letter is signed: "A group of members from the B'nai Amoona." This is perhaps the greatest irony. B'nai Amoona means "Children of Faith." What is that faith that we and all Jews are children of? "Children of the faith," which taught the equality of man to Western civilization, to begin with. "Children of the faith," which has given the world more martyrs than any other in history. "Children of the faith," which produced a Moses, whose own wife was an Ethiopian woman and which recorded that leprosy was inflicted upon those who objected. That B'nai Amoona's name should appear as part of the signature of that letter—this is the greatest irony!

I said a while ago that I didn't accept the theory that members of B'nai Amoona wrote this letter and sent it to me. I take it back because you, the members of B'nai Amoona, did write that letter, and so indeed, did I.

We all wrote that letter. For, even though I do not believe that a member of B'nai Amoona penned it with his own hand, we are part of the society which allowed it to be written. We have been content to live in a country and state which has no public accommodations law. We live in a country in which there is strong doubt that Civil Rights legislation, guaranteeing the most elementary rights to Negroes, will pass. We live in a land where governors bar the doors to state universities and high schools, where dogs are turned upon citizens exercising their American right of free assembly. We are the first to flee neighborhoods which threaten to become integrated.

We support business enterprises which are based upon a policy of discrimination. We even attend Synagogues where the great social message of our faith is squelched in favor of other, no more important and probably less important, aspects. We wrote the letter alright, and we must bear our shame.

Yes, may God forgive us—we wrote it! This is the season of repentance. During this season, we must, each one of us, make amends for that letter and for the persecution and narrowness which it symbolizes. We must make *Teshuvah*, forthrightly, quickly, and we must do so actively and not passively. Let us be in the forefront of the effort to end discrimination in housing and jobs. Let us abolish inequality in educational opportunity and in every public establishment in this land. Let us uproot every form and vestige of bigotry from our hearts. Let us obliterate every trace of this sinister prejudice which afflicts our soul and the souls of our children and friends.

Again, in the words of Heschel: "Our concern must be expressed not symbolically, but literally; not only publicly, but privately; not occasionally, but regularly." Our tradition says that the first man, Adam, was created on Rosh Hashanah. It was Rabbi Halpern who was fond of quoting the Midrash which says that God used three kinds of earth in creating Adam—white earth, black earth and red earth. In that same place, in the Midrash, there is another rabbinic statement which reads as follows:

"God's grace and loving kindness towards Adam revealed themselves, particularly in His taking, in addition to the three kinds of earth, one spoonful of dust from the spot where, in the time to come, the Temple alter would stand. God said, 'I shall make man from the place of atonement that he may endure.'"

On the High Holidays, this is perhaps the question which is uppermost in our minds: "Will we, and will this civilization, of which we are a part, endure?" Within each of us, there is one spoonful of dust taken from the place of atonement which may yet tip the scales in our favor. The time has come for us, and for all America, to atone for that letter and for the sins it represents. The time has come for us, and for all America, to march in Washington and in St. Louis and across the length and breadth of this land. To march forward in love and in fraternity, that we and our Negro brothers, and all of God's children, may live and endure, now and forever more. Amen.

To Obey God's Law or Man's—I Broke the Law in Selma

June 7, 1973 - Shavuot, Yizkor

One of the most difficult problems which people in society face is the problem of ultimate allegiance. To whom does a person owe his greatest loyalty—to his country or to his God? Let no one think that this is an easy problem, by any means.

When everything is going along smoothly, it is relatively simple to keep both loyalties in balance. But let there be a conflict, let a person be confronted with mutually exclusive or even mildly antagonistic demands between the two, and he has a problem. Which should he obey: society's law or God's law? What are the criteria of choice? What are the consequences of choice, both for him and for society?

These are some of the questions which have been emerging in my consciousness as I, like every other person here, have been confronting the awful and frightening disclosures of Watergate. What indeed were the obligations of President Nixon's aides during his first term of office, and subsequently in the campaign of 1972? Was their ultimate allegiance to him and to the country? Or did they have an obligation to some sort of "higher law?" What were the obligations of the president, himself? Was the security of our country, as he saw it, of first importance? Was the protection of individual rights, as embodied in the First Ten Amendments to the Constitution, of first importance? What were the obligations of ordinary citizens, like you and me, whose will was expressed at the polls? What were our ultimate allegiances? What were the criteria by means of which we chose? And what now are the consequences of our choice?

I know of no better time to invite your attention to these questions, and to share some of my thoughts about them, than today—Shavuot—the anniversary of the Giving of the Torah on Mount Sinai. The reason is that even though we might have some question in our minds about to whom a person owes his ultimate allegiance, there is no doubt in the mind of Judaism. A Jew owes his ultimate allegiance, says Judaism, to God and to His will as that will is expressed in the Torah and the body of literature which has emanated from it. I might as well tell you, at the outset, that I agree with Judaism, 100 percent. I believe that a person owes his ultimate allegiance not to government, not even to the American government; not to government heads, even if they be presidents; not to a political party, even if it be his own; not to the boss, whomever he may be; but to God and to His will. I believe also that, despite the fact that it is difficult at times to establish what God's will is, with study and with honesty and with the help of previous generations who have struggled to discover that will, it is possible to determine what it is. I believe that the consequences of giving ultimate allegiance to God are much to be preferred over giving ultimate allegiance to government, as the experience of America in the past ten years will, I believe, clearly show.

First, let me establish Judaism's position a bit more precisely. The Torah states that government, represented in its day by the king, was limited by divine law. Unlike other kings of that era, Jewish kings did not have unlimited power. Like everyone else, they were subject to the laws of the Torah and were publicly criticized and punished when they transgressed them. It was left to the Rabbis in a later age to expand the Biblical concept and to apply it much more widely.

For example, the Rabbis posed the issue of what happens when a subject of the king was ordered to do something which he knew to be contrary to the Torah. They stated, in no uncertain terms, that when confronted with such an order, a person had to refuse to carry it out, even if it meant a fall in his rank of status. The Rabbis also discussed the obligation of a person who became aware of an order by a king which was contrary to God's law. Was he permitted to close his eyes to it and disregard it? Once again, the rabbinic answer, in no uncertain terms, was that he must actively oppose the order and prevent its execution.

Finally, the Rabbis confronted the case of a person who voluntarily obeyed an order of a king which was contrary to God's law. They stated, once again in no uncertain terms, that he was guilty not only before God, but legally as well. He could not exempt himself on the grounds that he was an agent of the king. The principle is that there can never be an agent for wrongdoing. It was the *Rambam* who put the matter most succinctly in typical rabbinic style. He said that if the Master's orders (by whom he meant God) conflict with the servant's orders (meaning by man, including government heads), the Master's take precedence. It goes without saying, he continued, that if a king ordered a violation of God's commandments—even the slightest commandment—he was not to be obeyed (Laws of Kings 3:9). There you have it, just as clear as crystal.

In my own life, the closest contact I have had with this issue occurred during the middle '60s, when I participated, tangentially of course, in the Civil Rights Movement. I, like every thoughtful person at that time, was deeply concerned over the problem of governmental authority in conflict with what we regarded as divine authority. Let me remind you of the circumstances.

The whole South was engaged in a massive campaign to skirt the Supreme Court's decision regarding Integration, maintaining the segregation which had existed in that part of the country for more than 200 years. State governments, county governments, city governments, and whatever governments there were, set up countless—and, I might add, perfectly legal—road blocks in the path of integration.

One or two examples will suffice: Some counties in some of the southern states were populated ninety percent by blacks. Yet, in many of those counties, there was not a single registered black voter. The reason was that the black voters did not meet the so-called legal requirements for registration. That the requirements were set up precisely for the purpose of preventing their registration was regarded by many as being irrelevant. In many places, including one that I visited, called Selma, there was a law which made it illegal for three or more people to gather in a public place at one time. It was never found necessary to enforce this law against whites. I am sure I don't have to tell you how many times it was enforced against blacks, to prevent demonstrations.

Incidentally, when I marched in Selma in March of 1965, I knew that I was breaking the law and fully expected that I would end up in jail. Yet I, and many fellow marchers, considered our allegiance was to a higher law. That we were not arrested was a matter of luck. Many were, perhaps the more fortunate, because others were maimed or killed by the upholders of the law—the police.

Events moved swiftly in America around that time. President Kennedy was killed, and generally violence seemed to grip the country. The Civil Rights Movement spilled over into a variety of excesses: black militants burned the inner cities of America, and their white counterparts tore up the campuses of the country. Young people generally, as evidenced by the hippie and the anti-war movement, gave growing indication of their rejection of the laws of organized society.

At the same time, the crime rate increased perceptibly in every city in the United States. People began to ask questions. Many began to see a certain connection between the disregard of the law (that people, such as I, were guilty of) and these other manifestations of lawlessness. Permissiveness and softness; coddling of young people and criminals; the rebelliousness of certain elements within the religious establishment—all were seen as encouraging the disregard of the law.

A reaction set in. (Some called it a backlash). It could be seen to be growing during the Johnson administration, which began in 1964, and it could be seen to reach its full flowering in the campaign and election of Richard Nixon to the presidency, in 1968. Americans seemed to be saying that we have had enough of this conscience business; enough of the demonstrations, the mobs, the flag desecrations, the draft card burnings, the crime, the disregard for law, that were rampant in America. What the country needed was a return to the traditional governmental institutions of our society. What the country needed, to use their phrase, was a return to "law and order."

Mr. Nixon regarded his election as a mandate; he opened fire on all of the individuals and groups who were considered the enemies of law and order. Indictments increased daily. Courts were filled with clergymen of one denomination or another accused of all sorts of wild crimes, as well as many young people who defied established authority in one way or another. The wide-eyed liberals, those who had marched with Dr. King some years earlier, as well as their successors in the anti-war movement, were thoroughly discredited. The thought, that in doing this Mr. Nixon was carrying out the will of the American people, was affirmed in the traditional American way by a landslide victory which returned him to the White House in 1972.

Only a few months have passed since then and the idols of the conservative reaction, as well as their lackeys, are known to have clay feet—and very brittle clay feet at that. Understand me, it is not my purpose to engage in vilification or to heap invective upon the President and his aides. In the first place, most are not convicted yet of any wrongdoing. Secondly, I am not their judge.

But we have to learn from what we are seeing. We have to learn, I think, that whatever the liberals, by their protests and sit-ins and demonstrations, may have done to the law; whatever those who were motivated by religious conviction may have done to the respect for property by splattering blood on draft files; whatever those driven by their consciences may have done to the sanctity of the Constitution and to the reverence for human dignity, through the destruction of government records; whatever these people and others like them may have done, has proved to be petty larceny, petty disruption, and petty everything, by comparison to what has been perpetrated against these honored institutions of society by those who claimed so loudly to be their protectors.

I know that there are all sorts of difficulties involved in trying to uphold God's law. It is not easy to know even what that law is. It is always very difficult to distinguish between His law and your own. There have been innumerable abuses perpetrated by people who make a pretext of following God's law, including fakes and charlatans. However, their potential for evil, and their actual commission of evil, is infinitely less than those who have come to consider themselves the repositories of law and order. It is very hard to think of any good that might come out of Watergate, but I like to feel that, when all the facts are in and the smoke has cleared, good will result. Not the least of it might be our being reminded of something we claim to know as a people and something we give much lip service to, but have obviously forgotten these past four years. That is that men, be they Attorney Generals or Presidents, are subject to the judgment of God, as are all of us. That God and His Torah, in the broadest sense, are the ultimate authority in human affairs.

The name "Watergate," as you may or may not know, was taken from the Bible. It was one of the gates of the ancient city of Jerusalem and is mentioned in the Book of Nehemiah as the place where Ezra, the great 5th century B.C.E. teacher of Judaism, attempted to teach the people the Torah that they had forgotten during the Babylonian exile. While I do not accept Scriptural verse as literal support for any message of mine, I feel that we can do no better than repeat today, on Shavuot, the action of Ezra, if not at the Water Gate, then because of Watergate, as told by the Bible (Nehemiah 8:1-3): ". . .all the people gathered themselves together as one man into the broad place that was before the Water Gate; and they spoke unto Ezra the scribe to bring the book of the Law of Moses, which the Lord had commanded for Israel. And Ezra the priest brought the Law before the congregation. . . And he read therein before the broad place that was before the Water Gate, from early morning until midday, in the presence of the men and the women, and of those that could understand; and the ears of all the people were attentive unto the Book of the Law."

Amen.

Metzora—Soviet Jewry

April 7, 1984

If all goes well, Harriet and I will be leaving St. Louis early Tuesday morning for New York, where we will spend the rest of that day and part of the next day, prior to our departure for Russia. I cannot tell you the exact departure schedule for the overseas portion of the trip because the tickets, visas and other details of the trip will not be in our possession until we reach New York. However, it is my impression that arrival in Moscow will be sometime Thursday afternoon or evening, April 12, where we shall spend Friday, Shabbat, Shabbat, Sunday and Monday, followed by the first two days of Pesach, including the two *Sedarim*. Then, probably on the 25th, Wednesday, which is the third day of Pesach, we shall take a train to Leningrad where we shall spend *Hol Haomed, Shabbas* and the last two days of Pesach. I think that the day after Pesach we are to fly back from Leningrad to Moscow, with the return to St. Louis, Thursday evening, April 26.

As I recount these travel plans, it all seems so simple. But I want you to know that deep in every word, implicit in every letter of every word, is a great deal of emotion, a great deal of deep feeling and if I am to be honest, some anxiety as well. (I believe that this will be the first Pesach in 32 years that I will have missed at B'nai Amoona.) I want to tell you therefore how it is that we come to make this trip. What we hope to accomplish on it and by it, and what some of the emotions are that accompany us as we do.

I guess the best place to start is with the feeling that has been growing in me over the years, that I, personally (and American Jews, in general, really), really do not do enough on behalf of Soviet Jews. It is no secret to anybody that systematic persecution of the Jews of Russia has been the rule in that country for that last 100 years or more. The persecution takes different forms in different years and with different faces, but essentially the Jews of the Soviet Union suffered greatly under the czars and have suffered equally as much, and in some ways even more, under their successors. I think I may have mentioned from this pulpit before that my mother was born in a place called Kishinev, which is in the southern part of Russia, near Odessa. She and her family were victims of the famous Kishinev pogrom which occurred the week before Pesach in 1903, the 81st anniversary of which will be next week. This pogrom resulted in the death and injury of hundreds of Jews, and caused my mother and her family's departure from there. Many is the time she recounted to me her most vivid recollections of that pogrom. How she saw Jewish babies splattered up against the walls of her house. How her father, my grandfather, whom I knew—he was a big strapping man—stood by the front door of their home with an iron pipe and bashed the heads of the attackers as they entered, while my mother and her siblings hid under the bed.

This pogrom, incidentally, was one of the major causes of the second *Aliya* to Israel, which began in 1903 and which turned out to be probably the most important of all the *aliyot*. It included people like Ben-Gurion and Ben Tzvi who were really the ideological founders, and in some ways the physical founders too, of the modern State of Israel.

At that time, some of the Jews of Russia went to Israel, then Palestine. Others came here—to America, my mother among them. If this was my impression of Russian treatment of the Jews during my youth, I soon grew up and had those same impressions of Russia's treatment of her Jews confirmed and intensified. Anti-Semitism, which is obviously endemic to that society, was used as much by the Communists as by the czars.

In 1917 and the years following, after using Jewish brain power and social activism to help formulate the promise of a world-wide socialist dialectic which would bring freedom and plenty to all, Russia turned upon its Jewish citizens, determined to destroy them Jewishly and otherwise. Without recounting the whole grizzly tale of how this was and is being done, suffice it to say that active Jewish life in the Soviet Union is regarded as a crime and Jews are tolerated only to the extent that they neglect or deny their Jewishness. The result, incidentally, which is not unlike Hitler's result, has been phenomenally successful. Not long ago we used to speak of three million Soviet Jews. Now the figure is somewhere in the neighborhood of two million. In this regard, I was reading about Rabbi Halpern, my predecessor and senior Rabbi of this congregation for 45 years—between 1917 and 1962 on Friday—because it was his *yahrzeit*, and I learned that the very first sermon he gave at B'nai Amoona, on the first day of Pesach in 1917, expressed the hope that with the overthrow of the czar, the Russian revolution would bring freedom to—and get this figure—the six million Jews of Russia.

Two things: first of all that this should have been his first sermon on Pesach, and second, that the figure should have been six million Jews, reduced as I say, now to two. There is no question that Russia has succeeded in effectively reducing its Jewish population to only a shadow of its former self. Yet in the past dozen or more years, as a result of pressure from the United States—trade pressure, political pressure, and the like—and pressure from other sources as well, Russia has made some grudging attempts to honor the human rights of Jews, not Judaism mind you, but Jews who are willing to stand up and assert themselves.

Specifically, according to the Helsinki Agreement, among others to which she is a signatory, Russia is obligated to allow specifically those families with relatives abroad to leave in order to be reunited. Once an invitation is received, Russian bureaucracy takes over with the result that, from 1968 till about a year ago, approximately one-quarter million Jews were able to leave Russia. More than half went to Israel and the rest came to the U.S. and other places. But for whatever reason—and nobody really knows the reason—even that very narrow avenue has gradually become narrower and narrower, to the point that today hardly any Jews are permitted to leave.

In 1979, the average per month was somewhere over four thousand. The average in 1983 was somewhere in the neighborhood of one hundred per month. Nor is this the worst of it. Jews who apply for exit permits, but who are refused—called in English, Refuseniks—then become special objects of Russian repression. They lose their jobs. They are harassed, physically beaten; in some cases exiled to remote parts of the Soviet Union and in other cases incarcerated or executed for trumped-up charges of one kind or another. I don't know how many Refuseniks there are. I have seen figures all the way from nine thousand to forty thousand. I do know, however, that there does exist a significant—small but significant—group of Jews, especially in the major cities such as Moscow and Leningrad, who, despite all of the efforts of repression, are resolved to live as Jews and who, without leadership, without books, without any real encouragement from the outside world from which they are effectively cut off, are succeeding in learning Torah, observing Judaism and biding their time against the day when they will be able to leave.

I have delivered speeches on this subject and participated in several vigils. I have talked about it with our Congressmen. I have sent letters, made some contributions, but I have always felt that I have not done enough on behalf of our coreligionists in the Soviet Union.

Then one day, not long ago, an invitation came from the National Conference on Soviet Jewry for Harriet and I to spend Pesach in Russia. The purpose—to visit and to try to raise the morale of the Refuseniks—to show that they are not abandoned, that there are those who care and more specifically to teach—me to teach Hebrew language—and in Hebrew the *Humash*, Rashi and some Bible, the Haggada and philosophy.

Harriet is to teach cooking, needlework, including making *kipot*, and aerobics to those Refuseniks who can see their way clear to take advantage of our visit. Incidentally, the aerobics has to do with the need of the Refuseniks to keep physically fit—in case they are exiled to Siberia.

My reaction to the invitation was, "Absolutely! As long as I can go to Kishinev!" I approached our president, the Executive Committee and the Board, and I am proud to say that they agreed that we should go. Rabbi Kula graciously agreed to cover, and plans began to be made for the trip. We began to assemble those things that the Refuseniks community wanted us to bring along with us. Incidentally, the way this is done is that people like ourselves who go in bring certain things and then return with information on what is needed; all of which, for obvious reasons, has to be in oral form. It is for that reason that we are going to New York a day early. We need to be briefed. Some of the sensitive information that we possess will need to be coded and what we are bringing will have to be carefully packed and repacked. Included, for example, is 15 pounds of matza, two pair of *tefillin*, *Talesim*, clothes, tapes, Hebrew books, medicines, glasses, vitamins, cheese, and sweaters. Things like that that the poor benighted Refuseniks cannot secure themselves and need in order to keep body and soul together.

To give you some idea of how we are going about this, Harriet's ball of yarn for *yarmulkes* will contain not only yarn. Inside will be *tzitzi* that will be used to make *Talesim*. My *tefillin* will contain not just the four sections which are normally found in *tefillin*, but eight, so that Refuseniks can cut them apart and make another pair of *tefillin* out of the one. I don't know how we are going to carry all the stuff but we are going to try! I want to tell you the pride that I feel in the way various groups of the congregation, particularly the *haverot* and the children in the school, have responded to our requests for things to take. We are using a separate room in our home to gather all the stuff together and I want you to know that the beds there are overflowing with all the things that we are taking. There has been such an outpouring of generosity and love on the part of our members that, when I think of it, it brings tears to my eyes.

Now, having said all of this, I don't know for sure that we will actually make it to Russia. You must know that I have not talked about this publicly until now because it is so close to departure that I don't suppose that what I am saying will get back to the Russians. This is what the National Conference at least has advised. They authorized only this one talk prior to our departure. But it is not impossible, to be sure, that we will get to the plane that is supposed to take us to Moscow and that we will be turned back or turned back at any point once we get in. I don't know if you have been reading the papers recently, but a number of people in our category have been expelled and even roughed up. Although the National Conference people tend to feel that those were younger than we. Apparently this head of gray hair is considered by them to be some protection against undue harassment. But, with it all, we must try and we are going to try.

Oh, I forgot to add that as the details of the trip began to be worked out, it became clear that Kishinev could not be in the itinerary. Too much time had to be spent on trains and planes—time that we would have had to steal from our contacts and our teaching. It was with considerable reluctance, therefore, that we let Kiev and Kishinev go and agreed to concentrate on just the two major centers.

Ladies and Gentlemen of B'nai Amoona, I am now completing thirty-three years here, and over the years it has become increasingly hard for me to sort out where my personal life ends and where my congregational life—if you want to call it that—begins. It has come to be almost that I am B'nai Amoona and B'nai Amoona is me. I have lost, if I ever possessed it, the art of distinguishing between the two. (Which incidentally is not all good—either for you or for me!) But I just want you to know that you are going to be in Russia, God willing, this Pesach with us. We are going to be thinking of you and carrying you with us. You are going to be participating in whatever it is that we will be doing. We certainly couldn't have done it without you. Most of what we will be giving away will have been given by you. More than anything, the sense of concern for fellow Jews, the commiseration and empathy which we hope to communicate, has been nurtured and deepened in us by you within these walls. So, we will be together there.

I take this opportunity then, on behalf of Harriet and myself, to wish you a *kosherin* and *frelichen* Pesach—a kosher and a happy Pesach. May your *Sedarim* be beautiful and meaningful, and may all the enslaved peoples of the world, chief among them our coreligionists of the Soviet Union, go into freedom soon. And now, in closing, please join me in reading this prayer together on the final page of your Shabbat sheets.

A Prayer for Soviet Jewry

May the blessings of Heaven—
Grace, loving kindness, and mercy,
Long life, ample sustenance,
And the joy of seeing their children
Able to be devoted to the study of Torah—
Be granted to our people
Who live in the Soviet Union.
May the Almighty bless them and sustain them.
May they be granted the courage to continue.
May the bonds between us be strengthened.
And may they be enabled to live in pride and dignity,
Freedom and honor.
May those who struggle

To join our People in
Their ancestral homeland
Be permitted to do so.
Until these goals are achieved,
May we be their voice.
May our prayers on their behalf be heard
In the councils of the nations here on earth,
And in Your Presence.
May our acts and deeds be worthy of their sacrifices.
Master in Heaven,
Be with them in their plight,
And let us say, Amen.

Judaism in America: Challenges and Prospects

The American culture—with its *aspirational* openness to diversity, freedom to choose ones way of life, equality of opportunity, democracy, separation of church and state, impartial judicial system and adherence to human rights and dignity—has allowed, and still allows, Jews to flourish socially, economically, and creatively. Judaism, on the other hand, is being challenged to remain a relevant and compelling way of life in such an open and free society. This is especially true when the culture encourages and focuses on immediate self-gratification and consumerism.

The five sermons in this section are reflections on the Jewish experience, in mid-20th century America—both the good and the challenging, and on the efforts of a congregational rabbi to provide wise guidance.

B'nai Amoona Presents a Torah

Each Shabbas and Yom Tov, the highlight of the Synagogue Service is the reading from the Torah. All of us delight in this part of the Service each week, but does it ever occur to us that there are some congregations of Jewish in the world which cannot perform this portion of the Service? The reason they cannot is simply that they have no Torah. There is no lack of desire on their part, but they do not have a Scroll and cannot have the official Torah reading at their Service. One such congregation is only a few hundred miles from St. Louis. It had no Torah Scroll—that is until now. I want to tell you the story of how this congregation received its Torah Scroll, and how it feels about its Torah Scroll.

The story starts about four months ago when, at a meeting of the St. Louis Rabbinical Association, a request from Rabbi Ernst I. Jacob, of Springfield, Missouri, was read. Rabbi Jacob, in addition to being the Rabbi of the United Hebrew Congregations of Springfield, is also the Jewish Chaplain at the Medical Center for Federal Prisoners in Springfield. The Rabbi explained that there are some 15 Jewish patient-prisoners at the Medical Center with whom he conducts a bi-weekly service. But, said Rabbi Jacob, there has never been a Torah Scroll at this service, and he would like to secure one.

When I heard this request I was very much moved. I took the letter and showed it first to the President, and then to the Officers and Ritual Committee of B'nai Amoona. It seemed to me that we at B'nai Amoona are very rich in Torahs, and that we could do no better than share our wealth with Jews who are deprived in this respect. I am happy to report—and it is to their great credit—that the Officers of our congregation, the Ritual Committee, and the Board of Trustees, when apprised of the request, decided unanimously to make available, on a permanent loan-basis, one of our Torahs for the Chapel at the Medical Center for Federal Prisoners in Springfield.

It was suggested that arrangements be made for a committee of B'nai Amoona officials to take the Torah to Springfield and to present it in ceremonial fashion to the Chapel. An exchange of correspondence with Rabbi

Jacob, as well as a series of notices to the Officers and the members of the Ritual Committee, resulted in the choice of Thursday, May 7, as the day on which we would journey to Springfield to present the Torah. The Committee was to consist of Rabbi Arnold Asher, Assistant Rabbi of Congregation B'nai Amoona; Dr. Manuel Zimmerman and Secretary of the Congregation; Messrs. Jules Dubinsky; Ben Goldblatt; and me.

I must say that May 7 started out very modestly. But it wasn't long before the drama and beauty of what was happening began to penetrate, in a gradual and imperceptible way, until each of us who were participating in this experience came to realize what a truly great moment we were involved in. We gathered at services in our Daily Chapel that morning and we davened with just a little bit more *Kavanah* than we normally do. We sensed that we would soon be on a rather "*kavanadik*" mission.

This feeling became intensified after the service and breakfast ended, when I approached Mr. Isadore Katz, Shammas of the Congregation, to ask him which Torah he had chosen. Although I had discussed the matter with Mr. Katz earlier, I did not particularly relish this moment. You really have to know Mr. Katz and his feeling about Torahs to understand why. Mr. Katz is a living legend in B'nai Amoona and in St. Louis. He admits to being 83 years old, but rumor has it that he is well into his 90s. Mr. Katz has been Shammas of B'nai Amoona for over 54 years, and this is not his first position. Of course Mr. Katz knows everybody in the congregation. In addition, he knows everybody's father, and grandfather and, in some cases, great-grandfather. He is always willing to share interesting and accurate anecdotes about the "old folks" whom "he knew when." Blessed with a phenomenal memory, Mr. Katz carries around in his head all of the *yahrzeit* dates and all of the Hebrew names of all of the families who have been in the congregation for any length of time! This is no small feat considering that the congregation has well over 1,000 member families!

Mr. Katz' domain through the years has been the Daily Chapel which, even now at his present age—not that it has ever been different—he rules with a mighty hand. In the Chapel, things are done his way or not at all. This is not to say that Mr. Katz has no compassion. He has compassion and has it in abundance. But he measures compassion out sparingly, which serves to make it a highly coveted prize for the person who receives it.

Mr. Katz' greatest love is reserved for his Torahs. To Mr. Katz, a Torah is not just a Scroll, or even just a religious object. To Mr. Katz, a Torah is a friend and a confrere, a close associate and beloved colleague. Mr. Katz treats his Torahs like one treats a friend and an associate. A Torah's greatest fulfillment is to be read, of course. So Mr. Katz has a rotation system for his Torahs, which results in each Torah being read an equal number of times during the year. He is concerned, also, that his Torahs not be neglected in other ways. They must look prim and proper, and they must be treated with all the dignity and respect with which one treats an old and respected colleague.

So I asked Mr. Katz which Torah was leaving and I did not look forward to what I suspected his reaction would be. Evidently he had steeled himself against this moment and, with all the ripe maturity and wisdom of his years, he fought back his emotions. He declared, unequivocally, that we were doing the right thing. However, if we had the time, he did want to tell us a little bit about the Torah which he had chosen for the presentation. He told us what had happened to the son and the mother who had donated the Torah, and how happy the old lady, who has long since passed away, would be in the knowledge of what we were doing. When Mr. Katz finished, he said "goodbye" to his Torah. He said "goodbye" to us, of course, but most of all, he said "goodbye" to his Torah.

There was something anomalous about the trip to Springfield. We drove in two modern cars, over a dual-lane modern highway, at a rate of 70 or more very modern miles an hour, carrying with us our people's oldest and perhaps most modern document. The car in which the Torah was being transported was classified as a synagogue. Skull caps were worn throughout, and the same "No Smoking" ordinance in force in our Sanctuary was in force in the car. For some unexpressed yet instinctively felt reason, the conversation was circumspect and on a very high level. After all, we were in the shul—a traveling shul perhaps, but a shul.

We were met in Springfield by Rabbi Jacob and some fifteen of his leading *balabatim*. They had prepared a luncheon-reception for us which really gave us the feeling that we were honored guests. It was at the luncheon that Rabbi Jacob spoke and told us a little bit about the Medical Center for Federal Prisoners in Springfield. He explained that this institution is the hospital prison which serves all of the federal prisons of the United States. Of course he thanked us most profusely, and he told us that, at the presentation ceremony which was scheduled for early that afternoon, we should probably meet people such as Morton Sobel, Mickey Cohen, and a Gilbert individual, all of whose names are quite well known. When I spoke, I made the point that we deserve no particular credit for presenting this Torah, because the Torah, in truth, doesn't belong to any single congregation of Jews—not B'nai Amoona or the Medical Center—it belongs to all Jews and in a larger sense, to the whole world. We were simply *shluchei mitzvah*, messengers charged with performing a Mitzvah, a pious act. The Mitzvah itself is thanks enough.

By far the most moving thing we heard at that meal was the story, told by Chaplain Read, the Protestant Chaplain and the Chief of Chaplains at the Medical Center, about how the Center came to seek a Torah in the first place. Herein lies a wonderful tale which deserves to be shared.

Chaplain Read told us about a certain prisoner named Gerald, the product of a mixed marriage, a Protestant father and a Jewish mother. The Chaplain, who counseled with the boy, frequently had the feeling that the source of Gerald's problem was his lack of identity which resulted from the mixed marriage. Gerald never knew who he was or to what group he belonged. As a result, he became an assaultive person and entered one reform school after another. Finally, he committed a major crime and was sent to a federal prison. When in the course of time he was transferred to Springfield, Gerald began to evince an interest in Jewish things. He began to come to services and, before long, proved to be one of the most faithful attendees at services. It was obvious to the Chaplain that Gerald was beginning to identify himself with the Jewish people. Then one day, Gerald came to Chaplain Read and said, "If this is a real Jewish Service that we are having here, why don't we have a Torah?" Chaplain Read was delighted to see this interest on the part of Gerald. It was the first time he had shown an interest in anything positive. The Chaplain encouraged him. But, he also told him, "Gerald, if you are really serious about having a Torah, Rabbi Jacob and I will try to find one for you." Gerald soon showed how serious he was. He designed a pulpit, and he designed an Ark for the Torah Scroll which would be theirs someday. He and his fellow inmates executed the designs and the result was a beautiful, very simple, Ark and pulpit.

Throughout this period, Chaplain Read, the Protestant Chaplain, was counseling with Gerald on his problems. He began to notice a gradual but steady improvement. Gerald had found a goal, a Jewish goal—his Torah. In the process, he was also beginning to find himself. It was then that Chaplain Read and Rabbi Jacob tried to find a Torah, in earnest. They wrote to numerous cities, pursuing all the contacts which they had. But in every case, no one responded—no one, that is, until B'nai Amoona responded. When the news came that, finally, a Torah was to arrive soon in Springfield, the Protestant Chaplain sat down with Gerald and drew a fascinating parallel.

Chaplain Read told Gerald that he, Gerald, reminded him of Moses—that Gerald and Moses were similar in many respects. It seems that Gerald had a speech defect, as Moses did. But, the greatest handicap which Moses had, said the Chaplain to Gerald, was his inability to identify either with the Egyptians or with his own people. This was also Gerald's problem. He was unable to identify either with his Protestant father or his Jewish mother. Then, Moses committed a major crime, as did Gerald. Following this, Moses went into the desert for an extended period, in order to seek a solution to his problem, as did Gerald. Finally, Moses found himself. He decided to identify with his people. He took them out of slavery and he gave them the Torah. Similarly with Gerald, by means of the Torah which he insisted be secured for the Chapel, Gerald found himself. He identified with his people and, as a result, he was well on his way to becoming a worthwhile, responsible person again.

The close of the story almost broke our hearts, as it will yours.

"And, the final parallel," continued Chaplain Read, "between Moses and Gerald, was that Moses led his people to the very gates of the Promised Land, but was not permitted to enter it. He had to ascend the mountain and witness the fruition of his dreams and his labors only from afar. Similarly with Gerald, Gerald had led this little congregation in Springfield to the fulfillment of its goal, the acquisition of the Torah. But he himself would not be permitted to witness the presentation of the Torah, for Gerald had been transferred to another prison just a week and a half before!"

I had the feeling, at that moment, and I have the same feeling now, that if our presentation does nothing more than what it has already done for Gerald, it was all worthwhile.

We went to the Medical Center for the actual presentation. After finishing with the standard security precautions, we went to the little basement Chapel where the Jewish inmates had gathered. You should have seen the faces of the inmates as the Torah was carried into the room. Each man stood—even the man in the wheelchair managed to lift himself up—and turned to the Torah. Each eye followed the Torah down the aisle and each hand extended itself towards the Torah, symbolic of the kiss, remembered from childhood.

Rabbi Jacob conducted a beautiful service. One of the patients acted as *Chazan* and sang the *Mah Tovu*. Each member of our group was honored with a part in the Torah service. The big moment came, of course, when Dr. Snitzer presented the Torah to the representative of Warden Harris on behalf of Congregation B'nai Amoona.

We visited with the patients for a half hour more, none of whom, I can assure you, gave any impression of being a hardened, incurable criminal. These are people, perhaps, who have made mistakes in their lives. But they are much in need of compassion and love and consideration, and the Torah, as we are. Perhaps, more so.

You can well appreciate that the trip home was a very sober and thoughtful one. Each of us, with all due modesty, had represented a lot of people that day: all the members of B'nai Amoona; Moses, who delivered the Torah for the first time; and Gerald, whose insistence caused it to be delivered a second time, at least in Springfield. As to what the patients of the Medical Center feel about that experience and about having the Torah, I can do no better than to share with you a letter I received from Mr. Simon M. Goldberg, who is chairman of the Jewish Congregation at the United States Medical Center for Federal Prisoners, at Springfield:

"Dear Rabbi Lipnick:

On behalf of the entire Jewish Congregation of the Medical Center, I wish to convey our heartfelt gratitude to you and your congregation for our Torah.

We shall, as will, I am certain, the future members of the Jewish Congregation of this institution, revere and render homage to this holy symbol of our faith.

I feel that you are sensitive enough to understand how much your interest in our spiritual welfare means to us.

Words may mean little and are easily affected, but I hope you will believe our sincerity when we say, God bless you and your Congregation for your generosity.

Gratefully,

Simon M. Goldberg and Congregation"

Amen.

The Revolt of Jewish Youth

Jews, especially young Jews, tend to be very demonstrative. I don't know the statistics. But, I am sure that a significantly larger number of young Jews, from a percentage standpoint, are to be found in demonstrations and picket lines, of one kind or another, than any other group. And, by and large, I have a great deal of regard for our young demonstrators. Still, I must admit to developing, over the years, a considerable amount of, I suppose "jealousy" is the right word. Our kids, you see, demonstrate on behalf of peace, civil liberties, university reform, clean air, and a thousand other liberal and radical causes. Yet, they never seem to find it within their little radical hearts to demonstrate on behalf of specifically Jewish causes in the sectarian sense. And, incidentally, the word "sectarian" is not a bad word, to me.

A week ago I went to a convention in Boston which, as I think about it now, probably constitutes an historical first in American Jewish life. For the first time in the history of the organized Jewish community of America, there were demonstrations—by Jewish kids and on behalf of a sectarian Jewish cause. I am ecstatic! Let me tell you about it just as it happened.

I have been working these past five years with the St. Louis Jewish Federation, on a project which gives promise of culminating in the establishment of a new agency in this community devoted to Jewish education. It is to be called the "Bureau of Jewish Education." The implementation committee, charged with bringing this new agency into existence and finding a man to head it, is chaired by Louis Zorensky, a member of our shul and a good Jew.

For a number of weeks, Louis had been urging me to join him and some very fine St. Louisans at the Convention of The Council of Jewish Federations and Welfare Funds, held, this year, in Boston. The Council is made up of 223 constituent Jewish federations of America. The federations are responsible for collecting and distributing, to local and overseas agencies, the significant monies collected by the Jewish communities of this country. It seems that a number of the sessions of the convention were to be devoted to our subject, Jewish Education. Also, some of the *"machers"* from the American Association for Jewish Education, who might prove helpful in finding a man for us, were expected to be present.

While I was mulling over the wisdom of making a 36-hour trip to Boston and back, a letter arrived from a student of mine, Debbie Rubin, who is now studying at Boston University. She apprised me of something that was going to happen at this very convention.

It turns out that there is a group of kids, called The Jewish Activist League, of which she is a member. It had just concluded a plan to crash this convention. They were going to submit a list of demands to the 2,000 of the country's top Jewish leadership who were expected to attend. They would, if they had to, grab the microphone in order to be heard on behalf of, of all things, Jewish Education! Well, this tipped the scales in favor of the trip. I wrote Debbie immediately and told her that I was coming to Boston for essentially the same reason. I suggested that if they had to grab the microphone from someone, not to grab it from me or from the others in the St. Louis delegation because we were already on her side.

I arrived at the Boston Sheraton toward the end of lunch on Thursday, just as the confrontation began. The dining room was filled to overflowing. I noticed a goodly number of young faces around; among them, Ronnie Kimelman, one of our former students and a senior at the Seminary, and his wife. Another rabbinical student, whom I had met at Ramah this past summer, sat across from me. There was an air of excitement!

This was the session, I learned, which had been turned over to the representatives of the Jewish Activists League. There would be two young speakers who would address the convention. The president of the Council of Jewish Federations and Welfare Funds, Mr. Louis J. Fox, led off. Among other things, he congratulated himself and the other framers of the program for having been able—and here I quote him—"to search out and involve young people in the deliberations of our convention."

One of the two youthful speakers who followed him slightly disagreed with Mr. Fox's interpretation of how it happened. He said, "At the outset, I must make one point clear. I am not a part of this convention. Neither was I, nor any young person, asked to speak at this time. I stand here because of pressure that we exerted upon the planners of this conference, to permit us to address you directly, knowing that we were given this opportunity only through threats of disruption." The speaker was Hillel Levine, a Seminary graduate and presently a graduate student at Harvard University, whose speech at that luncheon session set the tone for all that followed.

Let me give you a few of the points he made. Levine started out by blasting the mythology generally associated with the origin of Jewish philanthropy in America. It seems that Peter Stuyvesant, of New Amsterdam, required early Jewish settlers to promise to take care of their own poor and indigent before he would permit them to settle. The Jews agreed and have been in the philanthropy business ever since. Levine is amused by the repetition of this story. First of all, it has the effect of making Peter Stuyvesant the honorary founder of American Jewish philanthropies. Secondly and much worse, it implies that Jews have no Torah or tradition which would have required this of us, without Peter Stuyvesant. Still, Levine said, he sees the repetition of the story as an attempt to justify federations' secular, as distinct from specifically Jewish, concerns.

And, it is true! Federations in this country have been, and are, primarily concerned with Jewish adjustment to American life in one form or another—perhaps, with fostering a vague sense of Jewishness on a superficial level. Jewish education is of little concern to federations; the allocation figures clearly show that. Levine said, "From examining the response of most federations and of the Council of Jewish Federations and Welfare Funds—to the problem of Jewish education—one gets the impression that the situation is rather hopeless but not terribly serious; not serious enough to warrant concerted and creative responses." A very fine speech!

Nor did the young people leave it at those two speeches. The kids have learned. They have taken a leaf from our black neighbors. They know that talk is cheap, and listening to talk is even cheaper. So they handed out a sheet listing four demands. The preamble of these demands begins: "In affirmation of our Jewishness and our concern for Jewish survival, we feel we can no longer be silent." Any sheet of demands from kids that starts out that way has merit, as far as I am concerned.

After a fine preamble in the same general vein, it lists the actual demands:

Demand #1: "We demand that, while maintaining the generous level of support for Israel, all local federations undertake a drastic and immediate reordering of domestic priorities in their local communities, in order to improve the quality of Jewish education at all levels, and to stimulate the growth of Jewish cultural life on campus and in the community."

Demand #2: "We demand special recognition of, and increased support for, the problems of our brothers in the Soviet Union."

Demand #3: "We demand wider representation on all federation policy-making bodies, especially on budget and fund-allocation committees. This representation must include students, academicians, rabbis. . ." One line in that particular demand I just love: "Professional administrators and lay leaders must show their commitment to Judaism by participating in Jewish study." And if that is true of federation leaders, I might add in passing, how much more true is it of congregational leaders?

And, finally, Demand #4: "We demand that each federation establish, within one year, an independent foundation which will allocate funds, no strings attached, to new projects in the community." It then lists some very imaginative experiments in religious living and radical-type literature that many of these students are involved in—with former B'nai Amoona kids, I want you to know—prominently represented.

As we left the afternoon session, as well as later that evening, a goodly number of the 300 young people were arrayed in picket lines, both within the hotel and outside, carrying placards which encapsulated this same general message. One read, "Pay up for Jewish Education;" another, "More students on Committees;" one in particular that I liked, "Jewish Education is for children and other living Jews."

In addition, and most important, these young people stayed at the convention, attended individual workshops and continued to hammer home their major points. They exerted what was, undoubtedly, the single most significant influence on the convention and perhaps one of the most significant grass-root influences ever exerted upon this federation body. I am proud that I was there with the kids, both in body and in spirit. "Beautiful," as they would say!

Having said all of this, and having expressed my admiration for the kids and for the points they made, I would be less than honest if I did not add a caveat which I feel now, and indeed felt at the time. As happens in all demonstrations, the kids tend to oversimplify. Certainly, pressure of this kind can make a difference and ought to be applied. But real solutions to the problems of Jewish life in America will not come from such pressure on federation leaders, or even from a reordering of priorities designed to put Jewish education and other survivalist endeavors higher up on the list. What is lacking, and therefore what is needed ultimately, is a viable rationale for Jewish life in this country to which Jews, including federation leaders, will commit themselves.

To give an example of what I mean, let's say somebody were to make available tomorrow morning $100 million to Jewish schools, as one of the youthful speakers suggested. What would change? Certain obvious things might change. Better facilities; higher salaries; perhaps the beginning of some experimentation. But $100 million would do hardly anything by way of providing us with answers to, say, the relevance of the Bible to people today; the place of Hebrew; meaningful ritual for kids; the place of prayer in their lives, and in ours. What about other serious problems, such as why should we be Jews in America today, altogether? Why shouldn't we intermarry? How should we be Jewish in America, today?

These are the problems which grow like tropical weeds in the secular soil of America, and are at the root of our difficulty. The absence of answers to these problems is what causes federation heads to make the lopsided judgments that they make. And $100 million, or $200 million, is not going to make a whole lot of difference one way or the other. This is the work for theologians, philosophers and thinkers, and these we don't have. That friends, is the problem. These are considerations which are difficult to share with kids carrying placards, especially when you respect so highly, not just what they say, but the commitment which inspires them to say it.

In today's *sedra*, we are told the story of our patriarch, Jacob, who left his home and went to live in a foreign land with his uncle, Laban. He married, fathered a number of children and worked very hard for Laban. Twenty years passed by, and Jacob finally approached Laban with the news that he was going to leave. "You well know," he said to Laban, "how I served you and how your livestock fared with me. For the little you had, before I came, has grown too much, since the Lord has blessed you. . . And now, when shall I make provision for my own household?"

Jacob was beginning to grow up! We Jews are known as the Children of Jacob, or after Jacob's name was changed to Israel, as the Children of Israel. We came to this land—America—many generations ago. We married and established families. We also founded and supported some very fine institutions, such as hospitals and centers and all the rest, which were an important contribution to the general community and to ourselves. But there are abroad now, signs of a new maturity in the Jewish community, inspired by kids like Debbie Rubin and Ronnie Kimelman. They take our sectarian Jewish concerns quite seriously, and are telling us that our commitment to Mr. Stuyvesant has been paid in full. These Children of Israel say to the world what Jacob said, and in almost the same words: "You well know how we Jews have served the general community, and how the Lord has blessed it as a result. But now, when shall we make provision for our own household?" That is the question that the kids put to the Council of Jewish Federations and Welfare Funds last week. Upon the answers to the questions that we and a whole lot of other Jews around this country give, depends the whole future of Jewish life in America. That future, I hope and pray, will be long and vibrant, and always youthful.

Amen.

I Stake Out My Position on Feminism
and the Need for Egalitarianism

Rosh Hashanah 5737 (1976)

The time has come to deal with a subject that we at B'nai Amoona have avoided for too long a time. The subject is Feminism—that is, the position of women in society, generally, and in Jewish society, specifically. My reason for choosing Rosh Hashanah to treat this subject is two-fold. First, it has been my habit to discuss on Rosh Hashanah a theme large enough and important enough to engage our attentions all year long. Surely feminism is such a subject. It is many faceted and extremely far-reaching in terms of its implication and consequences. We might deepen and extend today's initial treatment of the subject, on whatever occasions, during the course.

Just as important, the theme of women belongs on Rosh Hashanah, this year, because Rosh Hashanah happens to be the anniversary of the creation of the first woman. Today, you see, is the beginning of the year 5737. Five thousand, seven hundred and thirty seven is considered by our tradition to be the number of years since the creation of the world. But the world, you recall, was created in six days; or seven days if you include the Shabbat. Rosh Hashanah, does not mark, interestingly, the beginning of the process. According to the Jewish tradition, Rosh Hashanah corresponds to the sixth day of Creation. The day on which God's creative energies reached their zenith. As He breathed the breath of life into the nostrils of the first human being whose name, incidentally, was "Adam and Eve." You heard correctly: not just Adam—but Adam and Eve. Let me quote the relevant passage. It is found in Geneses 1:26-28:

"And God said: 'Let us make Adam in our image, after our likeness; and let them' *(not him, but them)* 'have dominion over the fish of the sea, and over the fowl of the air, and over the cattle and over all the earth, and over every creeping thing that creepeth upon the earth. And God created Adam in

His own image; in the image of God created He him, male and female He created them. And God blessed them; and God said unto them: 'Be fruitful and multiply, and replenish the earth, and subdue it; and have dominion over the fish of the sea, and over the fowl of the air and over every living thing that creepeth upon the earth.'"

Notice that the Biblical author regards the first human being as having been androgynous—that is, a single creature incorporating within itself both sexes. It is obvious that the Bible here saw woman not only as the equal of man but almost contiguous with him. The Torah, at least in this spot, regarded humankind as one indivisible unit. Man and woman were created equal. One did not precede the other in the order of creation. One was not inherently better or worse than the other. Only, says the text, for the purpose of procreation were they divided into the two sexes. "Be fruitful and multiply and replenish the earth."

But unfortunately, this is not where the Torah left the matter. You see, there is a second account of Creation which follows the first (It is chapters 2 and 3 of Genesis, the very next chapters to the one I just quoted.) This account, which I would guess is more familiar to you than the other, saw God as having created a very male "male," named Adam, whose life proved to be rather lonely. For which reason God took a rib from his side and from it, He fashioned, as I have heard it described, a "female" woman, to be his helpmate. The Bible then, in a sequel to this second account of Creation, tells a most fascinating story which conveys a view of woman quite different from the one found in the first chapter. After creating Eve, God placed her and her husband in the Garden of Eden, instructing them not to eat of the tree of the knowledge of good and evil.

You will recall that soon thereafter Eve was enticed by the snake. And that she, in turn, enticed her husband to disobey God's command. The punishment which God meted out following her disobedience had far-reaching consequences. God decreed, for example, that humankind would henceforth be mortal—that is the point at which death entered human life. Also, man henceforth would have to struggle in order to earn his living, and woman was doomed to suffer great pain in childbirth. All because woman committed what came to be known as the "original sin." Like Adam said to God: "The woman whom Thou, God, gavest to me is the one who did it."

Two diametrically opposed views regarding woman and her relationship with man. One, as it appears in Genesis 1—the view that man and woman are completely equal, in total harmony with each other. Concerned solely about peopling the world and tending it. And the other, in Genesis 2 and 3, the East of Eden view, which sees woman as inferior to man and the origin of humankind's problems.

Now, all of subsequent Jewish history and much of the history of western civilization was fed by these two opposite traditions. Whereas the earlier one that I described was never allowed to disappear, the truth is that the latter one became the norm in Jewish society and much of western society. By and large, let it be said honestly and directly and without all the shilly-shallying which has long characterized pronouncements on this subject. By and large, we Jews have bought the view that women are inferior to men and the root source of human evil, from which followed naturally the view that women have to be dominated and that that domination had to be imposed by men.

In Jewish legal theory, for example, there is the basic conviction that woman is the possession of man. A girl literally belongs to one man or another—never to herself. First, of course, she belongs to her father and later to her husband, who acquires her by purchasing her from her father—which is the reason that the bride has little or nothing to say at the wedding ceremony. She is merely an object which is legally transferred from one male to another. It is for this reason, too, that in Jewish law divorce is almost solely at the discretion of and under the power of the husband. After all, if the woman is man's property, he is free to retain it or to dispose of it as he sees fit. It is for this reason too, that if a husband abandons his wife, her status, as his property, remains unchanged. She is an *agunah*—a chained woman—all of her life, if that is how long he is gone. Women, according to Jewish legal stipulation, are not permitted to engage in business without their husband's consent. Even giving charity requires the husband's consent. Everything she owns belongs to her husband. And her sons—not she or her daughters—are her husband's sole legal heirs (although rabbinic law did obligate sons to support their mother from their father's estate).

In Jewish law, there are three major categories of people who are disqualified as witnesses—slaves, minors, and, of course, women. In the religious sphere, similar disabilities have attended the position of Jewish women. Women have not counted in a minyan. They have not participated in a *mizuman* with men in the Grace After Meals. Traditionally, both in the Temple and in the synagogue, women have been segregated out of the view of men and barred from all contact with the Torah. Even the study of Torah, which is regarded by our tradition as the most important of all religious pursuits, historically was not accessible to women. Girls were not given an education in Judaism beyond what was needed to operate their household. The few exceptions that one can point to, prove, on closer examination, either to be non-exceptions or to be in the nature of exceptions which prove the rule.

Socially, women have suffered similar discrimination. The tradition advises men not to talk with women except under certain conditions. It regards conversation with women to be, at best, a waste of time, or lust-evoking at worst.

As to the organizational structure of the Jewish community, the same discrimination is evident. A number of studies have been done which show that women are almost totally absent from positions of importance in the management and direction of synagogues and other Jewish institutions, and have been for centuries. In all fairness, it must be pointed out that the tradition did give women important religious assignments—such as candles and challah. But by and large, the status of women in Judaism and in the Jewish community was, and continues to be, far below that of men. To the extent that women were respected and honored, it was primarily as enablers, that is, people who enabled others—usually male others—to do what they wanted to do or to do what they considered important to do.

Now, it should be obvious to anyone with eyes in his head that western society is in the midst of a great social upheaval on this subject. And so is the Jewish community, both as part of western society and in its own right. Shock waves from the Women's Liberation Movement are being felt with ever-increasing intensity. And if, as Jews and as members of B'nai Amoona, we expect to be part of this world, we had better decide what we think is right.

Let us consider, first, women's position in the general society. It should be clear that women ought to be treated equally in all respects. Women should be given the same opportunities as men. They should be paid the same wages for comparable work as men. They should in no way be subjected to inferior status either legally, economically, or socially. And if the Equal Rights Amendment will help to assure this, which I happen to think it will, then it deserves our support. But equality does not mean that women must relinquish their femininity. I feel that some of the militant feminists do harm to their own cause by denying female uniqueness. A woman has a uterus which a man does not have, and this fact alone determines one major role which is unique to women. That is mother, and chief figure in the home. Equality for women cannot mean either divesting women of the uterus or adding it to men. And don't laugh; I have heard it said that only the development of an artificial uterus will truly liberate women.

The point is that equality does not necessarily mean sameness, and whereas some women will no doubt choose careers and activities in what has heretofore been a man's world, most women follow their biological distinctiveness and continue to find their fulfillment in motherhood and homemaking. The real culprit in this picture is our society in which it is only paid work which is considered dignified work. There are perhaps a few exceptions, such as what has come to be called professional voluntarism. But, by and large, if a person doesn't get money for what he does, what he does is not considered important. This materialistic prejudice of modern society has caused all kinds of terrible effects. Not the least of them being the denigration of homemaking and mothering.

Homemaking and mothering should be raised to the status of a profession. It should receive both recognition and government provisions for economic security. After all, it is no small matter to be entrusted, as mothers and homemakers are entrusted, with the care of the children who are the future of humankind. There is no more creative or important work than guiding children to become human, and if there is a certain amount of drudgery and boredom in homemaking and disappointment in mothering, so is there drudgery and disappointment in every activity people engage in—including the professionals. Equality is not sameness. Women must be liberated as women. Not as imitations of men.

Many of the same considerations apply, I feel, to women and Judaism. Here too, I feel that equality does not necessarily mean sameness. Jewishly, I think that the most fulfilling role that a woman can occupy is that of mother and homemaker. I think that mothering and homemaking are good for women.

Lord knows the Jewish people are desperately in need of such a role which should be filled by our most dedicated and talented women. At the same time, however, it seems to me that equality dictates that women who do not opt for mothering have a right to choose Jewish pursuits which are more satisfying and meaningful to them.

Take the area of study, for example, in which the Jewish community has made a significant start, and we at B'nai Amoona have shared in the start. Not more than a generation ago girls received little or no Jewish education. There are in B'nai Amoona families who having internalized the prejudices of the past, that still do not feel it necessary to have their girls receive intensive Jewish education. It was about 25 years ago that we instituted Bat Mitzvah, both as an incentive to girls to study Judaism, the same as boys, and as a means of recognizing their achievement when they do. Yet there is much more that needs to be done in the congregation, as in the Movement generally, to enable Jewish women who desire to study to do so.

There are no female rabbis in the Conservative Movement, and I know no reason why there should not be. Aside from the facetious question of what to call their husbands, I see nothing wrong with—and a whole lot right with—qualified women becoming teachers of congregations and exercising spiritual leadership as rabbis. The Seminary has consistently ducked the issue and probably will continue to do so as long as certain faculty members remain in power. Meanwhile, several female teachers have joined the Seminary faculty, (one even in Talmud). Small advances are being made. Incidentally, B'nai Amoona has several young ladies studying at the Seminary. I only hope that if the policy is changed and girls are accepted for rabbinical study, the first will be one of ours. What I am saying is that, in the study of Torah, which has nothing whatsoever to do with biology but with ability only and personal achievement, women should be accorded the very same privileges as men.

When one moves from the study of Judaism to the service and to prayer, while one does not encounter biology as such, one does encounter a much more difficult subject, both from a legal—that is an *Halachic* standpoint— and from a social-psychological standpoint. I am not of the opinion that all distinctions between men and women with regard to the service ought to be removed summarily. Each of the matters involved in this complex subject has its own history and its own background and should be considered on an individual basis in terms of its own history and background.

For example, according women *aliyot* is one thing. Including them in a *muzumin* for the *bensching* is another. Having the women recite the Kaddish is one thing. Having them lead the service as *Hazzan* is another. It is precisely to the fine distinctions that we shall be directing our attention during the course of the coming year.

Nor am I ready at this moment to commit myself totally on any particular item beyond assuring you that each will be studied carefully. When the time for decision comes, there will be open and honest discussion.

For your information, we have already undertaken and approved the question of including women in a *bensching* quorum. Right now I am personally dealing with the question of including women in the minyan. For those of you who may not know, about two years ago the Law Committee of the Rabbinical Assembly, by a majority vote, approved including women in a minyan. Although I still need additional study, my guess is that in the near future I shall rule that women may be counted in a minyan. After which I look forward to the Congregation's approval of my action. My reasoning, as it seems to be developing, is that *Halachic* questions aside—for there are many points on both sides—I do not see how we can continue much longer to regard women as guests in the synagogue or in a house of mourning. They are persons in the fullest sense. Because of changes in our society, they have the same obligation to pray as men. And to do so at a public service which the tradition regards as a *sine qua non* to the religious life. They are persons, in other words, whose presence counts, which is what minyan means.

As I said earlier, there are two traditions in Judaism regarding women which is, by the way, not an uncommon phenomenon. Very often you will find opposite views in Judaism. For various reasons one will be emphasized rather than the other, and different ones will be emphasized at different times. In the main, it was historical circumstances rather than innate truth which dictated the view that woman is a temptress and therefore needs to be repressed by man.

Modern influences and enlightened self-interest dictate a change in emphasis, and a change soon. Basing ourselves on the account of Creation which sees woman as the complete equal of man, we should enter upon a reevaluation and, if need be, a reinterpretation of our practices. We should pay full deference to all parts of the tradition, including the one which I feel to be the less worthy one. We should also pay full deference to our relationship with the rest of the Jewish community—in Israel and in the Diaspora—to the end, that we may both right ancient wrongs and assure a bright and vibrant future for our people.

In Judaism, *yahrzeit*, the day of the death of a forebear, is a sacred day. But there is a growing tendency to be aware also of the day of birth. Not just *yahrzeit* but also the birthday, and I rather like the trend. I especially like it in this case. The birthday of Grandmother Eve and Grandfather Adam, as described in Genesis, is instructive of the kind of relationship which they enjoyed for a time and which we should try to recover in our time. It is a relationship based upon equality, love and mutual respect. It is a relationship beautifully described in the Midrash by Rabbi Simlai in his attempt to square the two antithetical Creation accounts of Genesis. His words eloquently express what I hope and pray will be the outcome of our modest efforts in this connection in the year, and years, ahead. "Adam was created from the dust," said Rabbi Simlai, "and Eve from Adam, but henceforth it shall be in Our image—not man without woman, nor woman without man, and neither without the Holy Spirit."

Amen.

The Decline of the Family—"The Year of the Jewish Family"

May we all be inscribed and sealed for a good and a healthy year ahead!

Welcome also to this wedding anniversary celebration! Did you realize that today is a wedding anniversary celebration? Well, it is! Today, Rosh Hashanah, whatever else it may be, is the wedding anniversary celebration, conducted annually by the Jewish people, in honor of our great, great, great, great, great to the Nth power, grandparents—the 5,740th anniversary of the wedding of Adam and Eve—the first married couple in human history, and the *bubbe* and *zedye* of everybody here.

In case you think that this is a fanciful assertion, let me point out to you that, according to Genesis, God created the world in seven days. On the first day He created light. On the second the firmament. Until on the sixth day, He created Adam and Eve. "And God created the human being in His own image"... "Male and female created He them." Then apparently, Adam and Eve fell in love, love at first sight. They decided—or perhaps God decided for them—that they should marry.

There not being any other family available, obviously, God took it upon Himself to arrange the wedding, and what a wedding He arranged! According to the rabbis, the wedding was celebrated with a degree of pomp and joy that has not been duplicated in the whole course of human history. Now, according to the Biblical chronology, this wedding occurred late in the day, on the Friday of Creation, just before Shabbat. The wedding feast was held after the sun set. At the beginning, the Seven Benedictions, the most prominent feature of the wedding feast, were recited. After which, Adam and Eve retired to their chambers and consummated their marriage as God had ordered, beginning the whole long procreative process which resulted in the human family, including you and me, and something over three billion other children who are alive today. And it all started, like I said, five thousand, seven hundred and forty years ago today, on Rosh Hashanah, the anniversary of the first marriage in the history of this universe.

Now, from that time until this, marriage and the family it gave rise to, have been the most important and the most durable of all the institutions created by humankind. In primitive societies as well as in highly developed societies, family, in one form or another, has been the foundation of all interpersonal relationships. First, for procreative purposes, to perpetuate the race. But, for cultural purposes, to conserve the knowledge and the wisdom which has been created by civilization, and to pass that knowledge and wisdom on to succeeding generations.

But most of all, the family was created to provide warmth. This universe, as all of us know, can be very cold and very lonely. People need refuge from the cold, and love in order to counter the loneliness, and it is the family which, more than any other institution created by humanity, has provided that refuge and that love. This is particularly true about the Jewish family. If we Jews have any basis for pride over our long history, it has not been our scientific discoveries or our military might, or, for that matter, our wisdom. It has been our ability to produce exemplary families. Families which have reared good kids and cultured kids. Families in whose bosom the individual Jew found acceptance and warmth and love.

But alas, in recent years, far-reaching changes have begun to be evident in the structure of the family—among non-Jews and Jews alike. Some have gone so far as to say that the changes are so great that the family, as we know it, is doomed—finished! Others maintain that the family continues to be vital, albeit in different ways, and will never die. But whichever point of view you adopt, there is no denying that cataclysmic changes have occurred in the family.

For most of human history, for example as I have said, marriage and family were the bedrock of interpersonal relationships. Well, this is no longer the case. As of this moment, almost one out of four households in the United States is a one-person household! That is, one person living alone, by himself or by herself. Marriages, when they do occur, are now occurring later and later in people's lives. And are often childless by choice! Divorce, what was once anathema to most people, is becoming almost commonplace. As of this moment, one out of every four of all the children in the United States is living with one parent or with adults other than their parents. Even those who do marry don't seem to tolerate marriage for very long. As to the total family picture, the nuclear family consisting of only father, mother and children, has become the typical model of the American middle class. Extended families in which grandparents, uncles, aunts and other relatives lived nearby or in the same household is a rarity. The American family no longer, to say the least, is what it used to be.

When you look at the Jewish family, the changes seem to be even more far-reaching. They consist of the same changes that are present in the American family at large but to an aggravated degree. American Jews, for example, both men and women, tend to marry even later than other Americans. The American Jewish birthrate is far below that of the nation as a whole and is still declining. Divorce in the Jewish community has also reached crisis proportions. Among persons age 25–29 that are heads of households, fully 20 percent are separated or divorced. Parents without partners, it is reported, make up more than 30 percent of the constituency of Jewish Community Centers across the country.

In many ways, even more frightening are the figures on the extended family. Few Jewish households include grandparents like many once did. Few kids stay home for college or ever come back home to live once they leave for college. The result being that old and young are soon removed or remove themselves from the home permanently. Added to all of this is the over-riding painful problem of intermarriage which faces the Jewish community, which faces many of us in this sanctuary. I don't have to tell you what intermarriage means in terms of family relationships, between the couple themselves, and with respect to the larger family. Let me be clear. Not that each and every one of the changes which I have enumerated is an unmitigated evil. Some are. Perhaps even most are and some are not. But, at the very least, the fabric of family, as we know it, which has been the mainstay of Jewish life and pride these thousands of years, has been altered almost beyond recognition.

The time has come for us to deal with this issue and to do so forthrightly and deliberately. To understand the problems, to the extent and in the depth that we are capable of understanding them. Then to provide solutions, once again to the extent that it is within our power to do so.

Every year for the past number of years, at B'nai Amoona, we adopt a synagogue theme. That is, a subject of concern, which begins on Rosh Hashanah and serves to unify sermons, programming, study groups, and the like, throughout the course of the year. Recently, the officers of the congregation and the staff made a decision. That decision was to designate this coming year at B'nai Amoona, "The Year of the Jewish Family." A special group called the B'nai Amoona Jewish Family Life Council was appointed by the President. Its responsibility is to see to it that the theme is carried through in all our programming. The "Jewish Family," was chosen as the theme for this year because there was a gut perception on the part of everybody concerned that, as the saying goes, "this is where it's at!" This is the most important issue of all. This is the key challenge of our time. Family—vital, healthy Jewish family life—is the core. Strong, functioning Jewish families are the essence. There has been an instinctive, well-nigh universal realization that we have finally come upon the nub. That in order to assure a bright and worthwhile future for ourselves, our congregation, and our people, here is where we shall have to take our stand. Here is where we shall win it, or, God forbid, the opposite.

What I want to do with you today is to begin the treatment of the theme. Obviously, we are not going to exhaust the subject of the Jewish Family in one sermon. Nor, for that matter, are we going to exhaust the subject in one year. It is our hope that the emphasis upon Jewish family life and the effort to retain and, where need be to recapture, the values upon which solid Jewish family life is built, will become a permanent emphasis.

But start we must, and start we shall. We shall start with a plea. From this pulpit to every seat in this shul. From me to each and every one of you. The substance of that plea is, first, that as individuals we order or reorder our priorities so that family occupies the preeminent position that it deserves. So that family, with us, is out in front, ahead of everything else. Second, that we raise the quality of our family activity to the highest possible level. That we infuse our family life with the highest possible degree of understanding, and with ever greater sensitivity and beauty, and that we do all of this in the context of and with the assistance of Judaism and the synagogue. Let us look at each of these areas in turn.

I guess the best place to start to talk about priorities is with a story. I was once sitting with a man in his office (he shall remain nameless). He was fiddling through his desk looking for a paper or something, when he came across a picture. He pulled out the picture, looked at it rather quizzically and then handed it to me. As I looked at it, he said, "You know, Rabbi, who that is? That is a picture of me, my wife and four kids. It was taken about ten years ago. But you know what? I can't even remember the kids at that age or, for that matter, myself." He sat for a moment, silently, and he repeated. "I can't remember a thing that happened to me or to my wife or to the kids ten years ago." I really felt for the man. We got to talking, and right then and there he made a decision that he was going to gather his kids together—some of them were already scattered—and the whole family would go to Israel, as a family, that summer. Now this man was a successful businessman, a successful husband and probably a successful father, too. But, if he was like the rest of us, there were surely times—and maybe it is inevitable—that all of those various roles got mixed up—confused. Times when he wasn't sure what his real priorities were. Well, in that one moment, when he looked at the picture and realized that his kids would never be the same age that they were at that moment—that his wife and that he would never be the same age that they were then, it all kind of came together for him. He realized, he knew without any doubt, what really counted in his life.

Now, as difficult as it is for a man to establish that kind of priority in this day and age, it is even more difficult for a woman. The reason is that we are in the midst of a quiet revolution, and sometimes a not so quiet revolution, with respect to women's place in the scheme of things. There is a great deal of justice which motivates this revolution. Biology need not necessarily be destiny. Women, who for whatever reason, desire to leave the home and pursue a career, do have the right to do so. Still and all, I believe that there is a special role that women occupy with respect to the family. It is the woman's special role, I feel, to nurture, to feed, in the deepest sense of that term, the family. I am not talking about making dinner every night, but to feed the family with the substances and the nourishment which make for a successful family. Love, warmth, kindness, acceptance, sacrifice, and yes, food, too. It is women still, in this society, at this juncture of history who, if you will forgive the cliché, keep the home-fires burning—fires which provide illumination; fires which cook food; and fires which envelope all the members of the family in loving warmth. No, not necessarily all women and certainly not women who, for whatever reason, don't want it. But those women who are willing to make family their top priority. My first point is that as individuals, individual men and individual women, we should order or reorder our priorities so that family comes first, where it belongs.

Once having established that priority, the second thing we must concern ourselves with is with the quality of our family life. Putting family first is crucial, but not the whole story. We have to find ways of making the experience of family genuinely satisfying and worthwhile. Once having come home, in other words, we have to make our homes and the relationships among the people who live in our homes quality relationships. Communication, an ofttimes overused but nonetheless extremely important word, is an excellent place to begin. To what extent, for example, do we really listen to the members of our family? How willing are we to hear the members of our family—to hear their words, and to hear the message behind the words?

Do you remember that wonderful reading, written by Rabbi Riemer, in which he interprets the *Shema*: Judaism begins with the commandment: "Hear O Israel," but what does it really mean to hear? The person who attends a concert with his mind on business hears—but does not really hear. The person who walks amidst the songs of birds and thinks only of what he will have for dinner, hears—but does not really hear.

Or the man who listens to the words of his friends, or his wife or his child, and does not catch the note of urgency—"Notice me; help me; care about me," hears—but does not really hear.

The quality of our hearing must be improved. Or do you remember the one about the irate mother who, when told about the misbehavior of her son, said, "It's obvious that what that boy of mine needs is a good talking to." To which the teacher replied, "No, Madam, what your boy needs is a good listening to!"

Another way to improve the quality of our family life is to make the time that is spent together "quality time." Communication should lead not just to togetherness, but to togetherness with a purpose. If I had my way, for example, I would put all of the television stations out of business this minute, including the daily news programs, and most newspapers along with them. I realize that there are some worthwhile programs and that selective viewing rather than wholesale rejection is probably the better solution, but I can't think of one single object in modern civilization which has done more to separate members of families, even if they watch together, than television. It is, for the most part, bad, bad, bad. What I mean by quality time is time in which members of the family join, not to watch together but to do together, actively. On behalf of their home and on behalf of our community. Time spent in building together, learning together, recreating together.

Which brings me to the third point—namely the significant role that Judaism and the synagogue can play in the kind of family that I am describing. It is no big mystery why Jewish family life has been as successful as it has been over the centuries. It is because of the ennobling, uplifting influence of Judaism, Jewish values, Jewish ceremonials, and Jewish insights. Which, at one and the same time, arise from within the family and feed back into the family—supporting it, strengthening it, helping to make it the beautiful work of art that it can become. Can you in your wildest imagination think of a more family-enhancing, family solidifying meaningful activity for the family than a traditional Friday night table and service? Children and grandparents seated around the same table. The blessing of the children, all the members of the family joining to make happen something of real substance; with perhaps a guest or two at the table to share the bounty and the blessing of such a family. Can you in your wildest imagination picture a more uplifting family activity than shul on Shabbat in this Sanctuary? Where families have sat together literally for generations. Raised their voices in prayer and song. Joined together in solidarity and Jewish fellowship. If it is quality family activity that we are after, can you think of any more satisfying project than say, building a sukkah together on Sukkot? Or decorating the home for Hanuka? Or combining resources to run a substantial family Seder, at which tasty Matza-meal *knaidlach* and other goodies are served up? And lots, lots more! Judaism is still the best means ever devised to create solid, loving, communicating families which devote themselves to worthwhile purposes.

When you turn to the synagogue, it is a moot question as to just how much the synagogue—our own included—has done to enhance Jewish family life.

Suffice it to say that maintaining and strengthening the Jewish family has not been, and is not now, the top priority of the synagogue. But it has got to become such and it has to become such now.

The story is told of the Gerer Rebbe who once asked one of his disciples a question. "How," asked the Rebbe, "is Moshe Yaakov doing?" The disciple said, "I don't know." "What?" shouted the Rebbe, "You don't know? You pray under the same roof, you study the same texts, you serve the same God, you sing the same songs, and yet you dare to tell me that you don't know whether Moshe Yaakov is in good health, whether he needs help, or advice, or comforting? How is it possible?"

The same is true of the synagogue. Those of us who pray under the same roof, who study the same texts, who serve the same God, who sing the same songs, must know how each other is doing; must know who needs help, who needs advice, who needs comforting; must know who does not have a Shabbat meal to go to; must know who hurts and why; must know who lacks the warmth of family and then help to provide the meal, assuage the hurt, and supply, if not the family, the warmth.

We already have some ideas on how to go about it. Either later today or Monday you will receive in the mail an information sheet which you are asked to read carefully and fill out and either send back or bring back on Kol Nidre. It is designed to gather information on how the shul can be responsive to your needs and the needs of your family.

Sometimes at a wedding anniversary celebration, it is my custom to celebrate the event by singing or having the *Hazzan* sing the Seven Benedictions. In honor of today's wedding anniversary, I want to call to your attention one *Bracha* in particular, the third: "Blessed art Thou O Lord our God, King of the Universe, Creator of the human being." Do you realize that this is the only place in our entire liturgy where we bless God for creating the human being? We don't say the *Bracha* when we read the story of the creation of Adam in the synagogue. We don't say it even at a Bris or at a Bar Mitzvah or at a Bat Mitzvah. Only at a wedding! Or, like today, at the anniversary celebration of a wedding. Why? Because in Judaism, it is primarily in marriage, in the context of family, that the human being is a human being. It is primarily in the context of family that the human being has the opportunity to express fully that which makes him unique in all of creation. It is primarily in the context of the Jewish family that the Jew can approximate, as one of the earlier *Brachot* says, the true likeness of God in whose image we were created. It is primarily in context of family that the human being is fully human.

I hereby declare this year, 5740, to be the Year of the Jewish Family at B'nai Amoona. May we succeed in strengthening all of our families. May we succeed in strengthening the B'nai Amoona family. May such strengthening, as the prayer promises, help to usher in an era of peace and tranquility and blessed fulfillment in a world which will be ruled by the Messiah, the son of David. Speedily and in our day. And let us say, Amen.

Upgrading Our Commitment, Beginning with Shabbat

September, 1982 - Rosh Hashanah 5743

The *Akeda*, the Binding of Isaac, which forms one of the two Torah portions for Rosh Hashanah, has been understood in as many different ways as there have been scholars and students of Judaism. Each generation, and within each generation each individual, seems to interpret this moving account of Isaac's sacrifice at the hand of his father, Abraham, in accordance with what he sees as the mandate of faith in his own life at that particular time.

This year as I reread the story of the *Akeda*, it speaks to me with a similar message. It speaks that message in accents so forceful and so clear that I feel obligated to share it with you. The *Akeda* story speaks to me of commitment! To the need, which Abraham established right at the beginning of Jewish history, to respond with total commitment to what he perceived to be God's command; to respond with his whole being, completely and unequivocally—and then to transmit to his child, mostly by example, the need to do likewise in his life. Let's look at the story together and see perhaps why I read it this way!

"And it came to pass after these things that God tested Abraham." Tested him for what? It couldn't have been to see if Abraham believed in God. That was already established when Abraham broke with his father and with the Mesopotamian culture in which he was reared. The test couldn't have been to see whether or not Abraham would follow God's directives. That, too, was already established when Abraham obeyed God's command to journey to an unknown land that He, God, would show him. I contend that the purpose of the test, as revealed by the nature of the test, was to establish one thing—the depth of Abraham's commitment to God. Did Abraham really mean it? Was his commitment to God a total commitment?

In the second half of that same verse, just as the test is about to begin, God calls for Abraham, who answers with a powerful, single-word response, astounding in its simplicity and directness: "Here am I." Not, "Who's calling?" Or, "What can I do for you, God?" But, "Here am I."—all of me; totally present; totally committed. Then, true to his word, Abraham is given a chance to prove it. The test was not designed to be partial proof of a partial commitment. God asked Abraham for ultimate proof of an ultimate commitment. The life of his only, his beloved son, Isaac, to be taken by his—by Abraham's—own hand! As you think about it, it is kind of grotesque. But if we are talking about ultimate commitment, I suppose that there is one ultimate test of such commitment. Not, God forbid, to be carried out. Only the resolve to carry it out, if need be. This was it: The command for Abraham to take the life of his son, at God's behest, which he proceeded to do. . . right now. Says the text, "Early the next morning. . .!" It was this example which Abraham passed on to his son, Isaac. Forging the first link in the chain which, because of the strength of the commitment out of which it was fashioned to begin with, has bound us to God and to each other these past 4,000 years.

It is interesting to me that the dictionary definition of the word "commitment" is "to bind, as by a pledge." The *Akeda* is the Binding of Isaac, his binding, and the binding of all his descendants after him, as by a pledge—to God and to each other. In my estimation, many of the problems we face in Jewish life today are a direct outgrowth of a decline in commitment; commitment in general and Jewish commitment, in particular.

Today, to a greater extent than ever before, people's relationships with the world and with each other tend to be tentative and temporary. People today commit themselves up to a point. We are wary of becoming too deeply involved, over too long a period of time. One of the comedians recently spoofed the young man who proposed to his girlfriend by saying, "Would you please be my first wife?" They also tell the story of a salmon and a chicken who were walking along the street in a particular city, looking for work. They came upon a restaurant which advertised—it apparently was in a Jewish neighborhood—a special on lox and eggs. The chicken said to the salmon, "Let's go in and inquire!" "Nothing doing!" said the salmon. "Why not?" asked the chicken. To which the salmon replied, "I am not going into that place. From you all they want is a contribution. From me, what they want is total commitment."

I talk to young people I marry about where they intend to settle, and more and more the answer is that they are "mobile." Wherever the best opportunities present themselves, they tell me, they will move. They generally don't specify what they mean, but I gather they mean economic opportunities. Not opportunities to visit the old neighborhood and not opportunities to sit in a familiar seat in the synagogue. Economic opportunities!

Modern man seems embarrassed by the whole idea of commitment—either to places, institutions, ideals, for that matter, to other people. The biggest of all possible put-downs to a person is, "Something's really wrong with him. He ought to be committed!" What a sad commentary! And the greater the commitment, the greater the embarrassment.

Commitment conjures up in our minds the image of the Ayatollah Khomeini, or some other wide-eyed fanatic who is capable of doing anything to anybody. Indeed, total commitment sometimes does lead to dangerous extremism. On the other hand, extremism does not discredit commitment, as such. It only discredits particular commitments. Commitments that may be described as self-seeking, repressive, or vindictive. Commitment itself, as a condition for human progress and for the successful functioning of every human enterprise, is undisputed. Commitment is absolutely crucial to the achievement of every lofty goal and every worthwhile purpose to which human beings aspire.

What is true of life, in general, is true of Jewish life too. Our Jewish commitments, like the rest of our commitments, tend to be partial and tentative. We contribute money to worthwhile Jewish causes but, important as it is, a financial contribution represents a limited commitment. Some Jews express their Jewish commitment by lending their names and even their time to good causes. Some to the observance of this or that ritual of Judaism. To the espousal of this or that doctrine of Jewish belief. But all of us, almost without exception, pick and choose limiting ourselves in one way or another, stopping short of genuine total commitment.

There is no question in my mind that the biggest single problem afflicting Conservative Judaism is precisely this—the wishy-washiness of our commitment. Historically, and I think with a good deal of wisdom, Conservative Judaism has always followed a kind of a middle path. We have stood for the authentic study and practice of Judaism in creative interaction with our environment. "Tradition and change" has been our watchword. Bespeaking our goal of solid knowledge and the faithful practice of the essentials of Judaism, without at the same time neglecting the significant insights of culture and thought in the world around us. All outward signs point to the success of this approach.

The Conservative Movement is the largest Jewish religious movement in America, equal in size to the other two combined. Our synagogues are well-attended, and our programs many and varied, but if we are honest with ourselves, we have to admit that there are numerous signs of decline all around us. From my perspective of 32 High Holy Day celebrations in this very building and lots of experiences in between, I note a growing and alarming lack of knowledge of Judaism among our people. I hear it in private conversation. I see it at services. There is little familiarity with the prayers and with the melodies and even less familiarity with the other literary and musical treasures of Judaism—with the result that there is less and less dialog between our congregants and the ideas of Judaism. I have no way of measuring it, but I suspect that there is less and less dialog, too, between ourselves and God. I see a frightening decline not only in knowledge, but also in observance.

The three foundations of Jewish observance are prayer, *Kashrus*, and Shabbat. Regular prayer, private and public, is obviously in low estate. My guess is that allegiance to *Kashrus* has been relinquished by something like 90 percent of our people. And as to Shabbat, it, too, is honored more in the breach than in the observance. In general, our whole lifestyle is not determined, or for that matter greatly influenced, by Jewish ideals and Jewish practices and Jewish values—as much as by other forces and other systems.

But perhaps the greatest indication of what I regard as the crisis of Conservative Judaism, the biggest single indication, is our lack of ability to hold our children. Our children are not staying with us. True, membership in our congregation seems to be holding up. But that is only because of a large pool of unaffiliated people in the community, who choose to identify with us. Reach into your own experience and try to think of how many of our children have left us—identified either with other branches of Judaism or with no branch of Judaism. Obviously, there are many reasons for this, but one of them is that our children detect the superficiality of our commitment and they are put off. Like the chicken, they see our contributions but not our commitment!

Each year, at this time, I try to set out my goals for the coming synagogue year. And I want to do so today. For the last dozen or so Rosh Hashanahs, in this sermon I have established a synagogue theme for the year. The selection of a theme fills a need for me, personally. It provides me with a concentration, a major, around which my own enthusiasm can rally for the year. Towards which I can direct my thinking and perhaps the congregation's priorities, as well. Last year, of course, was our beautiful centennial. What I have in mind this year for us, and I definitely include myself, is up-grading our commitment to God and to what we perceive to be His will. Not to the point of sacrificing our children, like Abraham was prepared to do—perhaps we shall never reach that level of commitment. Maybe we shouldn't even try; I don't know. But with that example as the ultimate expression of Jewish commitment before our mind's eye, to move in the direction of enhancing, raising the level of, our Jewish commitment, and I am going to be on our necks all year to see that we do.

I want to start, not so much with prayer and not so much with *Kashrus*—although don't anybody think that I am down-grading their importance—I want to start with Shabbat. I want to tell you why.

First of all, I am inspired by the fact that Rosh Hashanah this year coincides with and begins on Shabbat. More than that, I feel that Shabbat, as an institution, contains more of the elements of meaningful Jewish loyalty than any other single Jewish institution. We are going to be talking about that in much more detail beginning on Yom Kippur and extending throughout the year. Suffice it to say for the moment that Shabbat, with its emphasis upon family, its emphasis upon the study of Torah and prayer and even its emphasis upon good food, seems to contain one of the elements of positive Jewish observance and thought than any other single aspect of Judaism. It is no accident, for example, that Shabbat is the only ritual Mitzvah dealt with explicitly in the Ten Commandments. Every other one of the Ten Commandments is non-ritual in nature. They all involve belief or relationships among people. The only commandment of the Ten Commandments having to do with Jewish ritual observance is the fourth commandment:

"Remember the Sabbath day to keep it holy." Therefore we are going to start with Shabbat.

Not just Shabbat in general, though, but two specific goals related to Shabbat. I am looking forward to every family of B'nai Amoona recapturing the beauty and the sanctity of Friday night at home with the family. The performance of the Shabbat table ritual. Candles, *Kiddush*, *HaMotzi*, *Zemirot*, *Benschen* and, in general, devoting ourselves on Friday night to rest and to spiritual regeneration, all within the context of family—biological family and/or extended family.

And the second goal is to have every member of B'nai Amoona join with the total B'nai Amoona family in communal prayer here in this sanctuary on Shabbat morning, where we pray, sing, and celebrate together the glory of being alive and being Jewish. No, these are not the only possible ways to raise the level of our Jewish commitment, but these are the two that I am going to be looking towards with you, with the auxiliaries, with the school and with our youth, during the coming year. If we are to make it as Conservative Jews, we have got to increase our commitment. If we are to increase our commitment, I know of no better place to start than with Shabbat.

The watchword of Jewish faith is "Hear O Israel, the Lord is our God, the Lord is One." And immediately thereafter we read: "You shall love the Lord your God with all your heart, with all your soul and with all your might." To which the commentators say "all" means even to the point of giving your life, if called upon to do so. Like Isaac was willing to give up his life at the start of Jewish history, I would like every person in this sanctuary to know that we, too, are being tested. Perhaps not as dramatically or as fully as Abraham and Isaac were tested, but tested nevertheless. There is a voice, a Divine voice, ringing out across the centuries—if we can but attune our ears to hear it—eager to know the depth of our commitment, the extent to which we are truly committed to God and to His commandments. The voice calls to each and every one of us, by name. It is my purpose, which I hope the congregation will come to share during the year ahead, that we shall respond, as Abraham responded, simply and directly, by saying and meaning, "God, here am I." A prayer to which I invite your assent by asking you to join me in saying, Amen.

Life Lessons and Reflections

A life well lived, a life devoted to others, a life in search of meaning, a life ever curious, ever energetic, ever reflective, is a life wherein wisdom may be found.

The six sermons in this section offer the reader a glimpse into the mind and heart of a humble and wise man.

The Best of the Second Raters

Kol Nidre - 1980

If there is one group of people for whom our society has little or no regard, it is the so-called "losers." On television, in sports, in business and in government, we are told that the world is made up of essentially two kinds of people, winners and losers, and if you are not a winner, then you are a loser. If you are a loser, you had better become a winner, and quickly. Whole sections in bookstores these days are set aside for the growing literature on what are supposed to be the components of winning. Books on how to make a million; how to win friends; how to "wow" the ladies; and in general, how to out-smart or out-muscle the opposition—which according to popular American culture, is what constitutes success in this life.

I have a book on my shelf by Robert J. Ringer entitled, *Winning Through Intimidation*. When I bought it originally, I thought it was a joke book. But it is not a joke book. It is dead serious. 'Assert yourself,' it says. 'Be a lion.' 'Intimidate a friend at lunch.' 'Walk! Talk! Wear your pocket handkerchief like a winner.' 'So you are greedy? Terrific! It is nothing to feel guilty about. On the contrary, follow your instincts.' 'Get filthy rich and flaunt it.' 'Look out for Number One!' 'Winning is everything!'

It was O. J. Simpson, who by anybody's standard is a winner, that put the matter very clearly. O. J., you'll recall, skewered an entire UCLA football team with a now-legendary 64-yard open field burst. It was that run which gave USC the whole glorious bundle—a 21–20 victory in the game's waning minutes. The Pacific Eight championship and the 1968 Rose Bowl bid. In any event, O. J. said, "Fear of losing is what. . . makes competitors great. Show me a guy who is a gracious loser and I'll show you a perennial loser."

Well, folks, I've got news for you and for O. J.! We are all losers! The approximately 1,500 people seated in this synagogue tonight, myself included, are losers. Yes, you have heard me correctly. All of us here are not winners. We are losers! We are losers in one area which, from the Jewish point of view, is the most important of all, and that is the moral, the religious area. The area of character—the quality of our humanity.

You see, our tradition says: "There is no one who is so righteous that he hasn't sinned." Whatever successes, therefore, we might credit ourselves with; and I am sure we all have our share. Whatever successes the world might credit us with. According to our tradition they are secondary to our moral quality. Yet we do not, by and large, measure up. Few of us are as pious as we might be or as decent as we might be or as loving as we might be; as considerate as we might be or as humble as we might be. We are all, to use a term which is not too popular these days, sinful—individually, and since we are part of a sinful society, collectively as well.

Which is why we came tonight; which is the reason we are together on Yom Kippur in the first place. We are here to acknowledge, before God and before man, that in life's most important area—the moral and religious—we are losers, and perennial losers. Perennial means year-long and indeed we are year-long losers. Most of us were here last year and most of us, God willing, will be here again next year. Why? Once more to acknowledge that in the really important areas of human endeavor—the moral and ethical and religious—all of us leave much to be desired.

So that is what I want to talk to you about tonight—winning and losing— as applied particularly to the realm of the moral. How we should look at winning and how we should relate to losing. What we should do with it. How, according to our tradition, we should handle it.

The first important fact about us losers, that Judaism conveys, is that not only are we here tonight, but that we are welcome here tonight. Now that's a big thing! Our tradition tells us that our moral insufficiencies, to the contrary notwithstanding, are not reason for our rejection. We are accepted, hopefully by other people, but if not by other people, then certainly by God. That is the meaning of the line in the 27th Psalm which the tradition has assigned for our study during this season: "Even if my father and mother forsook me, the Lord would take me under His care." That is the force, too, of the very first prayer that we uttered this evening, even before we recited the *Kol Nidre.* "By the authority of the heavenly Tribunal, and of the Court below, with divine sanction and with the sanction of this holy congregation, we declare it lawful to pray together with the . . ."losers." The very first prayer, the prayer that is designed to set the tone for what is transpiring here this evening, and what will transpire here tomorrow. What does it say? It informs us that as inadequate as you may be, I am permitted to pray with you. And as inadequate as I may be, you are permitted to pray with me. As bad as is the person sitting next to you, he or she and you and I have one thing in common, and that is that none of us has done well enough. The very first fact about us losers then is that, even though we are implicated, we are welcome. Even though we are all guilty, we have a right to be here. Or to put it more succinctly: I am not okay and you are not okay—but that's O.K.!

The second important fact is that though we are losers we are losers in a partial sense only. Obviously many of us have done not badly—even in the moral area. We are not, for the most part, bad people. Not as good as we might be, but certainly not as bad, either. But are our priorities on straight? Do we measure our win/loss ratio in terms of the quality—the moral quality—of our lives? Or do we perhaps let the little successes blind us to the need for the big ones, for example?

I don't know O. J. Simpson intimately. But I wonder if his personal life is as successful as that run he made. Whether his relationship with his wife and kids and friends is in the same category as his spectacular athletic achievement. I wonder what his relationship with his God is. I wonder what his relationship with himself is. I repeat, I don't know O. J., and I am certainly not casting aspersions.

But we do know about other so-called highly successful people. Their successes tend to be disproportionally limited, restricted to one, and often not especially significant, aspect of human existence. Take for example, Anatole France, the celebrated author. He tasted great achievement. He had hosts of friends, ample wealth. In short, a winner. Yet he is quoted as having said, "There is not in all the universe a creature more unhappy than I. People think me happy. I have never been happy for one day, not for a single hour." Some winner! Similarly, the so-called losers, their losing is also limited. Alfred Sutro wrote a play, called, *The Maker of Men*. The main character is a bank clerk who returns home after missing a promotion. He confronts his wife dejectedly and with head held low. And he says, "I see other men get on. What have I done?" And then his wife answers, "You have made a woman love you. You have given me respect for you and admiration and loyalty and devotion. Everything a man can give his wife, except luxury. And that I don't need. Shall you call yourself a failure who within these four walls are the greatest success?"

Most of us are winners and losers at the same time. The question is, do we win the big ones? In which case, even if we lose, according to the commonly accepted definition of the term, we win!

But perhaps the most important truth on this subject is the specific truth that is communicated by this Yom Kippur service, and that is that winning and losing are only tentative, temporary. That losing, in particular, need never be final. Certainly not in the moral area and not in the other areas of life either. That is what repentance is. That no matter where a person is on the moral scale, he can improve. The conviction that no matter how far a person has fallen, he can pick himself up again and return to his former self and to his God.

More than that, the loss that a person suffers is in itself, when viewed properly, the raw material out of which success can be and often is fashioned. I am thinking of a fifteen-year-old youngster who once stood sheepishly before the headmaster of a Munich school. The headmaster gave him a merciless tongue-lashing for his lack of interest in his studies which he concluded by dismissing the boy from the school. "Your presence in the class," he said, "destroys the respect of the students." The youngster then took an examination to enter the Swiss Polytechnic School in Zurich. But he failed the test. So he entered another school and finished his training. Then he applied for an assistantship at the Polytechnic. His application was rejected. He secured a position as a tutor for boys in a boarding house. But soon he was fired. At long last, he managed to obtain a job in the patent office in Berne and without going any farther, let me tell you that the man who compiled this impressive string of losses was none other than Albert Einstein.

Failures themselves, you see, can become stepping stones to achievement. They can teach us important lessons, if we would but heed those lessons, and leave us wiser, better and stronger for having failed. This is perhaps what the rabbis had in mind when they said that a repentant sinner stands higher on the moral ladder than a completely righteous person who never sinned. This is what Nietzsche had in mind, too, when he wrote, "What does not destroy me, makes me stronger." Someone once wrote that "failure should be cremated, not embalmed." True! But only if we have performed an autopsy. What caused the failure? What did I do wrong? After which we venture forth, determined to do it better and indeed equipped to do it better. Losing, says our tradition, especially in the moral arena, is only tentative, never permanent.

You know, it occurs to me that this subject should really be very familiar to us Jews. We happen to be members of a people who have known more failure than perhaps any other people in the history of mankind. Military defeat, burned temples, a destroyed homeland, exile, pogroms, deportations, and the crowning loss of all—the Holocaust. But when the Great Historian writes the history one day of our civilization, I have a feeling that the Jews will rate more than a passing reference, and that what may appear to have been a 'loser people' will turn out to have been the 'winningest people' of them all.

I can do no more than to wish all of us losers, when the time comes, a similar evaluation of our personal lives. Having acknowledged our lack of success and having realized that it is within our power to improve. That we shall indeed rise to great heights of moral achievement and excellence, this coming year and in all the years beyond. To which I invite you to join me in saying, Amen.

Into the Mountains

Behar - May 11, 1991

Mountains are very much on my mind these days. The reason is that, in just a little over a month and a half, Harriet and I will be leaving St. Louis in order to take up residence on a mountain called San Jacinto. The mountain is located in Southern California, about 100 miles due east of Los Angeles. The mountain itself goes up to a little under 11,000 feet. But we hope to build our house about halfway up the mountain, at the 5,400- to 5,500-foot level. It is no wonder then, that when I opened the *Humash* in order to search for a sermon idea for today, the title of the first of today's two *sedras* arrested my attention in a way that it never had before.

The title of the *sedra* is *Behar*, which means "in the mountain" or "on the mountain," referring to Mt. Sinai, where God and Moses had their encounter. Suddenly this word, "*Behar*," for the reasons I just mentioned, began, if I may use one of Harriet's favorite expressions, "to speak to me."

You know, I never realized just how deeply entwined Judaism is and has always been with mountains. For example, the Bible, right at the beginning, speaks of Mt. Ararat, which was the mountain on which Noah's Ark came to rest. Also in Genesis, Abraham's willingness to serve God at the ultimate price, that is to sacrifice his son, was tested on a mountain, Mt. Moriah. When Moses reached the Promised Land but was not allowed to enter, God afforded him a glimpse of the Promised Land, once again from the top of a mountain, Mt. Nebo. You will recall that the Prophet Elijah called upon his people to make a final and fateful choice, between serving God and worshipping idols. Where? On top of Mt. Carmel. Deborah met and defeated the enemy on Mt. Tabor. And, of course, the central religious drama in Israel's history, the revelation of the Torah, took place on top of a mountain, Mt. Sinai. Mountains have figured very prominently in Jewish experience and Jewish history.

Not just in Jewish experience and history though. From time immemorial, mountains have constituted a challenge to all people, of whatever race and creed. Mountains seem to symbolize people's determination to stand up to obstacles. To confront challenges of whatever nature and to overcome them. You'll recall what Sir Edmund Hillary said when he was asked why he climbed Mt. Everest. "Because it was there!" he replied. Not just in a physical sense, but in a psychological sense as well. Mountains suggest the rejection of that which is dull and mundane, commonplace and ordinary. Mountains suggest, rather, the willingness to exert the courage and the energy needed to overcome whatever difficulties lie in our path. Mountains suggest fortitude. The strength of pioneers, undaunted by the wilderness. They suggest the dreams of dreamers who are unafraid to act.

It was Dr. Ferdinand C. Lane, in the forward to his sensitive book, *The Story of Mountains*, who offered a penetrating, psychological insight into the statement from the Psalms, which says: "I will lift up mine eyes unto the mountains." Lane observed that the very act of lifting the face upward precipitates certain uplifting emotions—emotions which serve to elevate the soul of a person, above the sordid plain of the commonplace, to release it for wider horizons. "Up," he wrote, "has a thousand meanings to connote the desirable; 'down' as many in the opposite direction. Happiness is always linked with the ascending scale; misery with the reverse. God Himself is known as the Most High." In a word, mountains represent the need that active, proactive people have to overcome whatever obstacles lay in their path. The determination to scale the heights, no matter how high and how formidable. It seems to me, as William Blake once said, "Great things are done when men and mountains meet." Mountains suggest a second dimension, not so much of human experience as of human need. That is the serenity and the isolation that are so often lacking in our lives, but which are crucial for healthy living. It is on a mountain that we often find the quiet which is denied us on life's main street. On a mountain, withdrawn from the deafening clamor of life's obligations and burdens, we are generally in a much better position to think and to meditate. Not to mention the distinctive beauty which characterizes mountains. The beauty of the sky, the majestic rock formations, the trees, all of which combine to provide the perfect setting for the pursuit of serenity. I can tell you that whoever has not ascended mountains lacks significant knowledge of the great beauties of God's world.

Finally, mountains not only provide challenges and afford serenity, but they also provide us with a perspective on the world which is usually not available, certainly not in the same way, in any other setting. On top of a mountain we see more. We see farther. We see better. We see the whole forest as well as the individual trees. We see things in clearer relationship to each other. And observing the multicolored quilt of nature and civilization from on high, we are somehow given the perspective to see life steadily. To see it whole. To better understand our place in the scheme of things. Our relationship to other people and ourselves. To better understand our relationship to the maker of mountains, Himself. Yes, mountains symbolize challenges in life. Yet they provide serenity and beauty. They provide a perspective rare to those of us who have spent most of our lives on the plain.

Obviously, Harriet and I hope that our future on Mt. San Jacinto will provide us with all of these blessings. I can tell you that, so far, based upon our brief visits, "our" mountain has been all of these things to us and then some. The challenge of relocating and building a home at that level is indeed a great one, but we hope to accomplish it. The mountain is incredibly serene and beautiful—and isolated. We hope that a broader perspective on life, on ourselves, on God, will come in time. But having said that—and feeling every word of it most keenly—I have to tell you that I know that living on a mountain is not the only way to achieve these blessings. After all, what have we been doing until now? We haven't exactly been without challenges. Without some serenity and an appreciation of beauty. Or, for that matter, without a broad perspective.

What we have done until now is what Jews have always done. When we Jews had our mountains, we did our thing on them. The mountains inspired us, uplifted us. When we have not had actual mountains, we Jews have constructed mountains. Instead of mountains in space we made mountains in time. We constructed mountains of the spirit. You see, just as there are high places, so there are high moments. Moments when we accept challenges and are suddenly uplifted. Moments when our vision becomes clear and our perspective better. When life's haze suddenly lifts and there is revealed to us a glimpse of beauty or an insight into truth that we had not possessed before. When we Jews don't have actual mountains, we make mountains out of moments.

What is true of Jews individually is also true collectively. After all, that is what our holidays are, our sacred days. They are great peaks of the human spirit from which we obtain a sharper view of our lives. From the heights afforded by the collective wisdom and experience of our poets and prophets, psalmists and sages, distilled through our prayer book, we obtain a different and broader perspective on life and our relationships to one another. From the summits of these exalted moments—the holidays, especially Shabbat—we see many things that escape our view in the valley of daily living. The point is that as Jews, and as people, we need mountains—actual or simulated—in order to energize and uplift the spirit and the soul. I like to feel that actual mountains are perhaps a little more efficient in evoking the kind of responses I have been describing. But actual or simulated, the stimulation wrought by mountains is a crucial ingredient in living, Jewish and otherwise.

So let me express the hope and the prayer that those of us who will live on mountain tops, as well as those of us who will continue to live near sea level, will always have the satisfaction of significant challenge. That we shall have the serenity that we need and the opportunity to truly bask in the beauty of God's world.

Finally, I hope that we shall also achieve the perspective to see ourselves and all of reality, not in a limited, narrow way, but, if I may use one of my favorite phrases, that we achieve the perspective to see ourselves and reality "under the aspect of eternity." On Sunday, as part of the daily service, we daven Psalm 25, which poses the question: "Who is it who may ascend the mountain of the Lord?" If I may suggest my answer to the question, I feel it is those who are poised to meet life's challenges—those who truly appreciate the beauty of this world, and those whose perspective encompasses the whole wide range of Jewish and personal experience. These are they who will ultimately ascend the mountain of the Lord. And may each and every one of us be included among them. A sentiment to which I invite you to join me in saying, Amen.

Editor's Note: These were included as handouts at the sermon:

The Ten Tallest Mountains in the World
The following is a list of the ten tallest mountains of the world. They are found in the Himalayas. In fact, the fifty tallest mountains in the world are all found in Asia.

1. **Mount Everest** - China/Nepal - 29,035 feet (8850 meters)

2. **K2 - China/Pakistan** - 28,251 feet (8611 meters)

3. **Kangchenjunga** - India/Nepal - 28,169 feet (8586 meters)

4. **Lhotse - China/Nepal** - 27,939 feet (8516 meters)

5. **Makalu - China/Nepal** - 27,765 feet (8463 meters)

6. **Cho Oyu - China/Nepal** - 26,906 feet (8201 meters)

7. **Dhaulagiri - Nepal** - 26,794 feet (8167 meters)

8. **Manaslu - Nepal** - 26,781 feet (8163 meters)

9. **Nanga Parbat - Pakistan** - 26,660 feet (8126 meters)

10. **Annapurna I** (Annapurna contains six peaks) - Nepal - 26,545 feet (8091 meters)

The Seven Summits
The Seven Summits are the highest peaks on each continent:

1. **Mount Everest** (29,035ft/8,850m) Nepal, Asia, and the world

2. **Aconcagua** (22,840ft/6,962m) Argentina, South America

3. **Denali** ("Mount McKinley," 20,320ft/6,195m) Alaska, North America

4. **Kilimanjaro** (19,339ft/5,963m) Tanzania, Africa

5. **Mount Elbrus** (18,481ft/5,633m) Russia, Europe

6. **Vinson Massif** (16,067ft/4,897m) Ellsworth Range, Antarctica

7. The Seventh Summit is in some dispute: Indonesia's **Carstensz Pyramid** (16,023ft/4,884m) is Australasia continent's highest mountain. However,

some consider Australia to be the seventh continent as opposed to Australasia, in which case Australia's 7,000 foot walk-up **Mount Kosciuszko** is the seventh summit. Most climb both, just to be sure, making eight in total.

The Importance of Physical Contact, Hugging and Kissing

November 16, 2001 - Toldot

Tonight's sermon is dedicated to my mother, whose *yahrzeit* is today. She died on the second day of Kislev, 1959, which was 42 years ago, today. The sermon, incidentally, is one that she would have liked. The truth of the matter is that my mother would have liked any sermon I delivered. That's how uncritically partial she was to me. Still and all, beyond that, tonight's sermon would have been to her liking in a very special way. Because it was her example that provided me with the lesson that I am going to try to impart, and that lesson is the importance of touching. Physical contact; actual touching; and its most common forms, namely, hugging and kissing.

Actually, the whole subject was suggested to me as I read today's *sedra*, *Toldot*, which describes the blessing of Jacob by his father, Isaac. You recall the story. Esau, rather than his younger brother, Jacob, as Isaac and Rebecca's firstborn, was to receive the blessing of the progenitor. That is the double blessing and the double inheritance and, most important, the leadership of the tribe that was given to the eldest son. But the twins' mother, Rebecca, decided that Esau, even though he was the eldest, was unsuited to carry on the family tradition. She therefore arranged, deviously, to have Jacob, the younger son, take Esau's place before her blind husband and to receive the blessing in his stead; in Esau's stead. When Jacob entered the room with his father Isaac, Isaac immediately suspected that he was the object of a subterfuge. He asked his son to approach him so that he could touch what he knew to be Esau's hairy arms, and thereby verify that he was indeed his elder son, Esau. Now, that is the way we generally understand this part of the story. That Isaac was at first suspicious but was then taken in by his wife's ruse of covering Jacob's hands and neck with kid's skin to make them appear like Esau's hairy body. That after testing it by touching his son's arms, covered with the kid's skins, Isaac fell for the deception and thought he was talking with Esau. On the other hand, I am not so sure that this is what really happened. There is good reason to believe, I think, that Isaac knew all along what was happening. That he was not deceived at all. He made it appear as though he was—because, perhaps, of an innate weakness (which Rebecca did not share) to do what needed to be done. At this stage of emerging Jewish history, deep down, he may have agreed with his wife's judgment about Jacob's superiority to Esau. So, he allowed himself to be duped, or really, to appear to be duped—which would make the purpose of the touching by Isaac, not probing to see whether it was Jacob or Esau but simply touching for the purpose of touching and expressing love, as a prelude to the blessing he was going to confer upon Jacob. That this may well be what happened is indicated a little farther along in the text. After feeling his son's arms, Isaac ate the dinner which had been prepared for him, and then, as he was about to actually bless Jacob, he said, "Come here and kiss me my son." He came near and kissed him, and then he blessed him.

Now, this is far from the only example in Scriptures of the important place accorded to touching, specifically, hugging and kissing, among members of the same family and among good friends. Let me mention just one or two other examples.

Jacob grew up. This is long after he received the blessing. He lived with his father-in-law, Laban, for twenty years when he decided to leave and return to his home in Canaan. Which he did, somewhat precipitously, to say the least. When his father-in-law finally caught up with him, he rebuked Jacob in the following fashion: "You did not let me kiss my sons and daughters goodbye." Later on, too, when Jacob eventually reconciled with his brother, Esau, we read, "and Esau ran to meet him, and embraced him, and fell on his neck, and kissed him, and they wept." Many many examples, throughout Scripture of hugging and kissing, between parents and children, including fathers; between brothers and good friends. In the Bible, touching, physical touching, was regarded not only as acceptable behavior but as a prime means of expressing, and perhaps also of fostering, affection and love and trust.

Now, in our day, in American society as a whole and with many of us individually, there tends to be a good deal of, shall I say, confusion on the subject of touching. Many of us like it, but we are embarrassed by it. We do it but with hesitation. We respect it but we fear it. Has it ever struck you as strange that in an age which condones instant intimacy and casual sex, physical contact is reserved for parents with babies and teenagers suffering the throes of puppy love? Doesn't it strike you as odd that at the same time that half of the babies in this country are born out of wedlock, touching in public is regarded as ungentlemanly and unladylike? Perhaps if there were more touching associated with affection rather than with sex, we would not be guilty, as a society, of the excesses with which we are all too familiar.

Well, I remember a time, and it was not very long ago, when parents hugged and kissed each other and their children, and when children hugged and kissed each other and their parents. It didn't make any difference whether it was a father or a mother or a brother or a sister. I don't ever remember shaking my father's hand. He probably would have kicked me if I did. Our greeting was a kiss, like with my mother and my brother.

At a recent annual meeting of the American Ortho Psychiatric Association, in Toronto, Dr. Virginia Satir said, "Being able to have physical contact is very important." "Four hugs a day," she said "are necessary for survival. Eight are good for maintenance, and twelve are required for growth." Which I quite agree with. You surely remember Rene Spitz's famous study involving babies in a nursery who had no real loving care. That is, when they were untouched most of the day, despite the cleanliness of the nursery, they died. It has long been known that infants in premature nurseries who are handled fare much better than those who are not.

This wisdom is preserved not just in experimental studies and not just in the Bible, but also, interestingly, in the English language. Dr. Willard Gaylin, one of our nation's leading psychoanalysts, published a book called *Feelings*. He describes there how feelings are such an integral part of living, and then in a chapter called, "Feeling Touched," he describes the commonplace expression, "How touched we are... when or by the thoughtfulness of a friend, by an unexpected courtesy, by an unaccustomed act of kindness." He makes the point that the same is true of the word, 'contact,' that comes from the Latin, 'contractus,' which means 'touching'—which, in the wisdom of our language is the essence of communication between people. Indeed, what do we say when we take leave of a friend or a loved one? "Stay in touch!"

Which brings me back to my mother. I remember what I consider to be the biggest compliment that she ever conferred upon me. She used to introduce me—if you promise not to laugh—as her "kissing bug." I remember, too, that my biggest thrill as a young child was to be able to get in bed with my parents and "hug up"—although, I also remember once overdoing it with my Aunt Dora, from Philadelphia. I hugged her and broke three of her ribs, which brought an end to our hugging!

What I am saying is that we should all learn to touch and to be touched more—not indiscriminately obviously—overdoing anything, including this, cheapens it; but in general. Just as the body and soul are one, so should the spiritual and physical expressions of affection be one. If I may plagiarize an ad with which we are familiar, to a greater extent than we do presently, we should "reach out and touch" more; not just through voice contact, but actually touch those for whom we feel affection. That, like with Isaac, will surely be a source of blessing to them and to us.

Indeed, I do consider this one of the most important messages in today's *sedra*, and one of the most important lessons taught me by my mother, may her memory be for a blessing. To which I invite you to join me in saying, Amen.

Vegetarianism

October 19, 2001 - Noah

Last Shabbat, when we read the biblical account of the creation of the world, I commented that the Bible is of the opinion that human beings originally were intended to be vegetarians. That it was only much later, after Noah, when the tradition grudgingly permitted meat to be eaten. There was considerable interest in this comment on the part of several members, and I promised that today I would deal with the subject more fully. I will divide this presentation, therefore, into two parts: First, something of the biblical background for vegetarianism; and second, my reasons, personally, for becoming and remaining the vegetarian that I am.

In the first chapter of Genesis, at the end of the six days of Creation, we read "God said, 'See, I give you every seed-bearing plant that is upon all the earth, and every tree that has seed-bearing fruit; they shall be yours for food. And to all the animals of the land, to all the birds of the sky and to everything that creeps on earth, I give all the green plants for food.'" (Genesis 1:29) In other words, according to Genesis, Creation was so arranged that all living creatures, humans included, would have proper food to eat, and that food was to consist of plants, perhaps grain, and fruit, as well as what the Bible calls green plants. Notice that there is no mention of meat as food. Not for humans; not for birds and not for animals. All sensate life—people, animals, birds—were to eat plants, fruits and greens only. To use the technical term, all sensate life, when the world was created, was expected to be herbivorous, vegetarians.

Now, in this week's *sedra*, Noah, the situation changes drastically. Generations later, violence and corruption became rampant and God decided to destroy the world through a flood. Singled out to be saved, however, were Noah and his family, as well as representatives of the animal kingdom. Noah, being the most righteous person of that generation, was to restart the world after the flood would subside. After the flood, God sent Noah and the animals out of the Ark. He blessed them and then suddenly God declared, seemingly out of nowhere, "Every creature that lives shall now be yours to eat. Like I gave you the green grasses, now I give you all of these." However, the Bible adds, "You may not eat the flesh with its life blood in it." In other words, after Noah came out of the Ark, God changed the rules and granted permission to eat animal flesh, in addition to plants. Whereas vegetables and fruits only were the diet up until this point, from Noah on, meat was now permitted, rather all of a sudden.

So what had happened in between Creation and Noah to cause this change? Well, I submit that what happened, between Creation and Noah, is that sin had entered the world! Creation, as represented by Adam in the Garden of Eden, is the original, natural, sinless state of humanity, which subsisted on plants. The generation of the flood, on the other hand, Noah's generation, represents man's involvement in sin—and violence. This is what happened in the interim.

What this has to do with permission to eat meat I base on the insights of Rabbi Kook, who was Israel's first Chief Rabbi. He, himself, a vegetarian, Rabbi Kook declared that animal food was permitted to Noah and his descendants, once sin and violence had entered the world, in order to prevent cannibalism. To prevent people from eating other people. At some point after Adam, according to Rabbi Kook, human beings lusted, as an expression of their violence, after flesh. They wanted to kill for food in order to satisfy whatever needs, psychological and physical, that they had developed in their sinful state. They needed to commit violence against other sensate life. The worst form of which is violence against other people—in the form of cannibalism.

There really seems to be some solid textual justification for this view, since in the very next verse, after animals are permitted for food, we read that though animal blood may be shed, human blood may not be shed. (Genesis 9:6) "Whoever sheds the blood of man, by man shall his blood be shed." In other words, what the text is saying, says Rabbi Kook, is if you have to be violent and kill, do so. But limit your killing to animals, not people! Kill, if you have to, even for food, but make it animals, not people. The Torah is not completely comfortable with animals either—eat the animals but refrain from eating the animal's life.

That is one of the major purposes behind *Kashrut*—to avoid eating the animal's life which is its blood. You see, to the ancients, blood was equivalent to life. Simply because they saw that when a person bled, his life ebbed away. So again, if you are going to be violent, limit your violence to animals but even with them, make it kosher by not eating the life-part of the animal, which is its blood. Eat its flesh only.

So, it turns out that biblical Judaism sees a carnivorous, meat-based diet as being introduced to the world only as a concession to human sinfulness. Certainly not what was intended at Creation, and certainly not desirable, in any sense, since Creation.

Judaism looks forward to mankind perfecting itself in time, to the point where we will all return to an herbivorous diet. When we will put away meat entirely and not take even animal flesh for food. This is the force of Isaiah's prophecies for the "end of days." When the Messiah will come and the world will be perfected under the kingdom of the Almighty. You remember the prophecy: a lion will one day eat straw, rather than meat, as it presently does. The wolf will, in those days, lie down with the lamb. All of which will signal that the world will have returned to the bliss and to the sinlessness of the Garden of Eden and the original Creation.

The eating of meat turns out to be then, from the biblical perspective, an interim stage in the human drama. It was preceded, at the ideal beginning, by the eating of vegetables, greens, fruits, nuts—anything that grows from the ground, and it will return one day to the same condition. In between, imperfect human beings, as a concession to our violence-prone natures, as a concession to our sinfulness, may use sensate life for food. That is animal life. But only within the confines of *Kashrut*.

As to my personal reasons for becoming and remaining a vegetarian, I will make this very short and perhaps expand on it at another time. Very simply, I feel that vegetarianism is better for the animals; it is better for the world; and it is better for me.

As to why it's better for the animals, it is both obvious and not so obvious. What I am referring to is not just that the animals are killed in order to provide us with food. In this day and age, those animals are raised under inhuman, or in-animal, terribly cruel conditions throughout their lives, before they are finally killed.

On the factory farms where animals are raised for food, there is really only one motive, and that is profit. The image of the contented cow or the happy chicken is absolute dribble. The animals that end up on our plates never see a bucolic pasture. They see only the inside of crowded cages where they are fattened up, not for their own benefit but for ours—until they reach the point where they are brought to an unmerciful, and usually painful, end. Believe me; vegetarianism is better for the animals.

It is also better for the world. It may interest you to know that eight pounds of grain are needed to produce one pound of animal protein. That is, in order to produce one pound of beef, an animal has to eat eight pounds of grain. Whereas if a person eats the grain directly, he receives the same nourishment, including protein, that he derives from meat. It is obvious that there are millions of people starving all over the world. If we can stretch the world's food supply by a factor of eight, simply by eating grain and vegetables ourselves rather than routing it through animals, we would be way, way ahead of the game. This is not to speak of the terrible pollution to streams and to land caused by these animals that are being raised for food, as well as the destruction of the rain forests which are destroyed only to feed the European and American appetite for meat. Vegetarianism is definitely better for the world.

And, finally, I think vegetarianism is better for me. Every indication and every study that I have ever read says that vegetables and high-fiber diets are much healthier than meat, including fowl, although, admittedly, it is not quite as bad. Our stomachs were simply not made for digesting meat. Nor were our teeth made for chewing it. A vegetarian diet is better for people—no question.

So, what I am saying in summary, ladies and gentlemen, is that I think that the time has come for Jews to consider moving beyond *Kashrut* to vegetarianism. I think that the time has come for us to apply the insights of our tradition to the present condition of the world, to do our part to help speed the day when the wolf will lie down with the lamb; when lions will indeed eat straw and vegetables, rather than meat. When we, as human beings, will do likewise.

A thought I hope that you will consider by joining me now in saying, Amen.

Last Year as Rabbi of B'nai Amoona
What I have been trying to convey all of these years

Yom Kippur 1990

Several weeks ago, when I was searching for an idea for today's sermon, which I regard as the year's most important, someone offered me a rather intriguing suggestion. Knowing that this is my last Yom Kippur as Rabbi of B'nai Amoona, that person said, "Why don't you go through your files and pick out your best Yom Kippur sermons? Put their main ideas together and make that your Yom Kippur sermon!" Something like, if you will forgive the comparison, "The Best of Carson."

Well, the suggestion did have something to commend it, since I have kept rather complete files. It is never easy to decide what to talk about on this occasion. Yet, as I mulled over the suggestion, I concluded that even if the congregation would accept such a sermon, I couldn't. I don't know why, but it would make me feel kind of uneasy to do such a thing. Who was it who said, "The most difficult plagiarism to avoid is the plagiarism of the self."? Anyhow, past material somehow always ends up being dated, appropriate to a particular time and place, and inappropriate to the present. So I rejected the idea, but it did set me to thinking. What, indeed, after all of these years, have I said from this pulpit?

If indeed I were to distill the literally hundreds of Yom Kippur and other sermons that I have delivered over the years, if I were to boil them all down and try to condense them into one half hour, what would I say? What do I have to offer by way of summary on this, my last Yom Kippur in this pulpit? I began to put together in my mind a tentative list of ideas. Not being able to cover everything, I asked myself, "What is the core? What is the essence of Judaism as it has been given to me to try to understand it, and interpret it, during these past 40 years?" And you know what happened? As the list began to take form in my head, I realized that it was going to be made up of not very profound things at all.

The list, as it began to take shape, was going to consist of simple—I suspect even simplistic—thoughts as follows: Basic rules of conduct; fundamental guides to human behavior that everyone knows as well as I do. These are not the kind of weighty and involved maxims that one might associate with a rabbinical ordination and a university diploma—just plain down-to-earth, simple truths which underlie human life, which are known to everybody, Jew and non-Jew alike.

Jew and non-Jew alike! Then it clicked! Some months ago, I read a little book by Robert Fulghum, a Unitarian minister, which was on the Best Seller List for a long, long time. It is titled, *All I Really Need to Know I Learned in Kindergarten*, which is the title of one of the essays in the book. And I reread it. As I did, I suddenly realized that this Fulghum gentleman and I—though we stem from different traditions; though we have vastly different backgrounds, and pray in different languages—have come to many of the same conclusions. Though our starting points are quite different and our metaphors diverse, we both, after all is said and done, are at much the same place.

"Each spring, for many years," he wrote, "I have set myself the task of writing a personal statement of belief, a credo. When I was younger, the statement ran for many pages, trying to cover every base, with no loose ends. It sounded like a Supreme Court brief, as if words could resolve all conflicts about the meaning of existence. The credo has grown shorter in recent years—sometimes cynical, sometimes comical, and sometimes bland—but I keep working at it. Recently I set out to get the statement of personal belief down to one page, in simple terms, fully understanding the naïve idealism that implied." As I read these words again, it occurred to me that, today, you and I are involved in the same kind of exercise as he is.

We also are examining our commitments, composing statements of belief. That we are, in a manner of speaking, creating our own personal credos. His may be done each spring, and ours, following the lead of the Jewish tradition, is done in the fall. But the experience, at least for me and I suspect for us all, is very similar to his.

I know it is for me. In my younger days, the sermons that I delivered and the ideas that I expounded, were much more involved than they are now. As I reread some of them now, I see how I tried, like Fulghum, to cover every base, leaving absolutely no loose ends. I hope that the sermons did not sound exactly like Supreme Court briefs, but I know that I did attempt, in well-meaning but somewhat sophomoric fashion, to resolve all conflicts, religious and personal, about the meaning of existence. One thing is for sure. Years ago, the sermons were longer than they are now and they had a greater air of self-assurance, and, if you will forgive the word, authority.

I know whereof Robert Fulghum speaks.

But let me continue with him. After describing an incident with an old car he had, he says, "I realized then that I already know most of what is necessary to live a meaningful life. That it isn't all that complicated. I know it and have known it for a long, long time. Living it—well, that is another matter, yes? Here's my credo. All I really need to know about how to live and what to do and how to be, I learned in kindergarten. Wisdom was not at the top of the graduate school mountain, but there in the sand pile in Sunday School." Fulghum goes on to offer a series of short statements which are as eloquent a presentation as I know of the basic message of Judaism. Pretty nearly as I have tried to understand it and to communicate it all of these years from this pulpit. And I offer you now a selection of these statements—10 to be exact—together with my own brief comments which constitute, in a deep sense, the essence of all those sermons in the file that I was tempted to quote, but really have no need to.

The Rules:
The first rule is "Play fair." What indeed is the purpose of religion? The purpose of religion, the purpose of Judaism, is to teach us to play fair with one another. Now, I hasten to add that this is not the only purpose of Judaism. Judaism has a number of other bona fide, important purposes. But, were I called upon to name only one out of all the purposes that religion serves, it would have to be this one. One of the major purposes of religion, if not the major purpose of religion, is to teach people to play fair. Long ago, the rabbis said the same thing in different words: The *mitzvot* were given only for the purpose of refining, by means of them, human beings, and it

can't be said any plainer than that. The goal of life is not to get ahead of the other fellow. (Except perhaps on the racquetball court.) We should treat others with respect and consideration and with honesty. The same respect and honesty and consideration that we deserve for ourselves. Play fair! It applies even if you think you can get away with it. Because any other way is just not nice. And certainly not Jewish.

Another rule is "Don't take things that aren't yours." I take this rule to refer to the basic satisfaction with our lot that we ought to try to achieve. People take other people's things because they covet them. Because they are not satisfied with what they have. Well, we should certainly try to better ourselves. I don't deny that. But we should not do so at the expense of others. Like the rabbis said in the *Pirke Avot,* "Who is rich? He who is happy with his lot." As important a message as there is and absolutely as applicable to the adult world as to the world of children. What doesn't belong to you is not yours to take.

The next rule is "Clean up your own mess." It is only in recent years that we are beginning to be aware of how much damage we are doing to spaceship earth. We are systematically destroying the atmosphere. We are polluting the oceans. We are ravishing the land. The time has come to begin to clean up our mess because it is a fact that if we persist in the way that we are behaving now, the earth, to use the biblical expression, is simply going "to vomit us out." We made the mess. We've got to clean up the mess. There is nobody who is going to do it for us.

The next rule is "Say you're sorry when you hurt somebody." Not long ago, a popular definition of love was "not having to say you're sorry." Well that is utter foolishness. Sometimes we hurt other people. Most often unwittingly. But sometimes even intentionally. It is almost inevitable. But if Yom Kippur has anything to tell us, and if Judaism has any message, it is that if we hurt someone, we have to try to make amends. We have to seek that person's forgiveness. A good place to start is by saying that we are sorry. Obviously with sincerity. You have heard many times that Yom Kippur atones only for sins between God and human beings. Sins between human beings themselves have to be worked out jointly by them, and feeling remorse when we have hurt somebody, saying you're sorry, is a crucial first step in the process.

The next rule is "Share everything." Indeed this is the fundamental lesson of the Prophet Isaiah that forms the *haftarah* for today. Isaiah says that a major purpose of Yom Kippur, and indeed of all religion, is to teach up—"to loosen all the bonds that bind people unfairly;" "To let the oppressed go free;" "To break every yoke;" "To share," I repeat, "To share your bread with the hungry;" "To take the homeless into your home;" "To clothe the naked when you see him." And "Never turn away from people in need." The point is that "The earth is the Lord's and the fullness thereof." It is not ours. It is everybody's. We have to share it with everybody.

The next rule is "Warm cookies and cold milk are good for you." To me this conveys the important message that people should seek the simple pleasures of life. We don't need the complicated, flashy, expensive diversions that are, so often, touted as the secret of happiness. We should learn to take joy in the simple beauties of life such as milk and cookies. (Although, for some of us, not too many of the latter!) This to me is one of the main messages of the three nature festivals of Judaism that are like a tripod on which our calendar rests: Pesach, Shavuot and Sukkot. All of which bring us into contact with the world of nature and the simple pleasures of home and hearth which are available to us.

Another rule is "Live a balanced life—learn some and think some and draw and paint and sing and dance and play and work every day some." So many of the values of Judaism are contained in that line. From the emphasis on the Golden Mean which is found in the Book of Proverbs and which Maimonides emphasizes, to the need to develop as many of our talents as we can. Live a balanced life. Then, "Learn some." Do you realize that we are the only people, to the best of my knowledge, who call our house of worship a *shul*—which is simply the German word and later the Yiddish word for school. We are the only people that I know who put the study of a book at the center of our services. We are still a people who are entranced by learning. Have you ever heard of the Elderhostel program? That's a program where people 60-years-old and over go to college campuses all over America and the world, in order to study, to take courses, for a week. Well, I am told that whereas Jews are only 3 percent of the population, Jews constitute 35 percent of the people in the Elderhostel programs! And work every day! Some people don't work just in order to earn a living. People should work because good productive work is the source of some of life's greatest satisfactions. There is little that can compare with honest work, cheerfully undertaken and energetically completed. Drawing and painting and singing and dancing—and playing—when our work is done—is no less important. In a word, live a balanced, productive, varied life.

The next rule we learn in kindergarten is "When you go out into the world, watch out for traffic, hold hands and stick together." We Jews know a lot about loyalty, too. About sticking together as families, as fellow congregants, and as just plain Jews. Long ago, the liturgy declared, "All of Israel is responsible—one for the other." And this is the way Jews do act. Witness the difference in the way the world relates to the numerous refugees who are clogging the roads of our globe today. How, as a people, we are reacting to the plight of Soviet Jews. But at the same time, our antennae are out for signs of danger, particularly discrimination. We have learned the lesson well that hate, directed at any people because of their color, their religion or their creed, is a dangerous, corrosive force, which needs to be fought with all vigor. Prejudice is like a cancer that, unless it is excised, will end up maiming and killing. Indeed we hold hands. But at the same time, we watch out for the oncoming traffic that may, if we are not careful, run us down!

The next rule, the ninth, is "Be aware of wonder. Remember the little seed in the Styrofoam cup: The roots go down and the plant goes up and nobody really knows how or why, but we are all like that." You know, these words could just have easily been written by my teacher and one of the great theologians of the century, Rabbi Abraham Joshua Heschel. He contended that all true religion, in fact all worthwhile living, is rooted in wonder. What he sometimes called "radical wonder," or "radical amazement." Nobody knows how this business of life got started. Nobody knows for sure how or why it did, or for that matter where it is going. But we do know that real knowledge and that real insight begin with the wonder of it all.

Heschel wrote, "Wonder goes beyond knowledge. . .wonder is the state of mind in which we do not look at reality through the latticework of our memorized knowledge. . ." "Inquire of your soul what does it know, what does it take for granted, and it will tell you only that no 'thing' is taken for granted. Each thing is a surprise. . .we are amazed at seeing anything at all. Amazed not only at particular values and things, but at the unexpectedness of being as such; at the fact that there is being at all." It is at this point, according to Heschel that real religion begins. Not ends, but begins. As indeed it does! That is, if a sense of wonder is properly cultivated in us when we are small children, and then replayed and responded to during the remainder of our lives.

Finally, "Goldfish and hamsters and even white mice and even the little seed in the Styrofoam cup—they all die. So do we." *Yizkor*, which we are about to recite, is not easy. Not only because we remember loved ones who are no longer with us but because we see ourselves as one day being remembered in the same way that we now remember others. We become acutely aware at *Yizkor* of our own mortality. The fact is that at some subsequent Yom Kippur, God willing in the distant future, our names will be on the *yahrzeit* list. But there is at least one solace, and that is that the little seed and we and the goldfish and the hamster and the white mice are all in the same boat. We all live and we all die. It is the way of the world. Nobody is exempt. Nobody gets out of this world alive. As much as all of us hate to go, reality dictates that we shall. The reason is that we are all part of that great mass of being which ultimately will join with all other parts of being in God's eternal domain, and that we shall do so in His own good time. Which provides some comfort for me, like I hope it does for you.

And there you have it friends, by way of Robert Fulghum, and me. Everything you need to know is there somewhere. The Golden Rule, love, ecology, religious observance, politics and equality and sane living. No matter how old we are. When I was a student at the Hebrew University over 41 years ago, I had a wonderful teacher by the name of Professor Ernst Simon, head of the Department of Education. Professor Simon once discussed an idea which, at the time, made an indelible impression upon me. I remember wondering at the time if the idea would apply to me when the time came. After today I think that I can safely say that it does. The idea is "second naivety" which, briefly stated, is that a child begins life with naïve conceptions of the world and of his place in it. He displays a simple, trusting nature. Unsophisticated, ingenuous and credulous. Then he lives his life and things turn out to be much more complicated than he imagined. More devious, too. Things are not quite as simple as he thought when he was a child. There are two or twenty sides to every issue. Deep and even dark underlying causes. His trusting nature becomes somewhat jaded and he, himself, with perhaps prideful confidence—seeks to crack the puzzles. He strives and works and thinks and builds. He tears down and builds again, attempting to bring substance and meaning and order into the world and his place in it. By then life begins to pass him by. The end of the road is in sight and at that point he takes stock. What has he learned? What does he really know? After all is said and done, what does it all mean? Well, it is then, according to Professor Simon, when he reaches a stage called "second naivety." After all the searching and all the agonizing and all the Sturm und Drang, after all the planning and all the building and all the happiness and all the disappointment, he eventually arrives back at his starting point. He unabashedly realizes that all he needed to know really, in the final analysis, was what he knew from the beginning. What he had learned in kindergarten!

That is, I suppose, where I am at this moment. Not bitter, God forbid. Not despairing either; just wiser. A bit more of the man-child than I thought I was. Like we all are, I suppose, deep down.

So it is these lessons that I have concluded are the essential ones and that I commend to your attention. Play fair. Don't take things that aren't yours. Clean up your own mess. Say you're sorry when you hurt somebody. Share everything. Warm cookies and cold milk are good for you. Live a balanced life—learn some and think some and draw and paint and sing and dance and play and work every day some. When you go out into the world, watch out for traffic, hold hands and stick together. Be aware of wonder. Remember the little seed in the Styrofoam cup: The roots go down and the plant goes up and nobody really knows how or why, but we are all like that. Goldfish and hamsters and white mice and even the little seed in the Styrofoam cup—they all die. So do we.

I pray that we shall be given the years and the strength to absorb these insights, earlier rather than later. That the lives we fashion by means of them will prove a blessing to us, to our loved ones, to our people and to our God. A sentiment to which I invite you to join me in saying, Amen.

The Final Sermon—Walk Humbly

June 29, 1991 - Balak

Well, folks, this is it! My last sermon from this pulpit as the active Rabbi of Congregation B'nai Amoona. As of Monday, July 1, I become Rabbi Emeritus and if it is ever my pleasure to speak from this pulpit again, it will be in an entirely different role.

So what do I say to you at this time? I remember Harry Golden, of the *Carolina Israelite*, once did a study of the final statements of famous people. People like Einstein, Freud, and Mozart. What it is they said just prior to their deaths. After all, these people had made significant contributions to the world in the fields of science and culture. Surely on their death beds they had something momentous to convey to their listeners and to us! They uttered statements like, "Would you please close the window?" Or "Get me a drink of water." Or "What day of the week is this?" The truth of the matter is that final momentous utterances do not exist. Last utterances tend to be like much of life itself. For the most part, ordinary, commonplace, and rather mundane. The fact is that if you haven't said it until now, forget it—it's too late!

Yet, I have delivered literally thousands of talks and written probably a like-number of articles and columns during the past four decades. I wonder to myself what wisdom, what insight can I convey to you in this final message? Words which will encapsulate what it is I have tried to express to you during these past forty years. Well, once again, the tradition—which has never failed me yet—steps in to lend a hand. Here is a statement in the Talmud attributed to Rabbi Simlai which speaks directly to such an effort. Let me quote what he said. Rabbi Simlai said, "Six-hundred-and-thirteen commandments were given to Moses; 365 negative commandments and 248 positive commandments. Then David came and reduced them to 11. Then came Isaiah and reduced them to 6. Then came Micah and reduced them to 3." "It has been told thee, O man, what is good and what doth the

Lord require of thee, 1) only to do justly, 2) and to love mercy, and 3) to walk humbly with thy God."—Which happens to be the last line of today's *haftarah*!

In other words, everybody knows that the Torah stipulates 613 commandments which a Jew is to observe. Still, the rabbis realized that not all 613 of those commandments are of equal strength. There must be some underlying principle, they figured, some reduction in the direction of a distilled essence which animates them all. Indeed, there is.

According to David, there are 11 such. According to Isaiah, there are 6. And according to Micah, there are 3 which constitute the climax of today's *haftarah*. As far as I am concerned, it is the climax or distillation of my whole message these past forty years. In the interest of accuracy, the Talmud goes on to say that Isaiah further reduced the number to 2, and that Amos and Habakkuk even reduced them to 1. But it is the 3—Micah's formulation of the three underlying principles of Judaism—which engages my attention today. Not just because it is in today's *haftarah*, but because, in my opinion, there has never been and will never be a more succinct and beautiful summary of Judaism, and specifically the Judaism that I have tried to teach during my tenure as your Rabbi.

"It has been told thee, O man, what is good and what the Lord doth require of thee, only to do justly, and to love mercy, and to walk humbly with thy God."

Let me set the stage for understanding Micah's message by pointing out that the period in which he lived, during the 8th Century, B.C.E., was much like our own. Judea was extremely prosperous. There was a good deal of military and political success. On the surface all seemed well. Yet beneath the surface there was tremendous corruption. Social ills abounded. Disregard for human suffering was rampant. Thus, the rich built large estates in cahoots with crooked judges. At the very time that across the tracks there were slums and grinding poverty. Outwardly things looked fine, but inwardly there was considerable moral decay.

Micah looked at this condition and called upon his people to repent. Unless there was a change, he said, destruction would be visited upon their land. Jerusalem, the capitol, would be destroyed. The people, hearing his message, were, of course, greatly afraid. They turned to the prophet and said, "What can we do in order to avert this disaster?" "Shall we, perhaps, increase the number of sacrifices that we bring to the temple?" "Shall we bring a thousand rams or maybe 10,000 'rivers of oil'?" (Oil being a sacrifice, which was also brought to the temple.) "Or, perhaps God wants us to offer our children as sacrifices. Maybe that would do the trick?" "No," said Micah, "You are on the wrong track. No additional sacrifices of any kind will help. It has already been told you what is good and what the Lord requires of you. Only to do justly, to love mercy, and to walk humbly with God."

Let's look at the statement more carefully. First, "it has been told thee, it has been told you, O man." You know Micah could have said, "It has been told me." Or, "It was told to Abraham," or to Moses. But he didn't say that. There are no big secrets about what God expects of us. God's requirements are not found in some esoteric incantation available only to priests and to scholars. Not at all! What God expects of us is right out there. For you and for everybody else to see. "It has been told you!" Notice he says "O man," which really means human being. The message is not designed for Jews only. Or for men only. Or for women only. The message is designed for human-kind, humanity, all people. Notice, too, the juxtaposition of "the good" and "what God requires"—"It has been told you, O man, what is good and what the Lord requires of you." In reality what is good and what God requires of us are one and the same. God doesn't require anything of us which is bad. Only that which is good. We are not dealing with some capricious God who wants His back rubbed or His shoulders patted. Real religion and morality are one and the same. Indeed, it has been told you, O man, what is good and what God requires of you.

And what are those three things that are good and that God requires? First is justice—to do justice. It should be rather obvious that whatever else true religion involves, the very first thing it involves is justice. It has got to be right. It has got to be just. People, simply because they exist, have rights, the protection of which constitutes justice. The ability to confront an accuser; the right to redress before the law—administered, obviously, by honest judges and by honest courts. Justice for all—irrespective of color or creed—is the foundation of all human society.

If I might digress for a moment, this coming week we shall celebrate the 4th of July, the anniversary of American independence. Whatever else America may be and may have been at its birth; it has aspired to be a society based upon justice. "We hold these truths to be self-evident, that all men are created equal, that they are endowed by their Creator with certain inalienable rights, that, among these rights are life, liberty and the pursuit of happiness." Justice is the foundation of human society. Justice is the foundation of American society. Justice is the first of the three basic components of real Judaism.

Obviously, that is not the whole story. Justice needs to be tempered with mercy. I am reminded of the story of the man who needed a photograph in a hurry. So he said to the photographer, "For God's sake, I hope you will do me justice." To which the photographer, after looking at him, replied, "Mister, you don't need justice, what you need is mercy!" Well, we are all in the same boat. We all need mercy, kindness, charitable acts, and our tradition is very specific about what mercy consists of. Clothing the naked. Nursing the sick. Comforting those who mourn. Burying the dead,—known in our tradition as *"gemilut hasadim."*

It is told that when the Temple was destroyed, Yohanan Ben Zakkai bemoaned the fact that, from then on with the abolition of sacrifices, there would be no means of expiating human guilt and sin. But in a moment of great affirmation, he realized that this was not the case. There is another avenue, just as efficacious as sacrifices. That, he said, is *gemilut hasadim*, the performance of deeds of loving kindness.

The rabbis once posed a question about how God spends his time. After all, after creating a self-generating world, what does God do with Himself? One of the suggestions is that He spends three hours each morning sitting on the throne of justice. The next three hours He moves over and spends sitting on the throne of mercy. Shuttling back and forth, as it were, between the two, which is the model for how we should behave. Notice another thing. We do justice, but when it comes to mercy we love mercy—not *do* mercy, but *love* mercy. You see, we don't need especially deep emotion for justice. Just do it the way it ought to be done—justly. But when it comes to mercy, it has to be done with love or it isn't mercy.

And then, finally, the third part of the formula, "And walk humbly with your God." Humility, of course, is one of the most desirable of all human qualities. In many ways it is the underlying attribute of every attempt to lead a truly religious life. We can't know everything in advance. We can't anticipate all of the eventualities, but if we approach life with humility and avoid the sin of pride, things kind of fall into place. Someone once said, "Whenever I see a self-made man, I realize how poor a job he has done." Because nobody is self-made. We are all dependent upon one another and upon God. It is this awareness that puts our lives and our relationships with other people and God into proper perspective.

So that's it folks! These are my final words, in this my final sermon. "It has been told thee, O man, what is good and what the Lord doth require of thee, only to do justly, and to love mercy, and to walk humbly with thy God." So may it be, for you and for me, forever!

Amen and Shalom.

Epilogue

By Dr. Ron Wolfson

I don't know about you, but having read these magnificent words of our dear beloved, Rabbi Bernard Lipnick—*zichrono li'vracha*—may his memory always be a blessing—I feel elated, enriched, and *exhausted*. "Exhausted" because, for anyone who knew "Bernie," as he was called by his closest family, friends, and lay leadership, this was a man who leapt into life head first, with no hesitation, no fear, with nothing but indefatigable enthusiasm.

How did he do it all? Here was a man who stood at the intersection of the most monumental, historical moments of his time on earth. Volunteering at the founding of the State of Israel. Walking with the Reverend Martin Luther King, Jr., in Washington and Selma. Traveling to the former Soviet Union to meet with Refuseniks. Witnessing the "takeover" of the 1969 Jewish Federation conference in Boston by young Jewish activists demanding more attention and funding for Jewish education. Bernard Lipnick was not the kind of rabbi who holed up in his study; he was a passionate activist for social justice, for learning, for Jews and Judaism.

I, like you, adored this extraordinary human being. Yes, he could break your hand when he shook it, his hand strengthened by endless games of racquet-ball. Yes, he had a heavy foot when driving a car, always in a hurry to dive into the next experience. Yes, he gave us these beautifully crafted sermons, meticulous in their design to both connect us to the Torah portion at hand and to touch the hearts of his congregants. Of course, anyone who was present for one of Bernie's sermons cannot but hear his gorgeous baritone, enunciating the words as if singing at the Metropolitan Opera. Has there ever been a more sonorous, beautiful voice booming from a pulpit? I dare say, not a chance.

Yet, for this Epilogue, if you permit me, I would offer an exclamation point about the man, not simply the rabbi.

I first heard of Rabbi Lipnick in November, 1963. I was fourteen-years-old and a new member of my synagogue's youth group, BILU United Synagogue Youth, at Beth El Synagogue in Omaha, Nebraska. A youth educator had recently come to Omaha from, of all places, Congregation B'nai Amoona in St. Louis, Missouri, to become the educational director of our congregation. His name—Jack Molad. "Mar Molad," as we kids liked to call him, was a "pied piper" of enthusiasm for Judaism, a trait he undoubtedly learned from Rabbi Lipnick. He convinced a busload of us Omaha USY'ers to travel all night to St. Louis for the Regional Convention of EMTZA USY over Thanksgiving weekend that year. Getting off the bus at the Chase Park Plaza Hotel, I met kids from B'nai Amoona who were there to greet us: Marvin Goodman, Linda Kranzberg, and others. They became wonderful friends during the weekend. But the highlight of the convention, by far, was the keynote address by a dynamic young rabbi—Bernard Lipnick. He gave a riveting speech that had the 500 kids on their feet for a standing ovation. He called us to take charge of our own Jewish learning and experiences. He encouraged us to be activists. He made you want to live Jewishly.

Fast forward to 1967. I am a freshman at Washington University in St. Louis and decide to walk the few blocks from campus to that amazing building on Trinity to meet Rabbi Lipnick. You see, I had been elected the Regional President of EMTZA USY and had a few months left in my tenure. I'll never forget it. First stop was the desk of Miriam Friedman, the long-serving secretary, gatekeeper, and completely devoted protector of Rabbi Lipnick. When he was ready, I was ushered into the "holy of holies" at B'nai Amoona. Oh, you think the sanctuary and the ark were the most sacred places in B'nai Amoona? Well, perhaps, but Rabbi Lipnick's wood-paneled, darkly lit, and totally enveloping study was a close second. After asking about my studies, he offered me my first position at the congregation—a youth advisor for Kadimah USY, the pre-Bar/Bat Mitzvah kids. It was great fun.

The next year, on the third day of Sukkot, I received an urgent message from Mrs. Friedman to come to the study at precisely 3:00 p.m. As you know, when Rabbi Lipnick summoned you to do something, he usually got his way. Rabbi Lipnick asked if I had been in *shul* the day before. "Yes," I replied. "What happened to the *Hazzan*?" He said the *Hazzan* had left the employ of the synagogue. I asked: "What does that have to do with me?" "Well, Ron, we have some Bar Mitzvah and Bat Mitzvah kids who now need a tutor. Would you like the job?" I was a sophomore in college, taking a huge load of courses in order to accelerate my studies, knowing that I faced another six years in rabbinical school post-BA. (At least, that was the plan.) "Rabbi, I really don't think I would have time to do this. I'm living at the Hillel House on Forsyth as a caretaker and I have more than twenty credits of coursework. I really must decline."

Never one to hear "no" for an answer, Rabbi Lipnick began to pick apart my argument. "Ron, I know you told me you know how to do a *haftarah*. You had your own Bar Mitzvah, didn't you?" "Yes, of course," I answered." "And did you chant a Torah portion?" "Yes, I chanted my entire *parasha*." "Wonderful, have you ever taught someone to *layn* (chant) Torah?" "As a matter of fact, last summer I taught my brother Doug his portion." "Well, see, you can do this! We need you, Ron. I need you, Ron. Please accept my invitation to take on this very important position here in the congregation."

I had been "Lipnicked." I thought a moment, and then gave in. "OK, Rabbi. I'll give it a try. How many kids are there?" "Forty-five," he replied. "Forty-five!" I cried, already beginning to regret my decision. "When do I start?" Rabbi Lipnick looked at his watch, looked at me, and said: "4 o'clock." After I exhaled, he walked me to the *Hazzan's* study, patted me on the back, and said: "You're hoping to be a rabbi. This will be great experience for you. You'll do fine!"

How was I to know that this was the beginning of a life-long friendship with the senior rabbi of B'nai Amoona? The next year, Rabbi Lipnick invented the *Vov* Class experiment you read about in his sermon "The *Vov* Class," and I became a co-teacher with the wonderful Obbie Price in that first year. And then in the autumn of 1970, as I was just beginning to lead the *Vov* Class on my own—my first solo teaching experience—Rabbi called me into his study again. "Ron, I am taking a sabbatical from the congregation to finish my Ph.D. in Education dissertation at Washington University." "Wonderful, rabbi! And what will you study?" "Your class," the booming voice announced. "It's a methodology called non-participant observation. I will sit in the back of your class and on the weekend retreats and take notes on what I see. You will take notes on your lesson plans and reflect on what happens in each session and give those notes to me. And, I'll try to make sense of what transpires." I was mortified, but somehow intrigued that the senior rabbi of the congregation was going to be observing me in every single class session and on every one of the nine-weekend retreats. "Will you be giving me feedback?" I asked. Rabbi paused. "Only at the very end of the academic year; otherwise, I could influence the outcome." There was no discussion of this; it was a *fait accompli*. Ironically, the kids in that *Vov* Class watched as their rabbi sat quietly in class and on Shabbat weekends, observing what was transpiring, saying nothing but the occasional "Please pass the pepper" at the dinner table. They came to adore Rabbi Lipnick, even though he uttered not one significant teaching, not one sermon, hardly one word.

Near the end of that *Vov* Class, the kids marched into Rabbi Lipnick's study to demand a continuation of their group into the *Zayin* Class year. He immediately agreed, and on the final night of the final weekend retreat, he finally broke his silence. "We've agreed for the class to continue with Ronnie and Susie. What do you want to do in the coming year?" Frank Yawitz was first to speak: "What if we went as a group to Israel?" This was the moment the rabbi had been waiting…and hoping…for. He talked with the kids about what they would want to do and then went about creating the most impressive immersive experience of Israel ever known in Jewish education. With the guidance of his teacher, Professor Moshe Davis of Hebrew University, Rabbi Lipnick showed up in modern Orthodox *moshav* Nir Galim to convince the *haverim* of the community to welcome his kids. They had never seen a beardless American rabbi, but Bernie spoke to them in impeccable Hebrew about their responsibility as Israelis and as Jews to impart a love of Zionism and Jewish living to these pilgrims from B'nai Amoona. Susie and I had the privilege of being the first counselors for the program, an experience I documented in my Ph.D. dissertation. It changed the lives of those kids. It changed the lives of the Israeli families who hosted them. And, it changed my life, as well.

We plan; God laughs. We plan; Bernie Lipnick has other ideas. I had been on the list to enroll at the Jewish Theological Seminary rabbinical school for three years, with the intention of becoming a Conservative rabbi. Bernie changed all that. I remember him advising me: "Ron, there are many excellent rabbis. We need excellent Jewish educators. You can be one. But, you need at least two years of further Jewish studies if you're not going to the seminary." When I found an eight-page mimeographed brochure from the University of Judaism in Los Angeles, I brought it to my rabbi. "David Lieber is a good man. You can learn from Elliot Dorff and David Gordis," he said, approving of our decision to head west. "And when you've finished your master's degree in Jewish studies, there is always a position waiting for you at B'nai Amoona."

I loved my seven years at this great sacred community and I truly thought that is where I would spend my career. I don't know if Bernie was disappointed we never returned to St. Louis; if he was, he never let on. In my many years at the University of Judaism—now the American Jewish University—I consulted with Bernie on every major decision. His good counsel was the wind behind my back.

In his retirement, Bernie and Harriet became wonderful beloved friends, staying with us on their trips to California and encouraging us as we built our family. It was then that I saw another side of this man. Quite simply, he loved everything he put his inquisitive mind and his embracing heart into. I remember the day he and Harriet drove up to our home in Los Angeles in that ginormous RV the congregation bought for him as a retirement gift. No exaggeration: he spent a full two hours showing us every function, every part of that magnificent machine. In the midst of building their gorgeous home on Mount San Jacinto, he insisted Susie and I come up to Idyllwild to watch him cut boards and nail nails. When he became the Senior Rabbi of the S.S. *Rotterdam*, we would regularly receive postcards from the most remote places on the planet, all effusing about the sites and wondering how it was that a group of Jews on the world cruises would spend an hour every day studying Torah with him, when there was so much else to do. When Susie decided to create a cookbook of family recipes, Bernie painstakingly showed her how to make his hummus—and then handwrote the instructions for her book. We laughed when he always refused to eat dessert…and then took up a knife to "just even out the cake." We saw how he adored his "dolly," his Harriet—a love for the ages. And she loved her "Bern."

That love is demonstrated by this volume. Harriet was determined to publish a collection of Rabbi Lipnick's sermons which, by the way, he meticulously kept filed in his study. She recruited their devoted friends, Rabbi Jack and Sue Riemer, to help select and organize the talks, and B'nai Amoona congregant, Lester Goldman, to assist with the publication of this important book.

Bernard *"Barukh"* Lipnick did what all unforgettable teachers do: he transformed our lives. He was always there—to comfort us, to celebrate with us, to inspire us, to teach us, to encourage us, and to guide us into lives of meaning and purpose, belonging and blessing. He was our *rav*, first and foremost—our teacher. I tell my Ziegler rabbinical school students that the best compliment a rabbi can get is when someone says: "That's *my* rabbi." Because the word "my" indicates a relationship has been created. Relationships survive death; they are immortal. Bernie Lipnick will always be *my* rabbi, as he will be for many of the readers of this wonderful volume. And, even though he has left this earth, his teachings continue to enrich us—in our minds, in our hearts, and in our memories of this once-in-a-generation giant of a man. *Y'hi zichro barukh*—may the memory of Rabbi Bernard Lipnick forever be a blessing.

Dr. Ron Wolfson
Fingerhut Professor of Education
American Jewish University
One of Rabbi Bernard Lipnick's Kids

CPSIA information can be obtained
at www.ICGtesting.com
Printed in the USA
JSHW010852090620
6117JS00002B/5